Eisenhower for Our Time

People for Our Time

A collection of books from Northern Illinois University Press

A list of titles in this collection is available at cornellpress.cornell.edu.

Eisenhower for Our Time

Steven Wagner

Northern Illinois University Press
An imprint of Cornell University Press

Ithaca and London

First published 2024 by Cornell University Press

Library of Congress Cataloging-in-Publication Data

Names: Wagner, Steven (Steven T.), author.
Title: Eisenhower for our time / Steven Wagner.
Description: Ithaca : Northern Illinois University Press, an imprint of Cornell University Press, 2024. | Series: People for our time | Includes bibliographical references and index.
Identifiers: LCCN 2023024176 (print) | LCCN 2023024177 (ebook) | ISBN 9781501774294 (paperback) | ISBN 9781501774300 (ebook) | ISBN 9781501774317 (pdf)
Subjects: LCSH: Eisenhower, Dwight D. (Dwight David), 1890–1969. | Eisenhower, Dwight D. (Dwight David), 1890–1969—Political and social views. | Political leadership—United States—History—20th century. | United States—Politics and government—1953–1961.
Classification: LCC E835 .W24 2024 (print) | LCC E835 (ebook) | DDC 973.921092 [B]—dc23/eng/20230718
LC record available at https://lccn.loc.gov/2023024176
LC ebook record available at https://lccn.loc.gov/2023024177

In memory of my sister, Sharon Wagner

Contents

Acknowledgments

There are pros and cons to writing a book during a global pandemic. Although CDC recommendations removed many of the usual distractions and provided ample free time for research and writing, it was sometimes difficult to focus on the events of the mid-twentieth century when there was so much uncertainty in our own time. I feel privileged to have had the opportunity to spend my time in a way that kept me safe and healthy while others had no choice but to put themselves at risk.

There are several groups and individuals I would like to thank. Most importantly, Missouri Southern State University for approving my sabbatical request to pursue this project. My colleagues in the Social Science Department there did an outstanding job under very difficult circumstances while I enjoyed a year of research and writing. Megan Bever and William Delehanty provided timely feedback on several chapters. The Eisenhower Foundation awarded me a generous grant for research at the Eisenhower Presidential Library. Archivist Mary Burtzloff was especially helpful preparing me for my visit. Amy Farranto at Northern Illinois University Press suggested that Eisenhower would be an excellent subject in their People for Our Time series. Karen Laun and Deborah A. Oosterhouse at Cornell University Press provided valuable editorial assistance. Eisenhower historians Chester Pach and Richard Damms each read the entire manuscript and provided valuable feedback. Students in my upper-level seminar "Eisenhower and the 1950s" were an excellent sounding board for the topics covered in this book. Finally, as always, my wife and fellow historian Angela Firkus provided tremendous help and support throughout the project.

Eisenhower for Our Time

Introduction

GOOD JUDGMENT SEEKS BALANCE

On January 17, 1961, Dwight D. Eisenhower spoke to the nation for the last time. After eight years as president, Eisenhower wanted to do more than say goodbye and wish the nation well. Like George Washington had at the end of his presidency, Eisenhower hoped to pass on some of the knowledge and experience that came from a lifetime of service to his country. The United States, he said, had emerged from a half century of conflict as the most influential nation in the world. He cautioned, however, that military strength and material riches would not be enough to maintain this position of influence. What mattered was "how we use our power in the interests of world peace and human betterment." Throughout America's history, its basic purpose had been "to keep the peace, to foster progress in human achievement, and to enhance liberty, dignity, and integrity among peoples and among nations." In its continued pursuit of these interests, he warned, the United States would encounter many crises.

> In meeting them, whether foreign or domestic, great or small . . . each proposal must be weighed in the light of a broader consideration: the need to maintain balance in and among national programs. . . . Good judgment seeks balance and progress; lack of it eventually finds imbalance and frustration.[1]

These lines from the beginning of the Farewell Address have been overlooked by scholars who have focused almost exclusively on its warning about the dangers of the military-industrial complex. In this book, I will argue that the "need to maintain balance" defines the Eisenhower presidency. In the chapters that follow I will introduce readers to several significant events in Eisenhower's political career: his decision to run for president; his pursuit of a "Middle Way" for social welfare policy; his creation of a "New Look" for national security; his reluctance to intervene in the French-Indochina War; his handling of Senator Joseph McCarthy; his intervention in the Little Rock Central High School desegregation crisis; his response to the Soviet Union's launch of Sputnik; and his crafting of the Farewell Address. A common element in each of these events is Eisenhower's attempt to find balance. Balance between personal preference and civic duty; public responsibility and private enterprise; national security and economic prosperity; states' rights and federal responsibility; Democrat and Republican; liberal and conservative.

Readers familiar with Eisenhower will likely think of additional events that I might have included. The armistice that ended combat operations in Korea, the covert operations that overthrew the governments of Iran and Guatemala, and the downing of an American U2 in Soviet airspace are three others that I considered for inclusion in this book. In each of these situations, and many others, Eisenhower acted in a way that is consistent with my overall thesis that his presidency can be defined by his desire to find balance. Producing a concise book that would be accessible to students and the general public, however, required that I limit the number of topics.

Those who appreciate the value of studying history are fond of quoting Spanish philosopher George Santayana's aphorism,

"Those who cannot remember the past are condemned to repeat it."[2] For historians, however, using knowledge of the past to offer practical lessons for the present is fraught with difficulty. Historians may be authorities on the past, but we are unlikely to have a comparable expertise on the present. This is due, in part, to the fact that many of the sources we rely upon are not yet available. References to current events also risk dating our work too quickly. A well-researched work of historical scholarship will remain relevant until historiographical trends render it otherwise—decades if we are lucky. But if that work is filled with references to the time in which it was written, readers will dismiss it as soon as those references no longer seem timely. Finally, attempting to infer lessons from the past runs the risk of alienating potential readers who might find a historian's application of those lessons to contemporary issues too subjective. For these and other reasons, historians who believe that the subject of their research offers valuable lessons for the current day often leave it to their readers to make these inferences themselves. In the People for Our Time series, however, authors have been encouraged to make these references more explicit. The connections between Eisenhower's time and our own are so numerous that—as with chapter topics—I was forced to make some difficult choices. My intention was to make connections that, although timely, were also timeless. These connections offer lessons not just for our own time, but for the future. Eisenhower's pursuit of balance makes him a good fit for the series. In our time of political partisanship, Eisenhower's assertion that "good judgement seeks balance" is a valuable lesson.

In 1962, Harvard historian Arthur Schlesinger Sr. conducted a survey of seventy-five leading American historians. They were asked to rank the thirty-four former presidents of the United States based on their achievements while in office. Based on the results of the survey, Schlesinger placed the presidents in five categories: great, near-great, average, below average, and failure. Dwight D. Eisenhower, the most recent president to be included in the survey, was ranked number 21, near the bottom of the average category. This put him just below Benjamin Harrison and Chester Arthur, and just above Andrew Johnson, the lowest ranked "average" president. In a *New York Times* article summarizing the results of the survey, Schlesinger admitted that Eisenhower had been difficult to evaluate since his term had only recently ended. Eisenhower, he explained, had "received a few votes in the near-great category" but many more votes for below average and failure. A two-thirds majority had placed him toward the bottom of the average category. In explaining the average or, as he called it, the "mediocre" category, Schlesinger explained that it included twelve presidents who "believed in negative government, in self subordination to the legislative power. They were more content to let well enough alone or, when not, were unwilling to fight for their programs or inept at doing so."[3]

In 1982, a new survey of historians and political scientists conducted by the Siena College Research Institute ranked Eisenhower at number 11. By 2018, the Siena College survey, taken during the second year of the first term of each president since 1982, placed Eisenhower at number 6.[4] This put him behind only George Washington, Franklin Roosevelt, Abraham Lincoln, Theodore Roosevelt, and Thomas Jefferson. Although it is not unusual for a president's ranking to improve over time, Eisenhower's rise from twenty-first out of thirty-three to sixth out of forty-four is truly remarkable.

The first generation of historians to study Eisenhower's presidency took a primarily negative view of his performance. They portrayed him as a simple man, unprepared to deal adequately with the many complex issues that faced postwar American society. According to this view, Eisenhower delegated most of his duties to subordinates. If the 1950s was a time of peace and prosperity it was not because of anything that Eisenhower did, but rather because he had few critical issues with which to deal.[5]

Historians began to revise this interpretation in the 1970s. As the National Archives declassified documents, a different picture of Eisenhower emerged. Historians saw that he played the leading role in meetings of the cabinet and National Security Council. The minutes of these meetings show that while Eisenhower's subordinates may have received credit for major policy decisions, they made none without his explicit approval. Furthermore, historians came to realize that the decade was not a time when "nothing happened," but rather a period when important decisions and actions by Eisenhower prevented many events from escalating to the crisis stage. This realization had a powerful effect on historians who saw how unsuccessfully Eisenhower's successors were in dealing with the many challenges of the 1960s and 1970s. The Vietnam War, racial unrest, and a recessionary economy made many Americans nostalgic for the relative peace and prosperity of the 1950s.

Eisenhower revisionism gained momentum in the 1980s. Political scientist Fred Greenstein made an important contribution to the field with *The Hidden-Hand Presidency*.[6] Greenstein argued that Eisenhower was an active president who worked behind the scenes, deftly employing a "hidden hand" as a distinct leadership style. The hidden-hand thesis revolutionized the study of Eisenhower's presidency, and scholars found ample support for it in the records of the newly opened Eisenhower Presidential Library. Historians now accepted that Eisenhower was an active leader who took a personal interest in his administration. As time went on, however, they became more critical of his decisions.[7]

Synthesizing the work of the previous decade into a new interpretation of the Eisenhower presidency, historian Chester Pach concluded, "Too often revisionists mistook Eisenhower's cognizance of policies for brilliance and his avoidance of war for the promotion of peace."[8] Pach called his interpretation postrevisionist. "The postrevisionists," historian Richard Damms explained, "accepted some of the basic tenets of Eisenhower revisionism, that the president was intelligent, articulate, and fully in command of his own administration's major domestic and foreign policies, but took issue with the wisdom of his policy choices, the effectiveness of his decision-making, and the long-term legacies of his actions."[9] Most Eisenhower scholarship of the last thirty years can be categorized as "postrevisionist."

In this work I hope to reveal some of the attributes and abilities that have led historians to rank Eisenhower among the top tier of U.S. presidents. Some of these were thought by earlier generations of historians to be his weaknesses: executive ability, leadership, decision-making, and willingness to compromise. Others are often considered too subjective for historians to consider, but recent events remind us of their importance: duty, honor, integrity, and good character. The defining moments detailed here will show Eisenhower as an active president, intimately engaged in the decisions that defined the United States in the 1950s. Although his actions are not above criticism, on balance they place him among the most successful presidents to hold the office, and they provide us with many lessons to guide us in the future.

As his presidency came to an end, Eisenhower seemed cognizant of the fact that his hidden-hand leadership style had given many Americans the impression that he had presided over an eight-year period during which little of consequence had taken place. Reflecting on the relative peace and prosperity of the 1950s he said, with a hint of bitterness, "People ask how it happened— by God, it didn't just happen, I'll tell you that."[10] Most historians no longer doubt this.

1

Brief Biography

Dwight David Eisenhower was born in Denison, Texas, on October 14, 1890. He was the third of seven sons born to Ida Stover and David Eisenhower. In 1892, the family moved to Abilene, Kansas, a former cattle town at the northern terminus of the Chisolm Trail, which brought cattle from Texas to the Kansas Pacific railway for shipment to eastern markets. Although "Wild Bill" Hickok, the town's former marshal, was long gone before the Eisenhower family arrived, Abilene's "Wild West" past inspired Dwight's lifelong love of history.

After graduating from Abilene High School in 1909, Dwight spent two years working at the Belle Springs Creamery to pay for his brother Edgar's college education. At his friend Everett "Swede" Hazlett's suggestion, he then applied to the U.S. Naval Academy. Finding that he was too old for admission to Annapolis, he applied to West Point and was accepted. Ike, as he was commonly known, made the varsity football team his sophomore year but injured his knee midseason and was unable to continue playing. Eisenhower was not a stand-out student, and his occasional disregard of West Point's strict rules got him in trouble from time to time, but he persevered and graduated in the middle of his class. The West Point class of 1915 later became known as "the class the stars fell on"—fifty-nine of its members earned the rank of general.

While at his first post in San Antonio, Texas, Eisenhower met Mamie Doud, whose family owned a home there. He proposed to her on Valentine's Day in 1916, and they were married in Denver, Colorado, the following July. Ike and Mamie had two sons. Doud Dwight "Ikky" Eisenhower, born in 1917, died of scarlet fever when he was three years old. John Eisenhower, born in 1922, also graduated from West Point. Like his father, he had a career in the army, serving in Korea and retiring at the rank of brigadier general. President Richard Nixon would later appoint him ambassador to Belgium. John and his wife Barbara Jean Thompson gave Ike and Mamie four grandchildren: David, Barbara, Susan, and Mary.

When the United States entered World War I, Eisenhower requested an overseas assignment, but he was denied and spent the war at various stateside training camps. In 1918, the unit under his command finally received orders for deployment to France, but the armistice was signed a week before their scheduled departure. In the interwar years, Ike served under several prominent generals. These included Fox Conner, Douglas MacArthur, and George Marshall. Eisenhower was executive officer to Fox Conner in the Panama Canal Zone from 1920 to 1924. It was under Conner's direction that Eisenhower studied military history and theory. Conner called him "one of the most capable, efficient, and loyal officers I ever met."[1] It was on Conner's recommendation that Eisenhower attended the Command and General Staff College at Fort Leavenworth, Kansas, graduating first in his class. In 1932, Ike was assigned as chief military aide to Douglas MacArthur. It was in this capacity that he participated in the infamous clearing of the Bonus March encampment in Washington, DC. Eisenhower later accompanied MacArthur to the Philippines where he served as assistant military adviser to the Philippine government. Eisenhower returned to the United States in 1939.

As the country prepared for war, Eisenhower's superior officers recognized his abilities and rewarded him with greater responsibility. As a result of his successful participation in the Louisiana Maneuvers, a series of army exercises in 1941 designed to evaluate U.S. readiness for war, Eisenhower was promoted to the rank of brigadier general. After the Japanese attack on Pearl Harbor, he was assigned to the general staff in Washington, DC, where he served under the army chief of staff, General George Marshall. During his time in Washington, Eisenhower earned his second and third stars.

In November 1942, after a brief stint in London, Eisenhower was given command of Operation Torch, the American campaign in North Africa. Operation Torch provided Eisenhower with valuable combat command experience, something he had lacked. As the campaign reached its climax in Tunisia, Eisenhower was awarded his fourth star. After the defeat of Axis forces in North Africa, Eisenhower oversaw the invasion of Sicily and the Italian mainland.

President Franklin Roosevelt had intended to appoint Marshall the commander of Operation Overlord, the cross-channel invasion of northern France, but his top military advisers convinced him that Marshall's presence in Washington was too important to the overall war effort for him to be in the field. On December 7, 1943, returning home from the Big Three conference in Tehran, Roosevelt met with Eisenhower in Tunisia. "Well, Ike," he said as he was getting into a staff car with the general, "you are going to command Overlord."[2] Two months later, Eisenhower was appointed supreme allied commander, a position he held until the end of the war.

On D-Day, June 6, 1944, Allied forces under Eisenhower's command crossed the English Channel and launched a massive amphibious invasion of Normandy. Within two weeks, one million men had seized a stretch of beach sixty miles long and fifteen miles deep. By late August, Allied soldiers had liberated Paris. Soon after, Eisenhower was promoted to general of the army, becoming one of the first four men to wear five stars. Germany, however, was not yet defeated and launched a surprise counteroffensive in December known as the Battle of the Bulge. Although they sustained heavy losses, the Allies regained the offensive and by the spring of 1945 had taken the war into Germany itself.

After Germany's surrender on May 9, 1945, Eisenhower became the military governor of the American occupation zone. He held this position until November, when he was recalled to Washington to replace Marshall as army chief of staff. In 1948, there was a great deal of public speculation about Eisenhower's interest in running for president. Both political parties courted him as a potential candidate, but the general declined, saying that he was "not available for, and could not accept, nomination to high political office."³ This unequivocal statement removed him from consideration in 1948 but did not end speculation about his political future.

That same year, Eisenhower retired from active duty and became president of Columbia University. Holding a civilian job gave him the freedom to speak more openly on issues than he had been able to in the military. While living in New York City, Eisenhower published *Crusade in Europe*, his World War II memoir. The advance paid to him by Doubleday, the book's publisher, made him financially secure. While president of Columbia, Eisenhower spent a great deal of time in Washington advising the secretary of defense. Although the position had not been formally created, Eisenhower served as the de facto chairman of the Joint Chiefs of Staff.

In December 1950, President Harry Truman recalled Eisenhower to active duty, appointing him supreme allied commander of European forces. Ike took a leave of absence from Columbia and went to Paris to undertake the difficult work of building the North Atlantic Treaty Organization. He remained there until June 1952, when he returned to the United States and again retired from active duty to pursue the Republican Party's nomination for president of the United States.

After securing the Republican nomination, Eisenhower went on to defeat Adlai Stevenson, the Democratic Party candidate, by an Electoral College vote of 442–89, winning 55 percent of the popular vote. Eisenhower was reelected in 1956 by an even larger margin, defeating Stevenson 457–73 with 57 percent of the popular vote. The Republican Party won control of the House and Senate in 1952 but lost both in the 1954 midterm elections and remained in the minority for the rest of Eisenhower's presidency. This made Eisenhower dependent on support from Democrats to advance his legislative agenda. Despite his party's difficulties, Eisenhower's public approval ratings were consistently above 70 percent.

Eisenhower was a hard-working president. Unless he was out of the country or recovering from illness, he met with the cabinet and the National Security Council (NSC) on a weekly basis. In contrast to those of his recent predecessors, Eisenhower's cabinet meetings were deliberative, rather than merely informational. Members were encouraged to offer their opinions not only in their own area of expertise, but on any subject before the cabinet. Although he spent much of his time listening, there was never any doubt about who was running the meeting. If there was a decision to be made, Eisenhower made it himself. Meetings of the NSC were handled similarly, but Eisenhower was more comfortable with the subject matter here and was more likely to speak up during meetings.

Eisenhower also met with his economic advisers, Republican legislative leaders, and the press on a regular basis—on average every two weeks. Regular meetings with his economic advisers demonstrate the importance Eisenhower placed on fiscal conservatism. The secretary of the treasury and the director of the budget were even included in meetings of the NSC. Eisenhower did not enjoy meeting with the Republican leaders, but he understood the importance of their support for his legislative agenda and kept the meetings on his calendar even though they often frustrated him. When legislation related to foreign policy was on the agenda, he often included the Democratic leadership as well. Eisenhower also gave regular press conferences, averaging twenty-four a year. Unlike his predecessors', Ike's press conferences were mostly on the record. By 1955, they were also televised. These new elements meant that they required more advance work with his press secretary.

Preparation for and attendance at all these meetings required a great deal of Eisenhower's time. By meeting regularly with his top-level appointees, Eisenhower made them feel like part of his team. Allowing them to participate in deliberations also made them more likely to promote and support the resulting policies. These elements also engendered a great deal of personal loyalty. Most of Eisenhower's original cabinet stayed on the job for his entire first term, and two of them stayed the entire eight years. Only two cabinet positions had to be filled more than twice.[4]

Eisenhower's foreign policy was shaped by the Cold War. Like Truman, he committed his administration to containing communism. Eisenhower, however, believed that containment, as practiced by the Truman administration, was economically unsustainable. Hoping to find balance between military security and economic prosperity, Eisenhower initiated a national security policy called the "New Look." The New Look relied more heavily on nuclear weapons as a deterrent to Soviet expansion. Although nuclear weapons, and the research necessary to develop them, were expensive, they were less so than stationing American troops around the globe. After the Korean Armistice, signed just six months after he took office, Eisenhower kept the United States out of major conflicts for the remainder of his presidency.

Eisenhower's domestic policy was shaped by what he called the "Middle Way." According to Eisenhower, the Middle Way was "a liberal program in all of those things that bring the federal government in contact with the individual," but conservative when it came to "the economy of this country."[5] The Middle Way sought balance between the extremes of the political left and right. Those on the left, he said, believed people were "so weak, so irresponsible, that an all-powerful government must direct and protect" them. The end of that road, he warned, was "dictatorship." On the right, were those "who deny the obligation of government to intervene on behalf of the people even when the complexities of modern life demand it." The end of that road was "anarchy." To avoid those extremes, he said, "government should proceed along the middle way."[6] Eisenhower hoped that his Middle Way philosophy would appeal to moderates in both parties and help to change the direction of the Republican Party, which was becoming more conservative.

Eisenhower overcame serious illness on three occasions during his presidency. He suffered a heart attack in September 1955, making his decision to run for reelection the following year a difficult one. Nine months later, he had an attack of ileitis, a chronic inflammation of the digestive tract, that necessitated surgery. Then, in November 1957, after a particularly stressful period that included the Little Rock desegregation crisis and the Soviet launch of Sputnik, Eisenhower had a mild stroke. After recovering from his stroke, Eisenhower remained in relatively good health for the remainder of his presidency, but the serious nature of his illnesses highlighted the need for a constitutional amendment that would formalize a procedure for the temporary transfer of power to the vice president if the president was incapacitated. The Twenty-fifth Amendment, ratified in 1967, served this purpose.

Ike and Mamie lived in the White House longer than they had lived anywhere else. Their favorite getaways during the presidential years included Augusta, Georgia, where they stayed in "Mamie's Cottage," a home reserved for their use at Augusta National Golf Club; and Denver, Colorado, where they stayed in the home of Mamie's parents. During Ike's second term, Newport, Rhode Island, replaced Denver as their summer residence. Weekends were often spent at the presidential retreat in Maryland, which Eisenhower named Camp David, after his grandson.

Eisenhower played a minimal role in the 1960 presidential election. Vice President Richard Nixon lost to the Democratic candidate, Senator John Kennedy (MA), in the closest presidential election in history up to that point. Eisenhower, who saw the 1960 election as a referendum on his own presidency, considered Nixon's defeat his "principal political disappointment." He later recalled that one of his goals when he decided to run for president "was to unify, and strengthen the Republican Party." In this, he had failed. "Certainly," he wrote, "I did not succeed in the hope of so increasing the party's appeal to the American electorate as to assure a few more years, after 1960, of Republican government."[7]

Eisenhower was seventy years old when he left office, the oldest serving president up to that point. After Kennedy's inauguration, John Eisenhower drove his parents to the retirement home and farm they had purchased in Gettysburg, Pennsylvania. It was the only home that the two of them had ever owned. In March, Kennedy signed an act of Congress restoring Ike's five-star rank.

Eisenhower remained active in Republican politics, campaigning for members of Congress and, reluctantly, for Senator Barry Goldwater (AZ) when he ran for president in 1964. He also consulted with presidents Kennedy and Lyndon Johnson when they requested his guidance. The general wrote three more books: *Mandate for Change* and *Waging Peace*, his two-volume presidential memoir; and *At Ease: Stories I Tell to Friends.*

Dwight David Eisenhower died at Walter Reed Army Medical Center in Washington, DC, on March 28, 1969. He was seventy-eight years old. After laying in state at the Capitol for two days, his body was moved to Washington National Cathedral for his funeral, which was attended by President Nixon, former president Johnson, and official dignitaries from seventy-eight countries, including ten heads of state or government. After the funeral, Eisenhower's body was placed on a special train for transport to Abilene, Kansas. At his request, the general was buried in a simple government-issue coffin wearing his World War II army uniform, the army and navy Distinguished Service medals, and the Legion of Merit. His grave is inside a chapel on the grounds of the Eisenhower Presidential Center, a short distance from his boyhood home and the Eisenhower Presidential Library and Museum. Buried alongside him are his son Doud and his wife Mamie, who died in 1979.

2

A Transcending Duty

On October 14, 1951, his sixty-first birthday, while serving as supreme allied commander of European forces (SACEUR), Eisenhower wrote a letter to U.S. Senator James Duff of Pennsylvania. Duff was part of a group promoting Eisenhower for the Republican Party's presidential nomination. They had reached the stage where they needed assurances from the general that he was a Republican and would accept the nomination if it was offered. In the letter he outlined what he said was his current attitude regarding the situation:

[1] I do *not* want any political office.... [2] I have been and am an adherent to the Republican Party and to liberal Republican principles.... [3] While on this job I shall make no political statement of any kind.... [4] Any American would have to regard nomination for the Presidency, by the political party to which he adheres, as constituting a duty to his country that would transcend any other duty.... [5] I shall say or do nothing to gain a nomination.... [6] If ... I should nevertheless be nominated by the Republicans I would resign my commission and assume aggressive leadership of the party.... [7] I will enter no objection of any kind to your pursuing whatever course ... you may deem proper in organizing like-minded people.[1]

Decades of Eisenhower revisionism displaced most of the scholarship that denied Eisenhower an active role in his own presidency, but one such interpretation went relatively unchallenged: his decision to run for president. This interpretation held that Eisenhower, due to the incredible popularity he enjoyed as a symbol of American victory in World War II, was the recipient of a genuine presidential draft, the first since George Washington. One popular biography of Eisenhower claimed, "There is not a single item in the massive collection at the Eisenhower Library prior to late 1951, that even hints that he would seek the job or that he was secretly doing so."[2] In 1993, however, the *New York Times* published Eisenhower's letter to Senator Duff, quoted above. It shows Eisenhower's active involvement in October 1951 and suggests that he was involved much earlier.

Eisenhower Decides to Run, by William B. Pickett, was the first significant reinterpretation of Eisenhower's decision to run for president published after the Duff letter became known. Pickett argued that Eisenhower "worked behind the scenes to encourage a popular movement for his candidacy." Although he would have preferred to stay out of politics, Eisenhower was concerned that the United States lacked the necessary leadership to preserve the ideals for which it had fought two world wars. "Far from remaining aloof and waiting for a draft," Pickett claims, "Eisenhower began to work closely with the partisan efforts" that resulted in his nomination.[3] Since the publication of the Duff letter and Pickett's book, historians have accepted that Eisenhower played a significant, although not public, role in the 1952 nominating campaign.

Eisenhower had no ambition to be president of the United States. After the 1948 election, however, he was unwilling to rule out the possibility entirely. This was due to his extraordinary sense of duty. He knew that if he could be convinced that it was his duty, he could not turn his back on the presidency. Ultimately, he was convinced by three factors. First, he believed that if Robert Taft, the leading candidate for the Republican nomination, became president, he would put the collective security of Western Europe at risk. Second, he believed that if President Truman, or another Democrat, were elected it would lead to the breakdown of the two-party system and perpetuate the centralization of power in the federal government. Finally, he became convinced that a significant number of people thought he was the best person for the job. This last factor was Eisenhower's biggest obstacle. He believed if the Republican Party nominated him as their candidate for president, it would present him with a duty to run. He felt no duty, however, to seek that nomination. Further complicating the matter was that when the campaign for the nomination began, he was on active duty as SACEUR. As such, he was prohibited by army regulations from engaging in political activity. For him to give up that duty, he would have to be faced with a transcendent one. Before he could make his decision to run for president, Eisenhower would have to overcome this final obstacle. Throughout the process, Eisenhower sought balance—balance between what others demanded of him and what he believed was his duty to his country.

The measure of an individual's sense of duty—in this case what an individual believes they owe to their country relative to the knowledge, experience, and skills they have to offer—is subjective. As such, it is a trait that historians are reluctant to praise when evaluating presidential candidates. Historians, however, show no similar reluctance to criticize candidates for pursuing the office in fulfillment of personal ambitions or partisan goals. It would be going too far to suggest that Eisenhower lacked these less desirable traits, but his sense of duty, a key factor in his decision to run for president, is worthy of praise. It is also an aspect of his presidency that is relevant for our time. The decision to pursue high political office is all too often based on a desire for personal power and partisan influence rather than on what one can contribute to the common good. As Eisenhower himself discovered, our nomination process no longer allows for the selection of a candidate who is not actively seeking the office, but his presidency suggests that we would do well to identify candidates who balance their personal and partisan goals with a similar commitment to duty.

The Finder Letter

It is not surprising that in the years following World War II Americans considered Eisenhower an excellent candidate for the presidency. His command of the D-Day landing of Allied forces on the beaches of Normandy had won him universal praise and his fifth star. After accepting Germany's unconditional surrender, he returned home to ticker-tape parades in New York City and Washington, DC, an invitation to address a joint session of Congress, and a celebratory dinner at the White House. No other individual was more closely associated with the Allied defeat of Germany than Dwight Eisenhower.

Talk of Eisenhower running for president did not bother President Truman, who told his wife Bess that a Democratic presidential ticket headed by Ike "was fine with him." In June 1945, during the Big Four conference in Potsdam, Eisenhower, now military governor of the U.S. occupation zone in Germany, took President Truman on a tour of Berlin. During the tour, Truman turned to Eisenhower and said, "General, there is nothing that you may want that I won't try to help you get. That definitely and specifically includes the presidency in 1948." The general was used to speculation about his future political plans, but he was taken aback by Truman's comment. "To have the president suddenly throw this broadside into me left me no recourse except to treat it as a very splendid joke, which I hoped it was," Eisenhower later wrote. "I laughed heartily and said: 'Mr. President, I don't know who will be your opponent for the presidency, but it will not be I.' There was no doubt about *my* seriousness."[4] After that awkward exchange, Eisenhower realized that he would no longer be able to laugh off questions regarding his political future.

In November 1945, Eisenhower returned to the United States, taking the position of army chief of staff (CSA). Although he insisted, both publicly and in his private correspondence, that he had no interest in the presidency, speculation continued in the press and among prominent individuals in both parties. His childhood friend Everett "Swede" Hazlett, with whom he had a lifelong correspondence, raised the issue with him several times during this period. In October 1945, Swede had written, "No matter what party you affiliated with . . . you could carry the country without even taking to the road." By the following February Hazlett had sensed his friend's disinterest. "I have an idea that you have no real interest in public office," he wrote. "Your conclusions concerning my attitude toward politics are 100 per cent correct," Eisenhower replied. "I cannot conceive of any set of circumstances that could ever drag out of me permission to consider me for any political post from dog catcher to 'Grand High Supreme King of the Universe.'"[5]

Eisenhower was unhappy in the position of CSA, and in 1946 he started considering his options for a postmilitary career. This was a difficult time for President Truman as well. In November, the Democratic Party lost fifty-five seats in the House and twelve seats in the Senate, losing control of both chambers for the first time since 1930. Truman's political future was very much in doubt. It was in this context that Truman again offered to support Eisenhower for president in 1948, this time offering an interesting twist. "I told Ike," Truman wrote in his diary, "that he . . . should announce for the nomination for president on the Democratic ticket and that I'd be glad to be in second place, or Vice President. . . . Ike and I could be elected and . . . [I] would be happy."[6] Eisenhower does not relate this conversation in his own diary or memoirs, and no record of it has been found in the papers at his presidential library. If the conversation took place as Truman describes it, one can only assume that Eisenhower brushed off the offer as he had the previous year.

Truman was not the only one who saw Eisenhower's potential as a presidential candidate. His personal correspondence during this period consists primarily of denials of interest written to those from both parties who sought his candidacy, and his diary entries are frequently punctuated by his exasperation with those who "don't want to believe a man that insists he will have nothing to do with politics."[7] On January 12, 1948, Leonard Finder, publisher of the *Manchester Evening Leader*, wrote to General Eisenhower:

> As you know, a movement has been launched in New Hampshire to elect on March 9 a slate of delegates pledged to you. At the same time that this announcement was made public, *The Manchester Evening Leader* came out with open endorsement of you as "the best man." For our actions, we have no apology, even though we are aware that you are not desirous of being involved in this political contest. We have acted consistent with our own belief, based on what we regard as best for the welfare of the nation.[8]

Eisenhower's carefully worded reply eliminated him from consideration in 1948 but left the door open for future possibilities. His letter got right to the point. "I thought that unqualified denial of political ambition would eliminate me from consideration in the coming campaign for the presidency, because that office has, since the days of Washington, historically and properly fallen only to aspirants," he wrote. "But my failure to convince thoughtful and earnest men, such as yourself, proves that I must make some amplification." Then came the general's most forceful rejection since the idea had first emerged: "I am not available for and could not accept nomination to high political office." He said that it had been his intention all along to say that he would not accept nomination, but he had refrained from making such a "bald statement." He now believed this omission to have been a mistake "since it has inadvertently misled" sincere Americans.

Next, he offered his reasons for refusal. The first was humility. He did not want to assume "that significant numbers of people would actively interest themselves in me as a possible candidate" or to appear disrespectful of the "highest honor American citizens can confer." The second reason was duty. This was a subject that Eisenhower felt very strongly about and, as we shall see, would define his response to demands that he run in 1952. He explained that he did not want to violate "that concept of duty to country which calls upon every good citizen to place no limitations upon his readiness to serve." On this point he said that he believed that "unless an individual feels some inner compulsion and special qualifications to enter the political arena," which he did not, then "a refusal to do so involves no violation of the highest standards of devotion to duty." This explanation left the door open for reconsideration prior to 1952.

Finally, Eisenhower stated that it was his conviction that "the necessary and wise subordination of the military to civil power will be best sustained . . . when lifelong professional soldiers in the absence of some obvious and overriding reasons, abstain from seeking high political office." In addition to ruling himself out, this last point had the added benefit of ruling out Douglas MacArthur, whose political ambitions he did not support. Eisenhower concluded his letter to Finder by stating that his decision was "definite and positive." He planned to make the letter public "to inform all interested persons that I could not accept nomination even under the remote circumstances that it were tendered to me."[9]

In 1948, Eisenhower retired from active duty and became president of Columbia University in New York City. Although the Finder letter put an end to serious talk of nominating Eisenhower that year, his transition to civilian life gave many individuals new hope that their desire for him to be president would one day be fulfilled. In the spring of 1948 Eisenhower, as the newly installed president of Columbia University, received twenty thousand political letters, postcards, and telegrams. An analysis by Columbia's Bureau of Applied Social Research determined that 89 percent of those who wrote wanted Eisenhower to run for president. Although 9 percent did not want him to run, three-quarters of those gave as their reason that they did not want him to risk his "unimpeachable position in the eyes of the American public."[10]

Eisenhower's public-speaking schedule and the content of his speeches would have done little to dissuade those who had begun to see him as a politician. Although he had not revealed his party affiliation, a careful listener would not have had difficulty determining it. In his inaugural address at Columbia in October 1948, for example, he warned that "a paternalistic government can gradually destroy . . . the will of the people to maintain a high degree of individual responsibility. And the abdication of individual responsibility is inevitably followed by further concentration of power in the state."[11] In that same month he made twenty speeches, a pace he kept up for much of the next two years. Many of these speeches took positions on the problems he believed America faced. When those problems were domestic, his positions were consistent with those of the Republican Party.[12]

In addition to honing his skills as a political speaker, Eisenhower's time at Columbia prepared him for his future in another way as well—he acquired a circle of wealthy and powerful friends and a significant amount of money of his own. Most important of these friends was William Robinson, publisher of the *New York Herald Tribune*. It was Robinson who, in 1947, persuaded Eisenhower to write *Crusade in Europe*, a memoir of his World War II years. Robinson introduced Eisenhower to executives at Doubleday Publishing, which advanced him over half a million dollars for publishing rights. For a career military officer, this was an incredible amount of money. Robinson also introduced Ike to Clifford Roberts, chairman of the Masters Tournament at Augusta National Golf Club. Augusta would quickly become Eisenhower's favorite place to get away and relax. As William Hitchcock, Eisenhower's biographer put it, "Eisenhower's friends . . . were not simply wealthy: they were among the richest and most powerful businessmen in postwar America." They had other things in common as well. One was a hostility to the expansive federal programs of the Roosevelt and Truman administrations. Another was a belief that Eisenhower should be president.[13]

With Eisenhower out of the running, Truman ultimately decided to run for election in 1948 and, despite a badly divided Democratic Party, he defeated Republican Tom Dewey, the governor of New York, in one of the biggest upsets in American political history. Eisenhower was troubled by the prospect of four more years of Truman's Fair Deal and the "trend toward governmental centralization" it represented to him.[14] He was also concerned that Dewey's defeat would allow isolationists under the leadership of

Ohio Senator Robert Taft to take control of the Republican Party. He continued to resist partisan politics, but his diary entries from this period reveal that his duty in this regard was constantly on his mind.

On January 1, 1950, Eisenhower wrote a long diary entry on the subject "to clarify [his] mind." His mind seemed clear on one thing: "I do not want a political career." But his sense of duty made him feel that an explanation was necessary. He saw his role as that of an elder statesman, one who transcended party politics. He believed that because the American system was "superior to any government elsewhere established by men," that his "greatest possible opportunity for service [was] to be found in supporting, in renewing respect for, and in encouraging greater thinking" about its fundamentals. In these fundamentals, he said, "there is no difference between the two great parties." The role of the parties was merely to provide a choice between "two different methods in the application" of those fundamentals. "Therefore," he said, "I belong to neither."

Eisenhower's loyalty to the army and to Columbia University affected his views on partisanship. "I have been a soldier—necessarily without political affiliation—all my life," he wrote. Having been educated and trained by his government to perform that role, he felt a duty to provide his counsel "no matter what political party might happen to be in power at the moment." Furthermore, he felt an obligation to assist in the "aspirations and the welfare of our veterans of World War II." Since those veterans were both Democrats and Republicans, he believed they would have greater confidence that he was doing everything he could for them if he refused party membership. Eisenhower also felt an obligation to Columbia. Having accepted the presidency, he wrote, "I do not believe it appropriate for me to proclaim a loyalty to a political party." At Columbia, and among its alumni and supporters, there were "men and women of all parties." He recognized that "joining a specific party would certainly antagonize some" and prevent him not only from serving the institution well, but from using the university's resources to promote his beliefs.[15]

Although Eisenhower gave equal weight to the army and Columbia in his diary exposition on partisanship, it soon became clear that his connection to the army was greater. As Eisenhower's biographers have demonstrated, the general had a difficult time adjusting to the academic world. Columbia University's board of trustees retained control of big-picture decision-making, leaving Eisenhower with the less familiar roles of fund-raising and entertaining, neither of which suited his strengths.[16] It was not long before his time and attention were once again on military matters. By early 1949, Eisenhower was commuting to Washington, DC, on a regular basis to consult with Secretary of Defense James Forrestal and the Joint Chiefs of Staff (JCS). He would continue this arrangement with Forrestal's successor Louis Johnson. The position of chairman of the JCS had not yet been created, but Eisenhower was essentially filling this role, and his responsibilities were about to expand dramatically.[17]

Supreme Allied Commander

On June 25, 1950, North Korea invaded South Korea, and President Truman quickly committed the United States to the defense of the south. The United Nations (UN) backed this commitment, and several member nations sent troops. With the United States at war, Truman relied heavily on his World War II generals. He put General Douglas MacArthur in command of UN forces in Korea and, a short time later, replaced Secretary of Defense Louis

Johnson with General George Marshall, who had retired in 1949 after serving as secretary of state. Truman also had a job in mind for Eisenhower.

On October 28, Truman discussed with Eisenhower the possibility of becoming SACEUR. The North Atlantic Treaty Organization (NATO) had been formed in April 1949, but the integrated military structure it envisioned had not yet been created and no commander had been named to lead it. Truman believed Eisenhower was the only one with the international prestige to succeed in this role. Eisenhower recorded his reaction in his diary later that day: "I am a soldier and I am ready to respond to whatever orders . . . the president, as commander in chief, may care to issue to me."[18] As for his feelings about the job of organizing NATO into a collective security force that could contain the Soviet Union, Eisenhower believed it was of the gravest importance. "I rather look upon this effort as about the last remaining chance for the survival of Western civilization," he wrote to Swede Hazlett.[19]

Eisenhower had several important matters to attend to before departing for the Supreme Headquarters Allied Powers Europe (SHAPE), located in Rocquencourt, a suburb of Paris. One was his presidency of Columbia. The board of trustees refused Eisenhower's resignation and granted him an indefinite leave of absence while he performed his NATO duties. Two others would be more complicated. "Since the announcement of my appointment to the Supreme Command, I had been pondering what I could do to stop once and for all the speculation about my possible candidacy for the Presidency," he recalled in *At Ease*. There was something else on his mind as well. "I felt I should try to persuade, in person, those opposed to our participation in the military defense of Europe."[20]

Most of the opposition to sending a large American force to Europe was within the Republican Party, and the leader of that opposition was Senator Robert Taft of Ohio, who had voted against U.S. participation in NATO. Taft was also the leading candidate for the Republican nomination for president in 1952. Eisenhower hoped "it might be possible . . . to kill two birds with one stone" by meeting with Taft. "My first purpose was to be assured that when I got to Europe, the United States government's position would be solid in support of NATO. If such assurance were forthcoming, from the chief spokesman of what seemed to be the opposition, there was a way to kill off any further speculation about me as a candidate for the presidency."[21]

Before his early February meeting with Taft, Eisenhower, with the help of two staff officers, wrote a statement that he would issue if Taft convinced him that he accepted U.S. participation in the collective defense of Western Europe. The statement "was so strong that, if made public, any political future for me thereafter would be impossible." When Taft arrived the two men had a long talk. Eisenhower asked the senator if he would "support the concept of collective security for the North Atlantic community." He explained that if Taft said yes, then he would be content to spend his "next years" at SHAPE. If Taft said no, then NATO would suffer and "I would probably be back." The implications could not have been lost on Taft, but despite Eisenhower's best attempt to persuade him, he would not commit himself. When Taft left, the general called in the staff officers who had helped him draft the statement and "tore it up in front of them." Without Taft's assurances, he wrote, "it would be silly for me to throw away whatever political influence I might possess."[22]

By the fall of 1950, a small group had formed with the objective of securing the Republican presidential nomination for Eisenhower. Among its founders were Brigadier General Edwin Clark, who had been a member of Eisenhower's wartime staff and was now an attorney in New York, Massachusetts senator Henry Cabot Lodge, and James Duff. These three men met with Eisenhower several times in November and December of 1950, before the general took up his position at SHAPE.[23] Another member of the group was New York governor Tom Dewey, the Republican nominee for president in 1944 and 1948. Dewey understood that public association with him would be a liability for Eisenhower, so he remained in the background, relying on Lucius Clay to relay messages to the general. Eisenhower had known Clay since the late 1930s when they both served in the Philippines under Douglas MacArthur. Clay had succeeded Eisenhower as the military governor of the U.S. occupation zone in Germany—a position he still held at the time of the Berlin airlift. Association with these men led historian William Pickett to state that "by the time Eisenhower departed for his new military command, he was deeply involved with individuals and organizations who yearned for his presidential candidacy."[24]

So, when Eisenhower departed for Paris in February 1951, he had left the door open to a future political career. Through that door came a steady stream of visitors and an abundance of mail. Each caller and correspondent attempted to convince the general that he should return home as soon as possible to run for president. Since Eisenhower had no personal ambition to be president, one might reasonably ask why he did not simply close that door. The answer requires an understanding of duty as Eisenhower understood it. Eisenhower felt a strong sense of duty to his current job as SACEUR. But if he were to be offered the Republican Party's presidential nomination, it would present him with a transcendent duty, and he would have to accept. Many of those who encouraged Eisenhower to run for president did not fully grasp his sense of duty and did not understand why he could not give them a straight yes or no answer.

In May 1951, Clay sent Eisenhower a detailed memorandum from Governor Dewey, who he referred to only as "our friend." In the memorandum, Dewey used a code to refer to others who were laying the groundwork for a presidential campaign. In this code Senator Duff was "A." At this time the code went only to "D," but it was eventually expanded to "S." The memo covered topics such as leadership, fund-raising, and the appropriate time for Eisenhower to return home and announce his candidacy. In his cover letter, Clay wrote "I hope you will let me know that it is satisfactory for me to proceed." He assured the general that the steps recommended by Dewey could be done "without direct commitment from you" but was adamant that "we must move . . . there will be no one else who can unite this nation."[25]

Eisenhower's mission as SACEUR—organizing the military establishments of NATO's twelve member nations into a unified force for the collective security of the North Atlantic community—was an exceedingly difficult one. But it was a job that Eisenhower was uniquely qualified for and one that he personally believed was vital to the defense of the United States and its allies. He also understood that partisan political activity would not only violate army regulations but put his mission at risk. It was within this context that Eisenhower responded to Clay. "It is obvious that I cannot serve in this complex and critical military post if I should make a declaration of party affiliation or political interest," he wrote on May 30. "As I have understood the reasoning of both 'Our Friend' and 'A,' they have separately concluded that there could develop circumstances that would leave me no opportunity of remaining aloof from all these problems. They seem to visualize a situation that would obviously represent a higher call to duty than does even my present job." But Eisenhower had a different idea of what would represent a higher call, or a transcendent duty. "I am sure that none of them could imagine me in the role of assisting, even remotely, in bringing about such circumstances." So, although Eisenhower believed that a presidential nomination would present him with a transcendent duty, he felt no duty to campaign for one. As for what the unnamed individuals referred to in the memo should do in his absence, Eisenhower wrote that they had a right to do as they pleased. "I am not going to make any comment . . . publicly or privately, on what they may or may not do in advancing what they believe to be the best interests of our country."[26]

In June 1951, a Gallup poll showed that Democrats preferred Eisenhower over Truman 43 percent to 18 percent and Republicans preferred Eisenhower over Taft 38 percent to 27 percent. In response, Eisenhower's suitors became more persistent. To save time, the general developed a standard paragraph that he used in replies to those who implored him to declare his party preference and enter the race:

> The job I am on requires the support of the vast body of Americans. For me to admit, while in this post, or to imply a partisan political loyalty would properly be resented by thinking Americans and would be doing a disservice to our country, for *it would interfere with the job to which the country has assigned me.* The successful outcome of this venture is too vital to our welfare in the years ahead to permit any semblance of partisan allegiance on the part of the United States Military Commander in SHAPE.[27]

The Duff Letter

On September 4, Lodge visited the general in Paris. According to Eisenhower, this was one of seventy-eight meetings devoted to politics in the fall of 1951. This one, however, stands out. Lodge reviewed the Democratic Party's success in the last five presidential elections. He believed that another Republican defeat would lead to the collapse of the two-party system, which was "vital to the ultimate preservation of our national institutions." In addition to the systemic damage, Lodge lamented other consequences of successive Democratic administrations: "Gradual but steady accumulation of power in Washington, increased 'paternalism' in government's relations with the citizens, constant deficit spending, and a steady erosion in the value of our currency." These were all fears that Eisenhower shared.[28]

Shifting the discussion to the shortcomings of the Republican Party, Lodge made an argument that resonated even more strongly with Eisenhower. It's leadership, he said, had been taken over by the "Old Guard." Isolationists like Taft, who opposed sending American troops to Europe for the purpose of collective security, "made the party appear unaware of the realities of the modern world." What was needed, he concluded, was a Republican candidate who could "achieve at least a partial reversal of the trend toward centralization in government, irresponsible spending . . . and at the same time avoid the fatal errors of isolationism." To be elected, this candidate would need to be popular enough to win not only Republican votes, but those of independents and discriminating Democrats as well. "You," Lodge said to Eisenhower, "are the only one who can be elected by the Republicans to the presidency. You *must* permit the use of your name in the upcoming primaries."[29]

By this time Ike was used to such demands, but there was something different about Lodge's visit. "He argued with the tenacity of a bulldog and pounded away on this theme until, as he left, I said I would 'think the matter over.'" At the time he said this, Eisenhower thought he was merely saying what he needed to say to get Lodge out the door. He did not feel as though he had changed his thinking about running "in the slightest." But as he looked back on this visit with Lodge, he thought of it as a turning point. "For the first time I had allowed the slightest break in a regular practice of returning a flat refusal to any kind of proposal that I become an active participant. From that time onward, both alone and through correspondence, I began to look anew—perhaps subconsciously—at myself and politics."[30]

Lodge's visit to Paris laid the groundwork for a request from James Duff, now representing Pennsylvania in the U.S. Senate. Duff, in a memorandum to those working to secure the Republican nomination for Eisenhower, wrote that he was convinced that Taft's wide support among party regulars, along with the party's procedures for selecting delegates, "almost necessarily eliminates the possibility of [an Eisenhower] draft either before or at the convention." It was imperative, he believed, for Eisenhower to give "definite and unqualified assurance" to a small group of people "that he will be a candidate on the Republican ticket" and "commit himself unqualifiedly to a campaign." Such an assurance would allow a national organization to be formed without members fearing that Eisenhower would, at some late date, issue a rejection of their activities on his behalf. "The preservation of the two-party system and the future and security of the nation" required Eisenhower's leadership. Clark agreed to go to Paris and seek such assurances.[31]

Clark arrived in Paris on October 13 and met with the general at SHAPE that afternoon. He explained Duff's request for something in writing that would provide the assurances his supporters needed. The two men later went to Eisenhower's home, the Villa-St. Pierre, in Marnes-la-Coquette and continued their conversation after dinner. According to Clark, he was able to convince Eisenhower to provide such assurances that evening, and the two of them made plans to draft a letter the following morning.[32] The letter, quoted at the beginning of this chapter, was addressed to Senator Duff. In it, Eisenhower confirmed that he was a Republican and that he would regard a presidential nomination by the Republican Party a duty that would "transcend any other duty." He said he would do nothing to gain such a nomination, but if it were given to him, he would resign his commission and campaign for the office. He stated no objection to the senator and other like-minded people organizing themselves for the purpose of securing such a nomination. In closing, Eisenhower said that the letter, marked "personal and secret," was for his assurance and not for public release.[33]

By the time Eisenhower and Clark had finished the letter a large group had gathered to celebrate Ike's sixty-first birthday. The general joined the celebrants, and Clark returned to New York where he showed the letter to Senator Duff. Afterward he put the letter in a safe deposit box. Presumably, Duff and Clark referred to the letter to assure others that Eisenhower was a Republican and would accept the nomination if it was offered to him, but the letter itself stayed locked up. Based on an interview with Clark, historian William Ewald reported the existence of the Duff letter in his 1981 book *Eisenhower the President*, but Clark never showed Ewald the letter. After Clark's death, Ewald contacted the executor of his estate, who found and showed him the letter. In 1993, Ewald published the letter in its entirety in the *New York Times Magazine*.[34]

Just two days after Eisenhower wrote the Duff letter, Taft declared his presidential candidacy and the race for the nomination began. It is tempting to interpret the Duff letter as a decision on Eisenhower's part to run for president. The letter was an important turning point for Eisenhower, but as with Lodge's September visit, he does not seem to have realized it at the time. He had given Duff and other insiders the assurances that would, for a brief time, satisfy them, but Eisenhower himself was still conflicted. Two weeks after the Duff letter he wrote a long diary entry laying out the pros and cons of running. Eisenhower had met that day with "several individuals who brought up the political struggle in the United States." Their presentation had provided the general with the arguments in favor of entering the race: (1) without serious opposition Taft would win the nomination before the convention; (2) Taft could not win the presidency—Truman would beat him easily; (3) four more years of Democratic government would put the country "so far on the road to socialism that there will be no return"; and (4) the only way to prevent this from happening would be for Eisenhower to return to the United States, enter the race, and win the nomination. In response to these arguments in favor of running, Eisenhower offered his own reasons why he should not: (1) "I do not want to be president of the United States"; (2) he currently held a job that he believed was very important for the future of the country; (3) while holding that job, he did not believe he had any right to engage in politics; and (4) he would not leave his current position to seek high political office "except in response to a clear call to duty."[35]

The conflict between number one, not wanting to be president, and number four, having a sense of duty that would require him to do something he did not want to do, defines Eisenhower's struggle during this period. On the same day as this diary entry, he wrote letters to his friend Bill Robinson and his brother Milton. Robinson had recently written an editorial for the *New York Herald Tribune* endorsing Eisenhower for the presidency. The reason he was writing, he told them, "is to let you know that there has been no fundamental change in my thinking over the past several years because you both have known that I have always been ready to respond instantly to anything I saw as a clear duty. On the other hand, you both have known my complete lack of desire or ambition for any kind of political career."[36] He let them know that he was planning a quick trip to the United States later in the week and would like to see the two of them. In a separate letter to Milton he added, "there have been a few small developments of which I think that you are unaware," likely a reference to the Duff letter.[37]

The official reason for Eisenhower's early November trip to the United States was to make the case for additional tanks and other equipment necessary for the six armored U.S. divisions he was preparing for NATO. To this end, during his day in Washington he spent the morning at the Pentagon, had lunch with President Truman, and met with the NSC. The press, however, was more interested in Eisenhower's political future, and they questioned him mercilessly about it. Given Eisenhower's determination to make no political statements while still in uniform, he found this very frustrating. Immediately after his meeting with Truman, rumors circulated that the president had again urged Eisenhower to run for president as a Democrat, an assertion that Eisenhower flatly denied.[38] Despite his refusal to discuss politics publicly, however, his political future was on the agenda for the trip. He had breakfast with political confidant Lucius Clay, and a three-hour meeting with Bill Robinson, Cliff Roberts, and Milton Eisenhower in his plane on the tarmac at New York's La Guardia airport. At these meetings Eisenhower confirmed the statements he had made in the Duff letter. He had taken another significant step toward candidacy.

In the days and weeks following his trip home the effort to make Eisenhower president of the United States became more organized. A suggestion from Cliff Roberts led to the creation of a personal advisory committee. Roberts, Bill Robinson, and

Milton Eisenhower would be the key members of this group that placed Eisenhower's personal interests above efforts to make him president. On November 10, Duff, Clay, and Herbert Brownell met with Tom Dewey to set up a formal campaign organization. They chose Lodge as chairman, put Brownell in charge of delegate strategy, and also created a finance committee and a Citizens-for-Eisenhower group. Dewey would continue to stay out of the spotlight, while Clay and Clark would act as liaisons between the official group and Eisenhower. Headquarters of the Eisenhower for President organization would be the Hotel Commodore in New York City. Eisenhower made personal recommendations for members of both groups.[39]

Having assured key individuals of his party affiliation and his willingness to run if drafted and having participated in the establishment of his campaign organization, Eisenhower may have hoped that he could leave politics to the professionals and focus exclusively on his duties as SACEUR until such time that he was the recipient of a draft by the Republican Party. Although he was already in violation of army regulations, he was determined not to jeopardize the success of NATO by publicly associating himself with the efforts to make him president. The politicians were only briefly satisfied, however, and it was not long before Ike was complaining to Roberts that they were trying to drag him into politics. He warned of an impending "head-on collision" between what the politicians wanted him to do—campaign for the nomination—and what he believed was his duty: to carry on as SACEUR until called to a transcendent duty. "Some of these political enthusiasts are trying to make it appear that I have a duty to *seek* a nomination," he wrote. "This is ridiculous."[40]

The head-on collision Ike feared turned out to be a near miss. On December 3, Lodge wrote to Eisenhower, telling him, "It is becoming vital that you appear and speak in various parts of the United States. People want to know what you think from your own lips. . . . Talk of a draft is no good anymore." He even warned that failure to do so helped Taft, who was being praised for his willingness to discuss the issues.[41] Eisenhower did not immediately respond, taking a few days to think it over. In his diary he wrote, "A day or so ago I received a comforting letter from Cabot Lodge. . . . He says that the project is hopeless without my active *pre-convention* cooperation! That settles the whole matter! . . . Since I cannot in good conscience quit here, my reaction is 'Hurrah.' I've just prepared a letter to Cabot saying that he and his friends must stop the whole thing, now."[42] In his letter to Lodge, he wrote "I accept, without reservation, your observations and comments on the political scene at home; you fully convince me of the impracticability of nominating an individual who, for any reason, must remain inactive in the political field prior to the national conventions. . . . Since my current responsibilities make pre-convention activity impossible for me, the program in which you and your close political associates are now engaged should, logically, be abandoned."[43] Lodge's response made clear that he had gotten the message. "Although some public word or intimation may well be eventually desirable," he wrote, "I have always understood the grave difficulties involved in having you participate actively in a political contest at this time."[44] Eisenhower's follow-up suggests his earlier letter may have been a bluff. He wrote that Lodge's letter "assures me that you clearly understand the position I shall maintain with respect to the effort you and your friends are making."[45]

This exchange of letters with Lodge, the chairman of the Eisenhower for President committee, is fascinating for several reasons. First, it shows that Eisenhower was serious about his unwillingness to publicly engage in politics while serving as SACEUR. Second, it shows that in both his diary and his correspondence he maintained that this was all happening without his participation, although we know this was not the case. Finally, it shows that Eisenhower did not believe that things had gone so far that he could not shut the operation down if he decided to.

On December 28, Eisenhower received a handwritten letter from President Truman. "Do what's best for the country," Truman wrote. "My own position is in the balance. If I do what I want to do I'll go back to Missouri and maybe run for the Senate. If you decide to finish the European job (and I don't know who else can) I must keep the isolationists out of the White House. I wish you would let me know what you intend to do. It will be between us and no one else."[46] If taken at face value, Truman sincerely wanted to know what Ike's intentions were, so that he could make his own plans. Eisenhower responded in kind. He wrote that he was "deeply touched" to have received such a letter from the president of the United States. Paraphrasing Truman's "if I do what I want to do" line, Ike said that he "would like to live a semi-retired life with my family. . . . But just as you have decided that circumstances may not permit you to do exactly as you please, so I've found that fervent desire may sometimes have to give way to a conviction of duty." As he had to others, he said that he felt no duty to seek a nomination and would not do so. Moreover, he would abstain from politics "unless and until extraordinary circumstances would place a mandate upon me that, by common consent, would be deemed a duty of transcendent importance." All of this, while obscuring Eisenhower's participation in the efforts of those seeking the nomination on his behalf, was consistent with what he had been saying all along. One line of his letter to the president does, however, stretch the truth a bit. "The possibility that I will ever be drawn into political activity," he wrote, "is so remote as to be negligible."[47]

Moving toward Candidacy

Readers unfamiliar with the mid-twentieth-century presidential nomination process will likely assume that January of an election year is too late to begin a campaign. It is true that the new year would make it more difficult for Eisenhower to conceal his participation, but he still had plenty of time. In 1952, only thirteen states held Republican primaries, and only 39 percent of the delegates were pledged to candidates before the national convention in July. In comparison, 96 percent of the delegates to the national convention were pledged before the July 2020 national convention.

On December 17, New Hampshire governor Sherman Adams had written a letter to Lodge inquiring about Eisenhower's party affiliation. By law, he explained, the names of individuals on the ballot for New Hampshire's March 11 primary "shall be printed solely on petition of New Hampshire voters of the same party as the prospective candidates." On behalf of the Eisenhower for President committee, and with Eisenhower's authorization and input, Lodge responded on January 4 that "during 1948, 1949, and 1950, while he [Eisenhower] was serving as president of Columbia University, we several times discussed with him subjects of political and economic importance to the nation. During these discussions, he specifically informed us that his voting record was that of a Republican." He explained that army regulations prohibited the general from engaging in any political activity and that the committee was "working to produce a clear-cut call to duty without participation on his part." He concluded by saying that the signers of the petitions to put Eisenhower's name on the ballot "are completely secure in their signed sworn statement that General Eisenhower is a member of their party."[48] At a press conference on January 6, Lodge made his response to Adams public, and his letter was printed in the *New York Times* the following day. On that day the *Times* also endorsed Eisenhower for the presidency. At his press conference, Lodge said that if reporters needed further confirmation, they should get it from the general.[49]

The following day, Eisenhower released a brief statement confirming what Lodge had attested to. Although the *New York Times* headline proclaimed, "Eisenhower Will Accept a G.O.P. Call," the general's statement did not resemble the declaration of an enthusiastic candidate. Eisenhower said that Lodge's announcement had given "an accurate account" of his political convictions and Republican voting record. He also said that he would not campaign or participate in any preconvention activities. He understood that Senator Lodge and his associates were attempting to place before him a duty that would "transcend" his present responsibilities. In its absence, however, he would devote his full attention to NATO.[50]

The same day he made his statement, Eisenhower wrote a letter to Clay expressing his annoyance that he had been forced to do so. "I was caught in a bit of a trap since the press representative *insisted* that Senator Lodge had said I was prepared to corroborate his statement," he wrote. He found this "puzzling" since it was his understanding that "nothing further would be required of me." He had resigned himself to the fact that the reporters would want him to confirm what Lodge had said but "was astonished to find that *apparently*, in response to questions, both senators [Lodge and Duff] had *urged* reporters to refer the whole matter to me."[51] In his diary, he added "I don't give a d— how impossible a 'draft' may be. I'm willing to go part way in trying to recognize a 'duty'—but I do not have to seek one—and I will *not*."[52]

Having taken the significant step of allowing his name to be entered in the New Hampshire primary, Eisenhower's personal correspondence and diary entries for the next two months lead one to believe that he regretted his decision and even resented those who he believed had led him to this point. In a letter to Robinson, he even wondered if Lodge and his associates were, perhaps, "inept," "stupid," "hopeless," or "futile."[53] It was not until mid-March that something happened to make him feel like the whole thing may be worthwhile. On February 8, an event billed as a "Serenade to Ike" was held at Madison Square Garden in New York City. Due to its 11:30 p.m. start—the event could not begin until the attendees of a boxing match had left the arena—city officials had not anticipated a large turnout. To their surprise, more than fifteen thousand people attended the "serenade." The rally was not an official Eisenhower for President event. It was organized by various citizens organizations and led by "stage, screen, radio, and television stars." According to the *New York Times*, the crowd "showed great enthusiasm with frequent shouts of 'I Like Ike.'"[54] One of the event's organizers, celebrity aviator Jacqueline Cochran, had arranged for a film to be made of the event and, as soon as it was ready, brought it to Paris. On February 11, Eisenhower reported that she had arrived and was "burning with enthusiasm and the spirit of a crusader."[55] Ike watched the film that night, and the next day he wrote in his diary that viewing it "developed into a real emotional experience for Mamie and me. I've not been so upset in years."[56] His correspondence over the next week includes many references to the film. To Clay he wrote, "I think for the first time, there came home to me something of what it means to be the object of interest to a great section of packed humanity. Both of us are deeply touched, not to say moved."[57]

Eisenhower's attitude toward the presidential race noticeably improved after Cochran's visit. It even seemed that he was giving some consideration to campaigning before the convention. In a letter to a member of his personal advisory group, he admitted that "it could be argued . . . if I were to feel it my duty to accept a nomination, that I owe it to the voters to give them something substantial on which to base their decision."[58] On the same day he wrote a long letter to Robinson, presenting his views on the long-term damage caused by high federal tax rates. This was in response to requests from Robinson and others that he make his positions on domestic issues known to the public. In letters like this he sought to clarify his own thoughts for a friendly audience, seeking advice and criticism.[59] "As you can see," he wrote in a letter the following week to Clay, "my attitude has undergone a quite significant change since viewing the movie of the Madison Square Garden show and listening to your day long presentation of the activities now going forward in the United States."[60]

The presentation Eisenhower referred to had occurred in London, where the general and Clay had both attended the funeral of King George VI. In his presentation, Clay had suggested a timeline of events that Eisenhower was more comfortable with than those previously offered. As of mid-February, Clay believed, Eisenhower and Taft each had about half of the committed delegates. Those remaining would not commit until June or July. Eisenhower, therefore, should stay in Europe and avoid the mudslinging that would accompany a futile struggle in the spring. He could then return in June, undamaged from a campaign, and capture most of the remaining delegates. Although Eisenhower had been adamant that he would not take part in any preconvention activities, he was beginning to accept that it would be necessary, and Clay's timeline held out the possibility that he could complete his duty at SHAPE before returning home. He "tentatively agreed" to Clay's timeline but reserved the right to determine his own date of return.[61]

On March 11, despite heavy rain and snow, turnout for the New Hampshire primary was excellent. Eisenhower won 50 percent of the vote, and Taft, despite hard campaigning during a three-day tour of the state, won only 38 percent. Eisenhower also won all fourteen of the states' convention delegates. On the Democratic side, Senator Estes Kefauver (TN) pulled off a surprising win over President Truman. Eisenhower received word of his New Hampshire victory on an airplane returning to Paris after a trip to Germany, but on his arrival, he told the reporters who surrounded his plane that he did not know how the primary had turned out. They were excited to share the results with him, offering their sincere congratulations and allowing the general to bask in his victory.[62]

Eisenhower benefitted from an even more impressive outcome the next week in Minnesota. There were only two candidates for the Republican nomination on the ballot. One was Harold Stassen, the former governor of Minnesota. Stassen believed that someone had to stop Taft and the isolationists from taking over the party leadership but had assured Eisenhower of his support should Ike decide to run. The other candidate on the ballot was Edward Slettedahl, a public-school teacher. Stassen won the primary with 43 percent of the vote. Eisenhower, without any organized effort on the part of his campaign, received an incredible 81,840 write-in votes, enough for 38 percent of the total and a second-place finish. Taft, also a write-in candidate, came in a distant third with 8 percent of the vote. Speaking to reporters at SHAPE the following day, Ike told them he was "astonished" by the result and said, "The mounting numbers of my fellow citizens who are voting to make me the Republican nominee are forcing me to re-examine my personal position and past decisions." He was delighted that some voters, perhaps unsure of the spelling of his name, had simply written in "Ike."[63]

On March 24, Brownell arrived in Paris, and the next day he spent ten hours with Eisenhower. Brownell had managed Dewey's

1944 and 1948 campaigns and had also served as chairman of the Republican National Committee. Brownell told Eisenhower that, in his opinion, he could win the presidency. But he also told him that "it was entirely unrealistic to expect a draft. He would have to fight for the nomination." Brownell explained that Taft already had 40 percent of the delegates, with the remaining delegates available for a moderate delegate like himself, Stassen, or California governor Earl Warren, both of whom were campaigning. "If Eisenhower did not soon declare publicly that he was a candidate," Brownell told him, "Taft would be the nominee." To be successful, he suggested that Eisenhower "return to the United States at least a month before the convention, declare himself a candidate, speak in various parts of the country on the issues, and above all meet personally with as many delegates as possible before and at the convention." Brownell later recalled that this appeared to surprise the general, and he believed that the conversation was an "important turning point for him."[64]

Brownell's visit may have been a turning point for Eisenhower, but the analysis he shared cannot have been too great a surprise. It did not differ significantly from what Clay had told him in London, and he had already told Clay and others that he would "attempt" a June 1 return.[65] He had also told the press that he would have to "rethink" his January 7 statement as a result of the New Hampshire and Minnesota primaries. After Brownell's departure, Eisenhower wrote Clay. "Mr. Brownell," he said, did not press too hard for a May 15 date, "although he was quite certain that June 1st would be just about the limit. . . . My thought is that your group should not commit me to anything during the month of May. To make my move home and get settled, I shall have to remain in uniform that long. . . . And during that period, I could make only the most non-partisan of talks." Following this typewritten sentence, he had added in his own handwriting: "Preferably none."[66] Eisenhower made his departure imminent on April 2 with a letter to President Truman. "I am requesting the Secretary of Defense to initiate action to bring about relief from my current post as Supreme Commander, Allied Powers Europe, on or about June 1st of this year," it began. He explained that although the work of SHAPE would not be finished by that time, "the special organizational and initial planning missions that were deemed critical in the late weeks of 1950 have now been accomplished." The June 1 date, he explained, would give him time to complete the projects that he was handling personally, orient his successor, and make a final visit to the capital of each NATO state. Although he did not specifically say that he was coming home to run for president, he did admit that "political incidents" had influenced the timing of the request. "In the event that I should be nominated for high political office," he added, "my resignation as an officer of the Army will be instantly submitted to you for your approval." By this time there is no doubt that Truman, who had just announced that he would not be seeking another term, understood Eisenhower was already running for president.[67]

Eisenhower announced his departure to the public on April 11 and spent the remainder of his time in Europe carrying out the duties that he had outlined in his letter to Truman. He did his best to avoid purely political activity during his remaining time in uniform but, nonetheless, appeared very presidential while meeting with the NATO heads of state. On Sunday, June 1, he arrived in Washington, DC, where he was greeted with a seventeen-gun salute. After two days of ceremonies and meetings, including a Truman-led tour of his future home, the newly remodeled White House, Eisenhower left the capital for his hometown of Abilene, Kansas.

It would be convenient to conclude a chapter on Eisenhower's decision to run for president by quoting a speech in which he made that long-awaited declaration: "I am a candidate for president of the United States." Interestingly, he never made such a declaration. In the speech he made in Abilene on June 4, Eisenhower spoke more openly about his political beliefs than ever before, and at a press conference the next day, he was even more overtly political.[68] But, although it was clear to everyone that he was now running for president, he did not announce his candidacy. When asked if he thought he could defeat Taft for the nomination he replied, "I haven't the slightest idea," but at least he had not rejected the premise of the question. In fact, he said that he had come home because "it was impossible for me to remain there and at the same time to carry on in the status that I had allowed to be set up for me in the United States." This was as close to an admission that he had participated in the creation of his campaign that he would make.[69]

During the month between his speech in Abilene and the Republican convention, Eisenhower spent the majority of his time in places that he would have had a reason to be regardless of the campaign: his residence in New York City, his farm in Gettysburg, Pennsylvania, and Denver, Colorado, where Mamie's parents lived. The few speeches he made, like the one in Abilene, were political, but they did not directly criticize Taft or Truman. This would allow him, and future historians, to claim that he had been the recipient of a genuine draft. But Eisenhower's nomination was not a foregone conclusion, and despite his insistence that he would never engage in preconvention campaigning, the general spent most of the month before the convention meeting with delegates. As John Robert Greene argued in *I Like Ike*, without the strategy put in place by his campaign committee, particularly Lodge and

Brownell, Eisenhower could easily have lost the nomination to Taft. If Eisenhower had not returned, even that strategy may not have been enough.[70]

Eisenhower was not drafted at the convention, as some early historians of his presidency claimed. Although he did not campaign for the nomination, he did give aid and encouragement to those who sought the nomination on his behalf. This type of activity is consistent with other aspects of his presidency that have been revealed by Eisenhower revisionists. Although some admirers of Eisenhower might prefer to believe that he was the recipient of a genuine convention draft, his participation in the campaign should not detract from his reputation. He decided to run out of an extraordinary sense of duty—he truly had no ambition to hold the office. He feared that if Robert Taft became president, it would risk everything he had worked for as supreme allied commander, both during the war and after. He also feared that if a Democrat were elected president it would lead to the breakdown of the two-party system and perpetuate the centralization of power in the federal government. Originally, he believed that only the nomination of his party would present him with a transcendent duty to run. However, when he realized that such a nomination was possible, but not assured, he made the decision to return to the United States and play a more active role. Eisenhower had found balance between what others were demanding of him and what he believed was his duty to his country. Eisenhower's presidency suggests that we would do well to identify candidates who balance their personal and partisan goals with a similar commitment to duty.

3

Pursuing the Middle Way

Early in his presidency, Eisenhower wrote a letter to his good friend retired brigadier general Bradford Chynoweth, in which he explained his philosophy of the Middle Way.

> We have those individuals who believe that the federal government should enter into every phase and facet of our individual lives. . . . These people, knowingly or unknowingly, are trying to put us on the path toward socialism. At the other extreme we have the people . . . who want to eliminate everything that the federal government has ever done that . . . represents what is generally classified as social advance. When I refer to the Middle Way, I merely mean the middle way as it represents a practical working basis between extremists, both of whose doctrines I flatly reject. . . . The generality that I advance is merely this: Excluding the field of moral values, anything that affects or is proposed for masses of humans is wrong if the position it seeks is at either end of possible argument.[1]

Eisenhower's pursuit of the Middle Way often put him at odds with the conservative wing of the Republican Party. This aspect of his presidency, however, was not appreciated by historians for nearly a generation. Early historians of his administration took note of Republican intraparty rivalries, but they did not identify the president as an active participant in them. This led them to conclude that he was a weak president and an ineffective party leader.[2] In the 1970s, revisionists began to challenge this interpretation.[3] Making use of materials at the newly opened Eisenhower Presidential Library, they suggested that if Eisenhower failed to solve the great problems of the day, it was not due to a lack of initiative on his part. Instead, it was due to the opposition of conservatives within his party.

By the 1980s, historians considered Eisenhower's fight with the party's Old Guard one of the primary themes of his administration.[4] Conservative opposition to the president's initiatives in social welfare, farm and labor issues, public works, and many other issues revealed their fundamental disagreement with the president over the proper role of the federal government. Eisenhower's position on these issues placed him squarely in the middle of the American political spectrum—to the right of liberals who had supported Franklin Roosevelt, and to the left of conservatives in his own party. Since he had no expectation of support from the liberal wing of the Democratic Party, his fight was with those to his right.

In American political culture those who describe themselves as moderates are often portrayed as unwilling to take a stand or lacking in political sophistication. This was not the case with Eisenhower. His Middle Way was a carefully considered political philosophy—an attempt to find balance between the fears of conservatives and the demands of liberals. Despite his intentions, Eisenhower's domestic policy proposals were often defeated by an unwitting alliance of conservatives, who sought to limit the role of the federal government, and liberals, who wanted the federal government to do more than he proposed. Eisenhower hoped that his policies would change the direction of the Republican Party, but this was not to be.

Opposition from conservatives in his party made it necessary for Eisenhower to seek Democratic support for his legislative agenda. This was a difficult strategy in Eisenhower's time, and increased political polarization in the years since has made it even less likely to succeed. Further complicating matters is the increased use of the filibuster by the minority party in the Senate. It is now assumed that sixty votes—the number required to defeat a filibuster— are necessary for nearly anything to pass in the Senate.[5] So, even a president with a majority in both houses of Congress cannot count on legislative success. The unlikelihood of either party winning sixty seats in the Senate makes moderation and bipartisanship more important than ever.

Securing the Nomination and the Presidency

The 1952 Republican presidential nomination was a long-delayed battle between two factions for control of the party. An attempt to compete with Franklin Roosevelt's immense popularity had led to a string of liberal Republican presidential nominations: Alf Landon (1936), a former Bull Moose Progressive who had endorsed many New Deal programs; Wendell Willkie (1940), a former Democrat who had voted for Roosevelt in 1932; and Thomas Dewey (1944 and 1948), who supported the New Deal but thought that Republicans could administer it more efficiently. These candidates' failure to defeat Roosevelt, and Dewey's particularly embarrassing loss to President Truman in 1948, had made party conservatives determined to run one of their own—Ohio senator Robert Taft—in 1952.

As we have seen, Eisenhower's decision to enter the campaign for the Republican presidential nomination in 1952 was based, in large part, on his determination to prevent the nomination of Taft.

His primary concern was Taft's refusal to support NATO and U.S. participation in the collective security of Western Europe. He also believed that Taft's conservative positions on domestic issues were out of step with the views of most Americans. Taft's nomination, Eisenhower believed, would assure another Democratic victory and the breakdown of the two-party system, perpetuating the centralization of power in the federal government. Although he would have preferred to stay out of the campaign for the nomination, Eisenhower was ultimately convinced by his political advisers that doing so would assure Taft's nomination.

Herbert Brownell's warning to General Eisenhower that he would have to fight for the nomination proved correct. The lead story going into the Republican National Convention in Chicago was the large number of contested delegates. Texas had the most with thirty-eight, but six other states plus Puerto Rico brought the total number to seventy-five. The Republican National Committee (RNC) temporarily settled the issue of contested delegates in Taft's favor. This made the preconvention delegate tally 527 for Taft and 427 for Eisenhower, with 604 needed for the nomination. The final decision regarding contested delegates, however, would be determined by a series of votes from the convention floor. In these votes, contested delegates could vote on the status of contested delegates from other states, but not their own. To improve their chances of winning those votes, the Eisenhower campaign introduced an amendment to the rules of the convention that they called the "Fair Play Amendment." The Fair Play Amendment would prohibit the contested delegates from being seated at the convention until the issue had been settled. More important than the contested delegates themselves were the uncommitted delegates and those pledged to Harold Stassen and Earl Warren. How these delegates voted on the Fair

Play Amendment would be a good indicator of who the nominee would be.

Throughout the complicated process, Eisenhower's convention team, particularly Lodge and Brownell, proved themselves more adept than the Taft forces at using parliamentary procedure to their advantage. They were also more mindful of the importance of maintaining the ethical high ground, which was an important factor for uncommitted delegates. In what proved to be a test vote for the Fair Play Amendment, the convention rejected—648 to 548—a motion by Taft campaign manager Clarence Brown to have Louisiana, one of the states with contested delegates, excluded from the Fair Play Amendment. The uncommitted delegates sided with Eisenhower in this vote. After the rejection of Brown's motion, the Fair Play Amendment was adopted unanimously. With the Fair Play Amendment in place and the uncommitted delegates on his side, Eisenhower's convention team successfully challenged the RNC's decision on the contested delegations from Georgia and Texas. The momentum had clearly swung from Taft to Eisenhower.

On July 11, the convention voted on the presidential nomination. At the end of the first ballot, Eisenhower had 595 votes, Taft had 500, Warren 81, Stassen 20, and Douglas MacArthur 10. Eisenhower was nine votes short of the number needed for nomination. Stassen released his delegates, prompting the head of the Minnesota delegation to rise and ask for the floor. Earlier he had cast nineteen votes for Stassen and nine votes for Eisenhower. He now wished to change his vote, giving all twenty-eight to Eisenhower—more than enough for the nomination.[6] The general had unexpectedly won a first-ballot victory.

Despite a hard-fought battle for the nomination, Eisenhower's first instinct was to mend fences. Disregarding objections from some of his advisers, Eisenhower phoned Taft and asked to meet him at his hotel. A surprised Taft agreed and in "a trip that proved to be far more difficult physically" than he imagined, Eisenhower made his way down to the lobby of the Blackstone Hotel and across the street to the Conrad Hilton. The mood was much different there with "the crowds noticeably sorrowful and even resentful."[7] After a brief meeting with the senator, the two men spoke to reporters. "I want to congratulate General Eisenhower. I shall do everything possible in the campaign to secure his election and to help in his administration," Taft said graciously. Eisenhower responded in kind: "I came over to pay a call of friendship on a very great American. His willingness to cooperate is absolutely necessary to the success of the Republican party in the campaign and in the Administration to follow." Eisenhower's statement "brought a chorus of cheers" from Taft supporters. This was a welcome change from the "mixture of cheers and boos" that had greeted his arrival.[8]

Eisenhower had won the Republican nomination by a slim margin, but his victory in the general election was a landslide by any measure. In the Electoral College, Eisenhower defeated the Democratic candidate, Governor Adlai Stevenson of Illinois, 442–89. In the popular vote, Eisenhower had 34 million votes (55 percent) to Stevenson's 27.3 million (44.5 percent). A record 62 million Americans had voted (63.3 percent of eligible voters). Of particular note was Eisenhower's success in the South where he won four states of the former Confederacy, more than any Republican since the end of Reconstruction.

The Politics of the Middle Way

Republican success in the general election masked intense factionalism within the party. Eisenhower would be the first

Republican president in twenty years, but he was at odds with a growing faction of his own party. Conservatives, who had a considerable base of power on Capitol Hill, were eager to overturn a generation of liberal domestic policies and internationalist foreign policies. Central to the factional differences was the role of the federal government. Conservatives preferred free enterprise and individual initiative to federal programs and the taxes necessary to support them. When government action was unavoidable, they favored state or local control in areas where the federal government had no explicit constitutional power. In foreign policy, conservatives had not reverted to the isolationism they espoused before World War II, but they had not completely converted to internationalism either. They virulently opposed communism but did not see the benefits of collective security alliances or foreign aid programs.

Eisenhower, despite some of his campaign rhetoric, supported a more active role for the federal government in both domestic and foreign policy. He supported the continuation, and in some cases the expansion, of popular New Deal programs. When new programs were necessary, however, Eisenhower supported those that would allow the federal government to act as a catalyst for change without adding significantly to its responsibilities. This would allow government to look after the welfare of individuals and still maintain fiscal responsibility. It was, according to Eisenhower, "a liberal program in all of those things that bring the federal government in contact with the individual," but conservative when it came to "the economy of this country."[9] Somewhat less enthusiastically, Eisenhower also supported federal legislation that would protect the economic interests of farmers and organized labor, and the civil rights of African Americans. On foreign policy issues, Eisenhower was a committed internationalist.

To conservatives, the promotion of active government, both at home and abroad, seemed like a mere continuation of the Democratic policies of the previous twenty years, but that was not Eisenhower's intention. The key to understanding how Eisenhower distinguished his policies from those of liberal Democrats and conservative Republicans is his philosophy of the Middle Way. After he had secured the Republican nomination, Eisenhower began to speak more frequently about the Middle Way. In an October campaign speech, Eisenhower warned his audience about the dangers of going too far to the political left or right. Those on the left, he said, believed people were "so weak, so irresponsible, that an all-powerful government must direct and protect" them. The end of that road, he warned, was "dictatorship." On the right, were those "who deny the obligation of government to intervene on behalf of the people even when the complexities of modern life demand it." The end of that road was "anarchy." To avoid those extremes, he said, "government should proceed along the middle way."[10]

Many of Eisenhower's domestic policy proposals provide examples of his Middle Way philosophy.[11] It is the field of social welfare, however, that provides the sharpest contrast between Eisenhower and Republican conservatives who opposed him. Conservatives referred to his proposals in social welfare as "creeping socialism," but Eisenhower believed that by addressing the problems that threatened American society his programs would stem—not encourage—the impetus toward socialism. Eisenhower saw these programs as a safety net, "a floor over the pit of personal disaster in our complex modern society." Unlike socialism, however, they did not create a "ceiling" that limited initiative and industry.[12] They did not interfere with "the right . . . to build the most glorious structure on top of that floor."[13]

The Department of Health, Education, and Welfare

Searching for the Middle Way in the field of social welfare, Eisenhower attempted to provide for the general welfare, as called for in the Constitution, without taking on the enormous financial burdens of an ever-expanding welfare state or significantly encroaching on the responsibilities of local government. He was continually frustrated when his moderate programs were opposed by conservative Republicans anxious to overturn the legacy of the New Deal and by liberal Democrats unwilling to settle for less federal intervention than they would like. Eisenhower's only first-term social welfare success came in Social Security, an area where a program was already in place. His initiative in health insurance, which required a new program, failed at the hands of conservative Republicans and liberal Democrats. Leading the way in the formation of policy in this field was the new Department of Health, Education, and Welfare.

During the 1952 campaign, Eisenhower promised to study the problem of federal waste and mismanagement and, if elected, make recommendations for government reorganization.[14] Eisenhower asked Nelson Rockefeller, grandson of John D. Rockefeller, to chair a new Special Committee on Government Organization (SCGO). The other members of the committee were the president's brother Milton Eisenhower, president of Pennsylvania State University; and Arthur Flemming, president of Ohio Wesleyan University and former director of the Office of Defense Mobilization. The SCGO had a broad mandate to study and recommend changes in the organization and activities of the executive branch in order to promote economy and efficiency. Eisenhower's Middle Way served as the blueprint for the committee's recommendations. "We have been guided by your own expressed determination to avoid any actions which tend to make people ever more dependent upon the government and yet to make certain that the human side of our national problems is not forgotten," noted the committee's report.[15]

The first recommendation of the SCGO was the creation of a new cabinet-level department to absorb the functions of the Federal Security Agency (FSA). The FSA, created by Franklin Roosevelt in 1939, had thirty-eight thousand employees representing the Social Security System, the Food and Drug Administration, the Public Health Service, and the Office of Education. Despite a budget of $4.6 billion the FSA lacked cabinet status. The creation of a new department, the committee believed, would be "an important milestone on the road to social progress," making clear that the Republican Party recognized that the government responsibilities embodied by the FSA were permanent, providing "an excellent example of the beneficial functioning of our two-party system."[16] On March 12, 1953, Eisenhower delivered a special message to Congress requesting approval for the creation of the Department of Health, Education, and Welfare (HEW).[17]

Republicans had opposed President Truman's attempts to elevate the FSA to cabinet status in 1949 and 1950. For many Republicans, health and education were not legitimate areas of federal concern. Placing the Public Health Service and the Office of Education under the supervision of a cabinet department, particularly one oriented toward welfare, would only strengthen the federal bureaucracy's claim to legitimacy in these areas. The SCGO overcame these objections through decentralization. The plan for HEW did not place all of the department's powers in the hands of the secretary. The functions of the Public Health Service and the Office of Education, for example, remained in those agencies, which were subordinate divisions of the new department; the secretary would have only supervisory control.

There was very little opposition from either party to the creation of HEW. The measure won bipartisan support, and Eisenhower signed the bill creating the new department on April 11, 1953. Although Republican congressmen participated in the creation of HEW, they did not see themselves as acquiescing in the creation of a permanent welfare state. Rather, they were admitting that Social Security, the Food and Drug Administration, and the other components of HEW were an accepted and popular part of American society. Only the most conservative Republicans still favored their elimination.

Oveta Culp Hobby, whom Eisenhower had appointed head of the FSA, became HEW's first secretary. Hobby was a registered Democrat from Texas, but she had endorsed Eisenhower for president on the front page of the *Houston Post*, which she and her husband owned. Her appointment would reward the many southern Democrats who had crossed over to vote for Eisenhower and solidify the bipartisan credentials of the new department. Nelson Rockefeller, who had served in the Roosevelt and Truman administrations, would serve as undersecretary. Rockefeller believed that it was important for the Republican Party, which was so often associated with preserving the status quo, to demonstrate that the social gains of the New Deal era had bipartisan support and would be not only retained but improved upon by the Republican Party. "A Republican administration couldn't be seen to be trying to turn back the clock," he later recalled.[18]

As Eisenhower asserted in his campaign statements, he was definitely not in favor of turning back the clock. "I believe that the social gains achieved by the people of the United States, whether they were enacted by a Republican or a Democratic administration, are not only here to stay but are to be improved and expanded," Eisenhower noted during an October campaign stop. "Anyone who says it is my purpose to cut down Social Security, unemployment insurance, to leave the ill and aged destitute, is lying."[19] Despite these general principles, however, it was unclear to Hobby and Rockefeller where Eisenhower stood on the specific domestic policy debates that concerned HEW.

Expanding Social Security

Among the issues up for immediate consideration was the expansion of Social Security. Throughout the campaign, Eisenhower had promised, if elected, to extend coverage to groups not currently eligible for benefits.[20] He repeated this pledge in his first State of the Union address on February 3, 1953.[21] What was unclear was whether Eisenhower favored expansion of the system in its current form or if he preferred the "pay-as-you-go" plan that the 1952 Republican platform said deserved a "thorough study."[22] Under the current system, benefits for the elderly were paid using the same framework that had been established by the Social Security Act of 1935. This act created a federally operated, compulsory, old-age pension program. Qualified workers paid for the program with a payroll tax matched by their employer. Proceeds were placed in a federal trust account. At the age of sixty-five, those workers became eligible for monthly payments relative to the amount they had contributed to the program over the years.

The pay-as-you-go plan, promoted by the U.S. Chamber of Commerce and endorsed by many conservatives, was an attempt to create a universal coverage, old-age pension funded by current revenues. Under this plan all employed workers would be subject to the existing payroll tax and all elderly persons would be eligible for a flat-rate pension, regardless of their employment history. The cost of starting up the program would be paid for with the existing trust account, and all future benefits would be paid from that year's contributions. In his 1953 budget message, Eisenhower had shown interest in the pay-as-you-go model.[23]

HEW, however, recommended expanding the system based on the current model. Hobby and Rockefeller argued that under a current financing system, such as the one proposed by the Chamber of Commerce, business interests and others seeking lower taxes would pressure Congress to keep the program's costs down, preventing future benefits from keeping pace with inflation. Eliminating the trust fund aspect of Social Security, they argued, created the possibility that it could be dismantled by future politicians who did not want the responsibility of collecting the taxes to pay for it.

On November 20, 1953, Hobby and Rockefeller outlined HEW's proposal for expanding the current system to Eisenhower and the cabinet.[24] This meeting is often credited with convincing Eisenhower to abandon pay-as-you-go plans and endorse expansion of the current system.[25] Other evidence, however, suggests that by this time Eisenhower may have already made up his mind. On October 7, 1953, in a letter to financier Edward Hutton, Eisenhower anticipated HEW's contention that eliminating the trust fund would ultimately lead to the dismantling of the system. "It would appear logical to build upon the system that has been in place for almost 20 years," he wrote, "rather than embark upon the radical course of turning it completely upside down and running the very real danger that we would end up with no system at all."[26]

On January 14, 1954, Eisenhower submitted the HEW plan to Congress.[27] He followed up with several public speeches. "We want to preserve and strengthen its [the Social Security System's] reliance on a contributory system, in which workers and their employers share the obligation to make payments," Eisenhower said the following month in New York City. "Equally firm in our thinking is the belief that the benefits paid to workers . . . should bear a definite relation to their earnings in their years of activity. To scrap either of these underlying principles would move the system in the direction of charity and undermine the social insurance concept."[28] Although many Republicans still preferred a pay-as-you-go scheme, most were reluctant to vote against expanding one of government's most popular programs. The administration's proposal was, therefore, overwhelmingly approved by both houses, and Eisenhower signed it into law as the Social Security Amendments Act on September 1, 1954. This act brought nearly ten million additional people under the protection of Social Security. These included self-employed professionals and small farmers, agricultural and domestic workers, employees of state and local governments, and U.S. citizens employed outside the United States. Another important provision was a 16 percent increase in benefits.[29] The *New York Times* proclaimed, "In strictly human terms this was perhaps the most significant achievement of the administration in the 1954 session of Congress."[30] Not only had the new Republican presidential administration refused to dismantle one of the New Deal's most popular programs, under Eisenhower's leadership it had expanded it.

Health Reinsurance

During the 1952 campaign Eisenhower continually stated his opposition to any form of federal compulsory health insurance, such as that proposed by President Truman in 1949 and 1950. These plans he condemned as examples of "creeping socialism."

Eisenhower believed that plans offered by commercial and non-profit insurance carriers, together with locally administered programs for those unable to afford insurance, could best meet the needs of the American people. "Any move toward socialized medicine is sure to have one result," he said. "Instead of the patient getting more and better medical care for less, he will get less and poorer medical care for more. . . . We must preserve the completely voluntary relationship between doctor and patient."[31] Eisenhower's stand clearly reflected the Republican Party line as stated in the 1952 platform.[32]

Eisenhower did admit that the existing system was in need of improvement, but during the campaign he did not offer any specific suggestions.[33] HEW brought the problem into sharper focus. In 1952 only 17 percent ($1.6 billion) of all private expenditures for medical care ($9.4 billion) were paid by insurance.[34] Insurance carriers were, understandably, reluctant to offer policies that would place them at great financial risk. Some of the specific shortcomings in coverage identified by HEW were the following: age restrictions that prevented elderly Americans from getting insurance; inadequate coverage of low-income families and those who lived in rural areas; the characterization of certain individuals as "uninsurable" based on a preexisting condition; total benefit limits that fell short in cases of catastrophic illness; limits on the number of days of hospitalization covered; exclusions that limited coverage to specific procedures and treatments; and coverage for early diagnosis and treatment of chronic disease.[35] With the help of HEW Eisenhower sought a middle way between federally sponsored health insurance—a system he thought of as socialized medicine—and the existing system, where insurance carriers covered only a small percentage of health-care costs.

Once again Rockefeller played an important role in Eisenhower's pursuit of the Middle Way. The answer to bringing adequate medical care within the means of all Americans, he argued, was not to institute federally sponsored health insurance but to provide incentives for health insurance companies to expand their coverage. Rockefeller came up with a plan to do that without committing the federal government to a predominant role. The plan was known as health reinsurance. Under Rockefeller's reinsurance plan, the federal government would insure commercial and nonprofit insurance companies against "abnormal losses" associated with offering policies to individuals not adequately covered by health insurance, or for costs not widely covered by insurance policies.[36] The plan would not pay benefits to individuals or reimburse companies for benefits paid to any individual policy holder. Nor would the plan reimburse companies for their overall losses. Rather, insurance companies would propose that a particular type of policy be eligible for reinsurance. If the policy promoted the overall goals of the plan, reinsurance would be offered at premiums set by the secretary of HEW. Insurance carriers could then offer these policies without fear that doing so would financially jeopardize the company. If the company did experience an "abnormal loss" associated with a reinsured policy, they could file a claim with HEW. The plan was meant to be self-supporting. An initial appropriation of $25 million would be necessary to get the program started, but after that it would be paid for by the premiums. To protect the principle of free enterprise, the plan was subject to a no competition provision. Reinsurance would be offered only if insurance was not available commercially at a premium rate comparable to that offered by HEW. Regulation of the insurance industry was not the purpose of the plan. Participants need only demonstrate that they were financially sound and operating according to the law and in a manner entitling them to public confidence.[37]

Eisenhower approved the reinsurance plan. Its delicate balance between government involvement and private enterprise appealed to his sense of the Middle Way. As he would later say, it allowed the federal government to "fulfill its responsibility for leadership in these matters but in such a way that demagogues could not make the government responsible for all activity in them."[38] He began preparing the way for an administration-backed health-care bill with a special message to Congress in January 1954 and a series of public speeches emphasizing that health care should be accessible to Americans of all classes and races and in both rural and metropolitan areas.[39] Although the reinsurance plan had the administration's backing, it was not without its detractors in the cabinet. Secretary of the Treasury George Humphrey, one of the most conservative members of the cabinet, and Budget Director Joseph Dodge were both against the plan but consoled themselves in their belief that it would not pass.[40]

The Department of Treasury and the Budget Bureau were not the only opponents of the health reinsurance plan. Like many Middle Way initiatives, an unlikely coalition of the right and left wings of the political spectrum opposed the administration's health-care plan. Conservative groups such as the American Medical Association (AMA) opposed the plan on the grounds that it was an "opening wedge" for socialized medicine and would lead to a decrease in the quality of medical care.[41] On the other hand, liberal groups such as Americans for Democratic Action (ADA) opposed the plan out of fear that it might prevent passage of compulsory national health insurance.

In an effort to win support for the bill, Eisenhower hosted a luncheon for insurance company executives on May 17, 1954. In his address, the president emphasized that the majority of Americans believed that the insurance industry was doing an inadequate job of meeting their needs. Of these, he pointed out, a substantial number, including organized labor and the ADA, were in favor of a national compulsory health insurance system. The reinsurance plan, he argued, was a way to help the insurance industry better meet the demands of the people. By stemming the tide of support for a compulsory system, reinsurance would save the insurance industry and, indirectly, the health-care providers represented by the AMA.[42]

Secretary Hobby, in addition to making a national television address, also met with AMA executives in an attempt to win them over with Eisenhower's lesser of two evils approach.[43] Hobby tried to convince the AMA representatives that reinsurance was in the interests of the doctors since it would provide a buffer against compulsory health insurance and because better insurance coverage would assure payment of doctors' bills.[44] AMA intransigence, however, continued. Dr. Walter Martin, president of the AMA, reiterated the association's fears that comprehensive care would lead to a decrease in the quality of medical care.[45]

Despite Eisenhower's personal backing, on July 13, 1954, the House rejected the health reinsurance plan by a vote of 238 to 134. Seventy-five of those who voted against the bill were Republicans.[46] Eisenhower did not take the defeat lightly. He asked his press secretary, James Hagerty, to get a breakdown of the roll-call vote and bring him the names of Republicans who had voted against it. "If any of those fellows who voted against that bill expect me to do anything for them in this campaign, they are going to be very much surprised," Eisenhower told him, referring to the 1954 congressional election campaign. "This was a major part of our liberal program and anyone who voted against it will not have one iota of support from me."[47] The next day he went public with his criticism. "The people that voted against this bill just don't understand what are the facts of American life," Eisenhower told the White House press corps. "There is nothing to be gained, as I see it, by shutting our eyes to the fact that all of our people are not getting the kind of health care to which they are entitled."[48]

Eisenhower did not limit his anger to House members. He blamed the AMA for waging a campaign to portray the bill as socialized medicine. When Senate majority leader William Knowland (R-CA) tried to defend the AMA position at a legislative leaders meeting, Eisenhower cut him off: "Listen, Bill. . . . We said during the campaign that we were against socialized medicine. . . . As far as I'm concerned, the American Medical Association is just plain stupid. This plan of ours would have shown the people how we could improve their health care and stay out of socialized medicine."[49]

Health reinsurance was an excellent example of Eisenhower's Middle Way. By using government resources to encourage the insurance industry to expand health coverage, it would act as a catalyst for improving the system without assuming primary responsibility for it. Eisenhower vowed to continue the fight: "I am trying to redeem my campaign promises, and I will never cease trying. This is only a temporary defeat; this thing will be carried forward as long as I am in office."[50] The Eisenhower administration's attempts to revive the reinsurance plan in the Eighty-Fourth Congress, however, failed.

Eisenhower Republicanism

Secretary Hobby blamed congressional Democrats for the failure of Eisenhower's social welfare proposals. She believed they were "attempting to ensure that this administration got no glory for any legislative accomplishments in this field."[51] Eisenhower, expecting no help from Democrats, blamed conservatives in his own party. Many of these Republicans were, indeed, unhappy with the policies proposed by their president. Senator Barry Goldwater (R-AZ), who became the leading conservative spokesman after the death of Robert Taft in July 1953, wrote: "It is obvious that the administration has succumbed to the principle that we owe some sort of living . . . to the citizens of this country, and I am beginning to wonder if we haven't gone a lot further than many of us think on this road we happily call socialism."[52] He later recalled that he was "deeply disappointed when the Republican administration under President Eisenhower, with a working majority in both houses of Congress, proposed to continue the old New Deal, Fair Deal schemes, offering only a modification in scale and no change in direction."[53]

The president could not even get a word of support from his brother Edgar who wrote that many of his friends could see "very little difference between the policy of your administration and that of the former administration."[54] The president replied: "Should any political party attempt to abolish social security, unemployment insurance, and eliminate labor laws and farm programs, you would not hear of that party again in our political history. There is a tiny splinter group, of course, that believes you can do these things. . . . Their number is negligible, and they are stupid."[55] Eisenhower's experiences in the field of social policy gave added meaning to a remark he had made to his secretary, Ann Whitman: "You don't have very many friends when you're walking a decent middle way."[56]

As Eisenhower contemplated whether to retire at the end of his first term, he feared that the conservative wing would capture the party in his absence. "If they think they can nominate a right-wing, Old Guard Republican for the presidency, they've got another thought coming," he told press secretary James Hagerty. "I'll go up and down this country, campaigning against them. I'll fight them right down the line."[57] Eisenhower believed that the political thinking of the party's right wing was completely out of step with the times. "I believe this so emphatically," he wrote in his diary, "that I think that far from appeasing or reasoning with the dyed-in-the-wool reactionary fringe, we should completely ignore it and when necessary, repudiate it.... They are the most ignorant people now living in the United States."[58] After a disappointing midterm election in 1954, Eisenhower said that aside from keeping the world at peace, he had just one purpose for the next two years: "to build up a strong, progressive Republican Party in this country.... If the right wing wants a fight, they're going to get it. If they want to leave the Republican Party and form a third party, that's their business, but before I end up, either this Republican Party will reflect progressivism, or I won't be with them anymore."[59]

In private conversations, Eisenhower contemplated further the possibility of leaving the Republican Party. "If the right wing really recaptures the Republican Party," he told his friend Gabriel Hauge, "there simply isn't going to be any Republican influence in this country within a matter of a few brief years."[60] After one legislative defeat, he discussed with White House Chief of Staff Sherman Adams whether he belonged in the Republican Party. He thought that perhaps the time had come for a new party that would accept a leadership role in world affairs, a liberal stand on social welfare policy, and a conservative stand on economic matters.[61] After a talk with the president on this subject Bill Robinson wrote in his diary that Eisenhower had said that if the die-hard Republicans fought his program too hard, he would have to organize a third party.

Later, according to Robinson, Eisenhower smiled and admitted that this was an impractical alternative, but that he was not willing to give it up entirely.[62]

In Eisenhower's attempt to revitalize the party, many of his friends and advisers urged him to use the term "Eisenhower Republicanism," but he was against it. He agreed that personalizing the effort would be the easiest and perhaps the most successful way to reform the party, but he feared that if the effort revolved around him then the movement would collapse in his absence. "The idea," he thought, "was far bigger than any one individual."[63] He wanted to broaden the party's appeal, not personalize it. Although he would later take up the term "modern Republican," the president resisted the use of any descriptive adjectives to define his wing of the party. His opinion on this issue is apparent in a letter to his brother Edgar, who had referred to himself as the only "real Republican" in the family. "I am a little amused about this word 'real' that in your clipping modifies the word 'Republican,'" the president wrote. "I assume that Lincoln was a *real* Republican—in fact, I think we should have to assume that every president, being elected leader of the party, is a *real* Republican. Therefore, the president's branch of the party requires, for its description, no adjective whatsoever." Rather, he believed, "the splinter groups, which oppose the leader, would be the ones requiring the descriptive adjectives."[64]

Eisenhower was convinced that the only way for the Republican Party to remain a vital force in American politics was for it to take a liberal approach to its domestic problems: "This party of ours," he explained to James Hagerty, "will not appeal to the American people unless [they] believe that we have a truly liberal program." He was convinced that "unless Republicans make themselves the militant champions of the Middle Way, they are sunk."[65] He had little sympathy for the reelection bids of conservative congressmen who did not agree. He could not understand why they failed to see that "the best way they can get re-elected is by supporting the liberal program we have submitted to them."[66] Eisenhower even expressed indifference as to whether or not conservatives were reelected to Congress, asking why he should bother campaigning for conservative Republicans when he was just as satisfied to have the Democrats in control.[67]

Eisenhower's attempt to find a middle way for social welfare policy was only partially successful. Like the majority of Americans, Eisenhower accepted the contributions made by Presidents Roosevelt and Truman to social welfare. In these areas, where programs were already in place, he sought to strengthen and expand upon them. In this he was successful. His creation of the Department of Health, Education, and Welfare gave cabinet status to the Federal Security Administration, and his amendments to the Social Security Act gave more than ten million additional workers access to retirement insurance. Where new programs were necessary, however, Eisenhower was far less successful. Eisenhower's proposal for health reinsurance was an attempt to use the resources of the federal government to encourage progress in this area. Eisenhower was seeking balance, a middle way between conservatives, who believed that health care was outside the scope of federal responsibility, and liberals, who would have preferred that the federal government accept primary responsibility for them.

Eisenhower ultimately failed in his attempt to change the direction of the Republican Party. His failure was due primarily to his belief that the change he desired could be achieved on the strength of his policies alone. Eisenhower believed so strongly in the Middle Way that he could not understand why others did not. For eight years he battled conservative opposition to his programs in Congress, which rarely gave him the opportunity to show what they might do. Without a body of successful domestic legislation, the Middle Way could never achieve the status of a New Deal or Fair Deal and, in doing so, change the direction of the party. Eisenhower's inability "to build up a strong, progressive Republican Party" has tremendous relevance in our time. The defeat of liberalism within his party, followed by the defection of conservative, mostly southern, Democrats to the Republican Party in the decades that followed, left the country with a rigidly ideological two-party alignment.

Opposition from conservatives in his party made it necessary for Eisenhower to seek Democratic support for his legislative agenda. This was already a difficult strategy in Eisenhower's time, and increased political polarization has made it even less likely to succeed now. The Pew Research Center has concluded that in Congress, "Democrats and Republicans are farther apart ideologically today than at any time in the past 50 years." Both parties have moved away from the ideological center, with Democrats becoming "somewhat more liberal" and Republicans becoming "much more conservative." By Pew's account, this leaves only two dozen moderate members of Congress amenable to bipartisan legislative negotiations.[68] Participating in such bipartisan activity, however, leaves members from both parties open to primary challengers.

Further complicating matters is the proliferation of filibusters in the Senate. In Eisenhower's time, when use of the filibuster required the minority party to hold the Senate floor during debate, filibusters were relatively rare. Since 1970, however, the minority party can impose a filibuster by merely submitting a letter to the chair. Initially, this rule change led to only a moderate increase in filibusters. After 2008, however, increased partisanship and ideological polarization caused a dramatic increase. It is now assumed that sixty votes are necessary for nearly anything to pass in the Senate. So, even a president with a majority in both houses cannot count on legislative success. Given the difficulty of one party achieving a supermajority, the need for moderation and bipartisanship has never been more apparent.

4

A New Look for National Security

On April 30, 1953, the one hundredth day of his administration, President Eisenhower began his press conference by reading a brief statement:

> I have always firmly believed that there is a great logic in the conduct of military affairs. There is an equally great logic in economic affairs. If those two logical disciplines can be wedded, it is then possible to create a situation of maximum military strength within economic capacities. If, on the other hand, these two are allowed to proceed in disregard one for the other, then you create a situation either of doubtful military strength, or of such precarious economic strength that your military position is in constant jeopardy. . . . The fiscal situation represented by these two extremes absolutely has to be brought into some kind of realistic focus, and the only way to do it is to have a completely new, fresh look without any misleading labels.

Eisenhower's refusal to go into detail in response to the questions he was asked at the press conference made clear that the formulation of his national security policy, which would come to be known as the "New Look," was in its beginning stages. Clear in the president's mind, however, was that with the nation "finding itself confronted with a crazy quilt of promises, commitments, and contracts," made by the Truman administration, it was necessary "to bring American military logic and American economic logic" into balance with one another.[1]

Based on his lifetime of experience, national security was the area where Eisenhower was most qualified to lead the country. Despite this, early critics of his administration believed that he abdicated his responsibility in this area to John Foster Dulles, his high-profile secretary of state. Revisionists dismissed such claims, arguing that Eisenhower's hidden-hand leadership style obscured his activities in this area as it did in others. He was not only an active foreign policy president, but he was also an effective one. "Tested by a world as dangerous as any that an American leader has ever faced," one historian wrote, "Eisenhower used his sound judgement and instinctive common sense to guide the nation safely through the first decade of the thermonuclear age."[2] Revisionists also lauded Eisenhower's attempt to balance the nation's military and economic security. Eisenhower's goal, argued one historian, "was to achieve the maximum possible deterrence of communism at the minimum possible cost." The New Look, he concluded, "appears to have met these objectives." Defense spending during this period went down as a percentage of the total budget and as a percentage of the gross domestic product (GDP), but these cuts did not reduce American strength relative to that of the Soviet Union.[3]

After the end of the Cold War, historians Richard Immerman and Robert Bowie wrote *Waging Peace: How Eisenhower Shaped an Enduring Cold War Strategy*. Immerman and Bowie begin their book with a bold claim: "The ending of the cold war, with the disintegration of the Soviet regime . . . gives special relevance to a fresh analysis of the origins of the basic strategy pursued by the United States and its allies for three decades, which contributed to that outcome. Credit for shaping that strategy belongs to Dwight D. Eisenhower." Eisenhower, they argue, believed that the nation's security required "an explicit and integrated grand strategy." This strategy would not provide answers to the specific questions that would arise as the nation waged cold war. Instead, it would establish the long-term priorities that would ensure consistency in how the United States answered those questions when they arose. Although the strategy was created through the mechanisms of the NSC, it would be Eisenhower who made the final decisions. Those decisions, they argued, "were molded by the values, beliefs, images, and pre-dispositions Eisenhower brought to the Oval Office and the impact on him of the advice, deliberation, and debate produced by the policy process."[4]

Eisenhower was intimately involved in the creation of his administration's national security policy. With the help of the previously underutilized NSC, Eisenhower developed a grand strategy for national security that perpetuated the Truman-era strategy of containment but, to balance the nation's military and economic interests, placed a greater emphasis on nuclear deterrence. Eisenhower also sought to balance risk and reward by rejecting high-risk alternatives to containment such as "roll back," which had been the position of the Republican Party since the onset of the Cold War. Eisenhower believed that pursuing absolute security would require economic controls that would destroy the very freedom the nation was defending. On the other hand, pursuing economic prosperity without due regard to security would place the nation at an unacceptable level of risk.

Eisenhower's formation of the New Look remains relevant for our time. Creating a grand strategy for national security is more difficult now than it was in Eisenhower's time, when America's determination to contain communism gave it an objective that transcended all others. However, the existence of competing, and sometimes contradictory, interests in our time makes the creation of a grand strategy more important than it has ever been. A bipartisan commitment to that strategy, like that which prevailed throughout the Cold War, should also be sought.

The National Security Council

During the presidential transition, President-Elect Eisenhower appointed Robert Cutler, one of his closest advisers during the campaign, as his special assistant for national security affairs. He asked Cutler to conduct a study of the NSC and make recommendations on how it might be better used to formulate national security policy. The NSC was created by the National Security Act of 1947 "to advise the president with respect to the integration of domestic, foreign, and military policies relating to national security."[5] President Truman had convened the NSC, but many of those involved did not believe he had used it effectively. Eisenhower wanted the NSC to be "the most important policy-making body in government."[6]

By law, the members of the NSC were the president, vice president, secretary of state, secretary of defense, director for mutual security, and director of the Office of Defense Mobilization (later changed to the Office of Civil Defense Mobilization). During the Eisenhower administration there was also a "standing request" for the participation of the secretary of the treasury and the director of the budget. Advisers to the NSC were the chairman of the JCS, the director of central intelligence (DCI), and the special assistant to the president for cold war planning. The legislation also called for an executive secretary to the council and the president's special assistant for national security affairs (in later administrations this position would be known as the national security adviser).

Cutler's most important contribution to the NSC was to take what was formerly known as the "senior staff" and transform it into the NSC planning board. The planning board consisted of representatives from the Departments of State, Defense, and Treasury, the Mutual Security Agency, the Office of Defense Mobilization, the JCS, the Central Intelligence Agency (CIA), and the Psychological Strategy Board. As special assistant to the president, Cutler chaired the planning board. The planning board had lengthy meetings three times a week to discuss recommendations submitted by the represented departments. It then prepared drafts of policies for the consideration of the NSC. Planning board meetings were known for their intense debates. The point was not to resolve differences. Rather, it was to clearly identify them in policy drafts, where they were known as "splits." Prior to NSC meetings, each planning board representative had a "standing and unbreakable" meeting with his department's NSC representative to brief him on the agenda for the meeting and to go over the policy drafts, focusing on "splits." Cutler briefed Eisenhower in similar fashion.[7]

The NSC met in the cabinet room on Thursdays at 10:00 a.m. Meetings lasted for two to three hours. After an intelligence briefing by the DCI, the agenda turned to consideration of the planning board's policy drafts. Eisenhower presided over the meetings himself and played an active role in the discussion. During NSC meetings Cutler acted as facilitator, keeping the discussion on track and clarifying points in the planning board's draft when necessary. He did not act as a policy adviser to the president. Cutler served as Eisenhower's special assistant for national security affairs for three years and nine months. During that time the NSC met 179 times. The president missed only six of those meetings.[8]

The NSC apparatus served Eisenhower's leadership and decision-making style well. His early critics believed that the NSC was a policy-making body and was, therefore, an example of Eisenhower abdicating his decision-making responsibilities to appointees. This was not the case. The planning board spared NSC members from the time-intensive study required to draft policy recommendations. Having been briefed by their representatives on the planning board, members could then discuss these drafts intelligently at council meetings, allowing the president to hear the opinions of his top-level advisers. But the NSC did not make policy. Eisenhower reserved all final decisions for himself. At times, he would announce a decision at the end of the meeting. Other times he would make a final decision later, either alone or in the company of one or two others. In an October 1953 NSC meeting, for example, the secretary of defense continued to advocate for a JCS proposal even after Eisenhower had rejected it. Cutler suggested that the document they were working on reflect this difference of opinion between the president and the JCS. Eisenhower, however, said that "he would tolerate no notice of JCS dissent" from his opinion. "The Joint Chiefs of Staff were, after all, his military advisors; he made the decisions."[9] This style of leadership not only ensured that Eisenhower made informed decisions, it made his advisers feel that they had been a part of the process even when they did not get their way, making them more likely to support and defend the final decision.

Operation Solarium

Shortly after the president approved Cutler's recommendations for the revitalization of the NSC, Secretary of State John Foster Dulles invited Cutler to his home in Washington, DC, on a Sunday afternoon. Also invited were Allen Dulles, the DCI and Foster's brother, Undersecretary of State Bedell Smith, and Special Assistant to the President C. D. Jackson. Foster Dulles said that he had undertaken a thorough review of the Truman administration's national security policy. "Now that the President has approved Bobby's proposed revival of the council," he said, "shouldn't we tackle a policy statement to fulfill our campaign ideas? I conceive three possible alternatives to choose from or to combine in part some way or another." According to Cutler, Foster Dulles spent the next hour laying out his three possible alternatives. Dulles's guests were very impressed with his presentation. Afterward, Smith suggested further study of the alternatives: "Three teams of crack fellows, expertly captained, each developing an alternative." The next morning Cutler met with the president and requested a time when Dulles could repeat his presentation and Smith could outline his plan for a staff study. "His plan seems to me a fine way to crank up our first comprehensive basic national security policy for the council," Cutler said.[10]

Eisenhower agreed to the proposal, and the group made plans to meet later in the week. To avoid interruption, they met late in the afternoon in the Solarium, a room on the third floor of the White House with floor-to-ceiling windows and a panoramic view of the Washington Monument and the Memorial Mall. Eisenhower was enthusiastic about the idea for a study of Dulles's three policy alternatives and asked Cutler to prepare a detailed written proposal for his approval. Cutler suggested that they call the project "Operation Solarium."[11]

On May 9, 1953, Cutler presented Eisenhower with a detailed proposal for Operation Solarium. Task Force A would study the alternative of containment, "the general policy toward the USSR and its bloc, which has been in effect since 1948." Under this alternative, the United States would prevent the spread of communism beyond its current boundaries while avoiding general war with the Soviet Union or Communist China. This strategy was defensive—it sought to deter Soviet aggression "until the Soviets shall decay from internal weaknesses inherent in despotic government." It believed that "time is on the side of the free world—that if we can 'last out' the Soviets will deteriorate and fail." Task Force B would study the alternative of deterrence. In this alternative, the United States would make clear that it has "drawn a line." The fall to communism of any country beyond this line would constitute grounds for the United States to "take measures of our own choosing, including offensive war" against the Soviet Union or Communist China. The use of nuclear weapons was an inherent aspect of this strategy. Task Force C would study the alternative of "roll back." In this alternative, the United States would undertake, by offensive action, to restore communist countries to the "free world." This alternative was consistent with the rhetoric of the 1952 Republican campaign and sought to roll back communism in Eastern Europe and East Asia. Of the three alternatives, it held the greatest risk of general war.[12]

Eisenhower approved the proposal and even chose some of the men who would serve on the task forces. The most interesting choice was George Kennan as the chairman for Task Force A.[13] Kennan had written the so-called long telegram, a 5,363-word telegram to President Truman's Secretary of State James Byrnes outlining what he believed should be U.S. policy toward the Soviet Union. The long telegram along with "The Sources of Soviet Conduct," an article that he wrote anonymously for *Foreign Affairs* magazine, were the basis of U.S. containment policy under Truman.[14] Eisenhower's choice of Kennan to lead this task force must have come as a surprise to Dulles. As Kennan later recalled:

"I derived, I must say, a certain amount of amusement from it. . . . Since it was only three months since he had fired me from the foreign service, this gave me a certain satisfaction, I must say."[15]

The "General Information and Guidance" provided to each Operation Solarium task force included a section on "U.S. National Objectives." Admitting that it was difficult to reduce U.S. objectives to a single statement, participants were instructed to see NSC 153 and Eisenhower's speech to the American Society of Newspaper Editors (ASNE) on April 16, 1953. NSC 153 was a document prepared by the new NSC planning board and approved by the NSC in June 1953. Its purpose was to combine and summarize all existing U.S. national security policy. It superseded NSC 20, NSC 68, and NSC 135 from the Truman administration, as well as NSC 149 that had been adopted earlier in the Eisenhower administration. It was, essentially, the set of policies that Task Force A was being asked to defend. In its first paragraph, under the heading "General Considerations," was the problem Eisenhower believed was most important. "There are two principal threats to the survival of fundamental values in institutions of the United States: a) The formidable power and aggressive policy of the communist world led by the USSR. b) The serious weakening of the economy of the United States that may result from the cost of opposing the Soviet threat over a sustained period. The basic problem facing the United States is to strike a proper balance between the risks arising from these two threats."[16]

Eisenhower's speech to the ASNE is worthy of further consideration. On March 5, 1953, just six weeks after Eisenhower had taken office, Joseph Stalin, the leader of the Soviet Union, died. Stalin's death set off an intense debate among Eisenhower's advisers regarding how the United States should respond. C. D. Jackson, Eisenhower's special assistant for Cold War operations, believed that "Stalin's death had provided the United States with its first significant and normal opportunity to seize the initiative" in the Cold War. He suggested that the United States "exploit Stalin's death to the limit of psychological usefulness." He recommended that the president make a speech as soon as possible, calling for a meeting of the "Big Four" to negotiate all the outstanding issues between the Soviet Union and the West.[17]

When collaboration between Jackson and the State Department on a speech reached an impasse, Eisenhower began working on one with Emmet Hughes, one of his speech writers. Hughes later told the story of how the president came up with the idea for the speech. "Look, I am tired—and I think everyone is tired—of just plain indictments of the Soviet regime," Eisenhower lamented. "What have *we* got to offer the world? What are *we* ready to do, to improve the chances of peace?" After a long pause during which Eisenhower stared out the window of the Oval Office, "he wheeled abruptly toward me and went on . . . 'Here is what I would like to say. The jet plane that roars over your head costs three-quarters of a million dollars. That is more money than a man earning ten thousand dollars every year is going to make in his lifetime. What world can afford this sort of thing for long? . . . Now, there could be another road before us—the road of disarmament. What does this mean? It means for everybody in the world: bread, butter, clothes, homes, hospitals, schools—all the good and necessary things for a decent living. So let this be the choice we offer.' . . . The excitement of the man and the moment was contagious and stirring."[18] The result of this exchange was "The Chance for Peace," a speech that Eisenhower made to the ASNE on April 16, 1953:

> Every gun that is made, every warship launched, every rocket fired signifies, in the final sense, a theft from those who hunger and are

not fed, those who are cold and are not clothed. This world in arms is not spending money alone. It is spending the sweat of its laborers, the genius of its scientists, the hopes of its children.

The cost of one modern heavy bomber is this: a modern brick school in more than 30 cities. It is two electric power plants, each serving a town of 60,000 population. It is two fine, fully equipped hospitals. It is some 50 miles of concrete highway. We pay for a single fighter plane with a half million bushels of wheat. We pay for a single destroyer with new homes that could have housed more than 8,000 people.

This, I repeat, is the best way of life to be found on the road the world has been taking. This is not a way of life at all, in any true sense. Under the cloud of threatening war, it is humanity hanging from a cross of iron.[19]

The speech mentioned all of the major outstanding differences between the United States and the Soviet Union, including arms control, but made no specific proposals. "The Chance for Peace" was broadcast on television and radio throughout much of the world. It was also translated into forty-five languages and printed in newspapers. Even *Pravda*, the Soviet state newspaper, carried an accurate translation. An article that ran in the same issue of *Pravda*, however, was not complimentary. Eisenhower, it said, merely wanted each of the outstanding differences he had mentioned to be settled in favor of the United States.[20] Eisenhower had reason to be disappointed by the Soviet response but remained open to negotiations and insisted that any policy adopted by the NSC retain that possibility.

After more than five weeks of work at the National War College, Operation Solarium's three task forces made their presentations to the NSC on July 16. The strategy put forth by Task Force A was to (1) maintain, over the long term, armed forces capable of providing security for the United States and vital areas of the "free world";

(2) assist in building up the economic and military strength of the free world; and (3) exploit the political, economic, and psychological vulnerabilities of the Soviet Union without increasing the risk of general war. Task Force A believed that time was on the side of the United States—that if it could build up and maintain its strength and that of its allies, Soviet power would deteriorate to a point where it no longer posed a threat to the security of the United States and the free world. Containing Soviet expansion would, however, continue to require the use of military force, such as in Korea. While these operations would run the risk of initiating a general war, this risk was "not high" and may be deterred in the future by the build-up of indigenous forces in areas of likely Soviet aggression. The United States should also consider "announcing that the U.S. will feel free to use atomic weapons in case of local aggression in the future." Task Force A believed that this strategy could be pursued within the general framework of existing U.S. policy without altering the cost or risk of general war.

The strategy put forth by Task Force B was that (1) "any advance of Soviet military forces beyond the present borders of the Soviet bloc be considered by the United States as initiating general war," and in such a general war, "the full power of the United States will be used as necessary to bring about the defeat" and "dissolution" of the USSR; (2) the United States should make clear to the Soviet Union in an "appropriate and unmistakable" way that the United States is determined to carry out this policy; and (3) the United States should reserve the freedom of action to, in the event that indigenous communists seize power in a country outside the current Soviet Bloc, "take all measures necessary to reestablish a situation compatible with the security interests of the United States." General war in this strategy was defined as a war in which the United States would apply "its full power whenever, however, and wherever necessary." This explicitly included the use of nuclear weapons. Although the United States expected that its allies would assist in such a general war, the policy was, "in final analysis," a unilateral one. Under "Alternative B," the United States would be required to maintain, "for the foreseeable future" a military capable of defeating the Soviet Union in a general war. Task Force B proposed its alternative "as a support, rather than a substitute for existing policies." Its primary contribution to existing policies was to deter Soviet aggression with the threat of general war—nuclear war. "Any suggestion is rejected that there is a place in the atomic age for a U.S. military establishment having less offensive power than that which the rulers of the Soviet Union must regard as an unacceptable risk in war." Because communist aggression would be deterred by the threat of general war, peripheral wars like the one in Korea would be eliminated. This would, in the opinion of Task Force B, reduce both costs and the risk of general war.

The strategy put forth by Task Force C was to (1) "increase efforts to disturb and weaken the Soviet Bloc" and to strengthen the "free world to enable it to assume the greater risks involved"; and (2) "create the maximum disruption and popular resistance throughout the Soviet Bloc." To the current U.S. policy of containing Soviet expansion, this strategy sought to add ending the USSR's domination of countries outside its borders, such as those in Eastern Europe; bringing down the "Iron Curtain"; and destroying communist parties in the "free world." Initially, the United States would engage in this intensified Cold War covertly, using "a national program of deception and concealment" so as to prevent the Soviet Union from gauging the "depth and extent of our challenge." Such a strategy would require a "departure from our traditional concepts of war and peace." To do so would mean public and congressional acceptance of the greater costs of a stronger military establishment, including universal military training and service. The United States, Task Force C believed, should also maintain its freedom of action by avoiding participation in any additional regional military alliances or disarmament discussions.[21] Alternative C would be the costliest and run the greatest risk of general war.

After the three presentations, Eisenhower rose and spoke extemporaneously for about forty-five minutes. "He spoke," according to George Kennan, "with a mastery of the subject matter and a thoughtfulness and a penetration that were quite remarkable. I came away from it with the conviction . . . that President Eisenhower was a much more intelligent man than he was given credit for being." Andrew Goodpaster, a member of Task Force C, concurred, saying that Eisenhower showed his "intellectual ascendency over every other man in the room on these issues."[22] After saying that he had never attended a better staff presentation, the president observed that he believed "the only thing worse than losing a global war was winning one." The American people, he said, had shown their reluctance to occupy conquered territory after a war to see that their interests were upheld, "What would we do with Russia, if we should win?" He also feared the demands being placed upon the American people by an ongoing and increasingly costly Cold War. "If you demand of a free people over a long period of time more than they want to give, you can obtain what you want only by using more and more controls; and the more you do this, the more you lose the individual liberty you are trying to save and become a garrison state."[23]

The president's remarks suggested that he was opposed to strategies that would be too costly or run too high a risk of general war. "In Eisenhower's summation," said Goodpaster, "one could see the demise of the policy of rollback." Eisenhower had put Goodpaster, in whom he had great trust, on Task Force C to make sure that the idea of rollback was studied thoroughly, but its presentation had convinced him to put this tough rhetoric from the campaign behind him, something he had been inclined to do anyway. As for the heavy-handed deterrence of Task Force B, Robert Bowie, a member of the planning board later said of that policy, "I don't think there was . . . any significant inclusion of the idea of drawing the line . . . in the sense in which it was used in Task Force B." Kennan, the leader of Task Force A, left the meeting with the impression that "in general he [Eisenhower] was prepared to accept the thesis we had put forward, that our approach to the problem of the Soviet Union, as it had been followed in the immediately preceding years, was basically sound."[24]

Although he may have favored the conclusions of Task Force A over those of B and C, Eisenhower said that he believed the similarities in the presentations were more important than the differences. He suggested a meeting of the three task forces to see if they could agree on the best features of each alternative to be combined into a unified policy. After the president left the meeting the task forces expressed their resistance to his suggestion.[25] "We were exhausted," remembered Goodpaster. The participants in Operation Solarium had been away from home for five weeks and had worked every day. "We started at 8 o'clock and broke for lunch briefly, and for dinner. We might have had an hour of exercise in the afternoon but then worked until about midnight." Besides the exhaustion, the task forces believed that their positions were incompatible.[26] When Cutler reported this back to the president "he seemed very put out" and told him to "work out what he thought best."[27]

If, after an exhaustive five-week study, Operation Solarium had led Eisenhower to the conclusion that containment, the policy the

United States had pursued since the onset of the Cold War, was the best alternative, had the project been worthwhile? "Plans are nothing, but planning is everything," Eisenhower was fond of saying. "The secret of a sound, satisfactory decision made on an emergency basis has always been that the responsible official has been 'living with the problem' before it becomes acute."[28] Solarium had provided the new administration with a complete reexamination of national security policy. The result would allow Eisenhower to justify the changes he wished to make to this policy and put to rest alternatives like "rollback" that had become popular with some in his party.[29] Also, the very process was an educational one for Eisenhower and, more importantly, for his national security team. But the process was not over. As we shall see, a great deal of work was yet to be done before the New Look would become official U.S. policy.

On July 30, the NSC met to discuss the written reports submitted by the three Operation Solarium task forces. Cutler believed that the next step should be to direct a special Solarium Committee of the planning board to synthesize these reports into a policy draft for the council's consideration. With this in mind, he had drafted a memorandum for the planning board, laying out the task. Although there was some disagreement regarding the memo—Cutler had gone beyond instructing the planning board and written a first draft of policy—the council agreed to put the work of drafting a policy in the hands of the planning board and accepted Cutler's instructions as general "guidelines" or "points for consideration."[30] These included Eisenhower's stated directives as well as elements from all three task forces. According to these guidelines, the new policy should maintain "at the lowest feasible cost" a U.S. military capable of both continental defense and nuclear retaliation; cultivate strong regional alliances; determine those areas into which an advance by Soviet forces would be considered an initiation of general war; allow for "selective aggressive actions . . . involving moderately increased risks of general war," to eliminate Soviet domination of areas outside its own borders; and reduce or eliminate indigenous communism in nations of the "free world."[31]

The Sequoia Report

On July 14, shortly before the planning board was given the task of drafting a new national security policy, Eisenhower met with his newly designated JCS. He told them that he wanted them to familiarize themselves with the entire military establishment. After doing so, he wanted them to "make a completely new, fresh survey of our military capabilities in light of our global commitments." According to General Mathew Ridgway, "He stressed the fact that he did not want a long exhaustive staff study (like Solarium). He recognized our great collective experience . . . and what he wanted from us was our own individual views, honestly and forthrightly stated."[32] Among the things that Eisenhower asked the JCS to consider was the implication of nuclear weapons. After completing a tour of American military installations, the JCS spent August 6–8 aboard the Navy yacht *U.S.S. Sequoia* writing their report.

The Sequoia report made two significant recommendations. The first was that the administration should announce "a clear, positive policy with respect to the use of atomic weapons." The second was that the United States "place in first priority the essential military protection of our continental U.S. vitals and the capability of delivering swift and powerful retaliatory blows. Military commitments overseas—that is to say, peripheral military commitments—would cease to have first claim on our resources."

By this, the JCS meant that American forces should be redeployed closer to home to prioritize the protection of U.S. vital interests. The report recognized that such a policy change could damage relations with U.S. allies and could cause difficulties with some members of Congress and the general public, but believed it was the only policy to offer a "reasonable promise of improving our general security position."[33]

The NSC discussed the Sequoia report on August 27 in the presence of the JCS. Eisenhower was in Denver, and this was one of the few NSC meetings that he missed. Vice President Nixon chaired the meeting. Nixon began the discussion by asking whether implementing the recommendations of the report would cost more than the current program. JCS chair Admiral Arthur Radford responded that on the contrary, once the corresponding redeployments of troops were made "it would be possible to effect substantial savings." Secretary Dulles, noting that the greatest impact of the recommendations would be the reduction of American forces in Europe and East Asia, said that he presumed this meant greater reliance on air power and atomic weapons. JCS members were reluctant to answer directly. Chief of Naval Operations Admiral Robert Carney stated that he did not believe that air and naval forces alone were a sufficient deterrent, and Admiral Radford said that U.S. allies would have to contribute more men for their own defense. But when Nixon asked whether he was correct in assuming that based on these recommendations, "in the event of a major conflict the United States would use atomic weapons in both the tactical and in the strategic realm," Radford said that "this was indeed the case." He added that "as he saw it, we had been spending vast sums on the manufacture of these weapons and at the same time we were holding back on their use because of our concern for public opinion. It was high time that we clarified our position on the use of such weapons if indeed we proposed to use them."

Over the course of the meeting, it became clear that the JCS was unanimous in its belief that the U.S. military was overextended and that the nation's "vitals" were at risk. It was this consideration, not budgetary concerns, that had led them to recommend that U.S. forces be reoriented to continental defense. When asked if their recommendation would be the same if money were no object, the majority answered yes. This reorientation of U.S. military forces was not comparable to pre–World War II advocacy of a "Fortress America," however. Despite their reluctance to give a direct answer to Dulles's question, it was clear that the JCS believed that the nuclear deterrent was more important than a conventional one. "Admiral Radford stated that after the outbreak of the Korean war in June 1950, we really did not know the enemy's ultimate intentions, so all we could do was build up our forces in all categories. This was sound. . . . The atomic factor, however, now looms much larger, and the problem of continental defense is now much more important than it seemed in the summer of 1950." As for the impact of such a reorientation on our allies, Dulles said they would have to change their thinking as well. The citizens of New York do not consider themselves vulnerable to attack because our troops are quartered in some other state, he argued, because they can quickly be dispatched to the danger zone. "We can defend all vital parts of the free world by applying the principle of concentration of forces," Nixon insisted. "This . . . was *not* the Fortress America of the past."

Secretary of the Treasury George Humphrey, no doubt seizing on the cost-saving aspects of the plan, said that the JCS report was "terrific . . . the most important thing that had happened in this country since January 20." He suggested that the planning board's study of the Solarium reports be suspended. While the other council members were impressed as well, they were not ready to move as quickly as Humphrey. Dulles suggested that the State Department study the impact of such a military reorientation on American allies. The other council members agreed, subject to the president's approval.[34]

On September 2, Cutler briefed Eisenhower in Denver. Eisenhower was enthusiastic about the Sequoia report, calling it a "crystalized and clarified statement of this Administration's understanding of our national security objectives since World War II." Warming to the idea, he instructed Cutler to take dictation as he paced the room: "From the beginning, people who really studied foreign and military problems have considered that the stationing of American troops abroad was a temporary expedient. It was a stop-gap operation to bring confidence and security to our friends overseas." The objective was always to produce among them "the morale, confidence, economic and military strength" to develop indigenous forces that could hold until U.S. troops arrived. "Any thinking individual," he said, "always understood that." He approved the State Department study that the NSC had recommended and requested that Dulles come to Denver to discuss it with him. He also said that the planning board should incorporate the Sequoia report into their synthesis of the Operation Solarium presentations. He reiterated several times to Cutler that the JCS report must not be presented as a new idea. It was instead, a "reaffirmation and clarification of what he had always understood."[35]

NSC 162

The NSC met on October 7 and October 29 to discuss the planning board's drafts of a new "Basic National Security Policy" statement. The document was laid out in two columns to show the areas of disagreement among the planning board staff. It was these "splits" that the council focused on in its discussion. The first of these disagreements concerned the nature of the Soviet threat, which was articulated on page one of the statement. On side A were those who saw a singular threat to the existence of the United States: Soviet hostility. Although they acknowledged the importance of a sound economy, they believed this threat must be met without regard to cost. On side B were those who saw a dual threat to the United States: Soviet hostility, and the long-term damage that countering this threat would do to the American economy and way of life. If the United States spent too much over a sustained period to contain the Soviet threat, then it would destroy the very thing it was fighting to defend.

This fundamental question—how much liberty should be given up in exchange for security—is as old as the republic itself, and the council's discussion of it was long and rather heated. At one point, "Cutler expressed concern that the meeting of the National Security Council was degenerating into a debating society." As the discussion went on, however, it became clear that the two sides were not as far apart as they seemed. Secretary of Defense Charles Wilson said that "if we ever go to the American people and tell them that we are putting a balanced budget ahead of national defense it would be a terrible day." He added, however, that "what we are really trying to do is ascertain and reach a reasonable posture of defense over a long period. If we can do this within a balanced budget, fine. If not, we will simply have to postpone balancing the budget." Secretary of the Treasury George Humphrey, in an equally conciliatory statement, said: "While we did not propose to balance the budget by sacrificing our security, we are nevertheless, making every effort to revise and perfect our defense establishment and to get it within the limits of the means available to us." Eisenhower, sensing an opening for compromise, suggested using language that appeared later in the document. The basic problem of national security policy, it said, was to "meet the Soviet threat to United States security" and "in doing so to avoid seriously weakening the United States economy or undermining our fundamental values and institutions." There was no objection to this wording. While the debate over the nature of the threat may seem semantic, the problem of balancing the demands of security with the need to preserve American values—a problem Eisenhower referred to as the "Great Equation"—informed the remaining disagreements.

The next disagreement concerned the redeployment of U.S. overseas forces recommended by the JCS's Sequoia report. Side A argued that "a major redeployment of U.S. forces from Europe and the Far East at the present time would seriously undermine the strength of the coalition." Side B argued that because American and Allied security was "weakened by the present over-extended deployment of U.S. forces, an early determination should be made whether, with the understanding of our allies, the redeployment toward the United States of the bulk of our land and other forces should soon be initiated." Dulles, to whom the Sequoia report had been referred for further study, said that he believed it to be "sound," but that breaking the news to American allies would have to be handled "with the greatest delicacy." Eisenhower repeated his view that "the stationing of U.S. divisions in Europe had been . . . an emergency measure not intended to last indefinitely." Humphrey remained enthusiastic about the proposed redeployment. Rather than emphasizing the potential cost savings that would accrue, however, he focused on the Sequoia report's notion of correcting the overextension of U.S. forces. Ironically, it was now Wilson and

Radford who expressed reservations about the JCS redeployment plan, believing that, perhaps, the idea had caught on too quickly. In the end, the NSC favored side B but retained some language from side A to emphasize the need to prepare American allies for the change.

The NSC also discussed a planning board disagreement over "rollback." Although Andrew Goodpaster believed that Eisenhower's summary comments on Solarium on July 16 had eliminated this option, rollback still enjoyed strong support in the Department of Defense and the JCS. Both Defense and the JCS recommended deleting the following three sentences from the policy draft: "The United States should not, however, initiate aggressive actions involving force against Soviet bloc territory. Limited actions within our capabilities would not materially reduce the Soviet threat even if successful. Moreover, they are likely to increase the risk of general war, would place strains on the coalition, and might well destroy the chances of agreement with the USSR on the more fundamental aspects of the Soviet threat." Eisenhower agreed, but not because he advocated that the United States engage in such actions. Rather, he said, that it was because "any proposal involving the use of force against such territory, whether overt or covert, would require a prior council decision." The matter of rollback was far from settled, however, as Defense and the JCS interpreted the deletion of the paragraph prohibiting the initiation of aggressive acts as acceptance of them.

The final NSC decision on planning board splits concerned U.S. policy regarding the use of "special weapons," meaning both atomic bombs, such as the fission bombs used against Japan in August 1945, and hydrogen bombs, the fusion bombs under development at this time and first tested by the United States in 1952. As ballistic missiles were still in the development stage, the United

States relied on conventional long-range bombers as its primary delivery vehicle for nuclear weapons. Many of these bombers were on bases located outside the United States, making allied cooperation critical to their use. Eisenhower therefore suggested that the document should specify that the "approval and understanding" of American allies should precede the use of special weapons. Defense Secretary Wilson argued that the military needed to know whether "we intend to use weapons on which we are spending such great sums, or do we not?" The president insisted: "If the use of them was dictated by the interests of U.S. security, he would certainly decide to use them." This, however, was not enough for the JCS. "Can we," Radford asked, "use these weapons from bases where the permission of no foreign government is required?" Eisenhower replied that "so far . . . as war plans were concerned . . . he thought that the JCS should count on making use of special weapons in the event of general war. They should not, however, plan to make use of these weapons in minor affairs." Dulles expressed dissatisfaction stating, "Somehow or other we must manage to remove the taboo from the use of these weapons." Eisenhower remarked that "there were certain places where you would not be able to use these weapons because if you did it would look as though the U.S. were initiating global war. If, however, we actually got into a global war, we would certainly use the weapons."[36] The final NSC wording reflected both sides of this discussion: "In the event of hostilities, the United States will consider nuclear weapons to be as available for use as other munitions. Where the consent of an ally is required for the use of these weapons from U.S. bases on the territory of such an ally, the United States should promptly obtain the advance consent of such ally for such use."[37]

The National Security Council approved NSC 162, "Basic National Security Policy," on October 29, 1953. Despite Eisenhower's previous admonition to Cutler, NSC 162 quickly became known as the New Look. Admiral Arthur Radford, chairman of the JCS, speaking to the National Press Club on December 14, said that "a New Look is a reassessment of our strategic and logistic capabilities in the light of foreseeable developments." The objective of this reassessment, he explained, was to achieve "the maximum military strength and security of our country that can be obtained by the intelligent expenditure of the funds the people of our country . . . are able and willing to make available." It would be impossible, he said, to place combat-ready troops everywhere that Soviet aggression might occur. "If we tried to do this, we could insure economic collapse." Instead, the United States would improve its combat effectiveness with "new weapons and new techniques." These included an emphasis on "modern air power" and a reliance on atomic weapons, which he said, "have virtually achieved conventional status within our Armed Forces."[38]

In their public comments following the adoption of NSC 162, Eisenhower and Dulles also emphasized the Great Equation. In his 1954 State of the Union address, Eisenhower said that the United States and its allies "have and will maintain a massive capability to strike back." The new weapons that provided that capability, he said, had created "new relationships between men and materials. These new relationships permit economies in the use of men as we build forces suited to our situation in the world today."[39] Speaking to the Council on Foreign Relations five days later, Dulles said that the Eisenhower administration sought "maximum deterrent at bearable cost." To achieve this goal, "local defense must be reinforced by the further deterrent of massive retaliatory power." The "free community," he said, must be "willing and able to respond vigorously at places and with means of its own choosing." This would allow for "more security at less cost."[40] Fearing that press coverage had made too much of his use of the phrase "massive retaliation," Dulles quickly followed up with an article that appeared in the next issue of *Foreign Affairs.* He explained that the doctrine he had described did not mean "turning every local war into a world war." Nor did it mean that "if there is a Communist attack somewhere in Asia, atom or hydrogen bombs will necessarily be dropped on . . . China or Russia." What it did mean was that "the free world must maintain the collective means and be willing to use them in the way which most effectively makes aggression too risky and expensive to be tempting."[41]

Eisenhower's national security policy sought to balance the nation's military and economic interests. Recognizing that the Cold War required a long-term commitment from the United States, he sought to make that commitment economically sustainable. There was a limit to how much the American people would sacrifice. Asking for more than this would eventually require the imposition of economic controls to promote military interests. Imposing a "garrison state," as Eisenhower called it, would destroy the very freedoms the nation sought to preserve. "The problem in defense," he said, "is how far you can go without destroying from within what you are trying to defend from without."[42] Finding the proper balance between the nation's military and economic interests was an attempt to solve what Eisenhower called the Great Equation.

Emphasis on the Great Equation led to the New Look being described as a national security policy that provided "more bang for the buck." This characterization focuses on the New Look's greater reliance on nuclear, as opposed to conventional, weapons. As we have seen, the national security policy laid out by NSC 162 was more complicated. It did call for the redeployment of overseas U.S. forces, but it did so rather tentatively due to belated Defense

Department hesitancy and concern for the objections of American allies. The American commitment to NATO, which Eisenhower considered essential, was not undermined. NSC 162 also called for a greater reliance on nuclear weapons, which Eisenhower said he would not hesitate to use in the event of a global war. But their primary importance was as a deterrent to such a war, and he did not contemplate their use in a smaller conflict. This effectively ruled out the kind of deterrence proposed by Task Force B in the Solarium Project. Also ruled out was Task Force C's "rollback" of communism in Eastern Europe, which had been advocated by the Republican Party since the onset of the Cold War. By eliminating these two high-risk strategies, Eisenhower, who recognized that winning a nuclear war was only marginally better than losing one, sought to balance risk and reward.

Creating a grand strategy is far more difficult now than it was in Eisenhower's time. America's determination to contain communism gave it an objective that transcended all other foreign policy concerns. With the collapse of the Soviet Union in 1990, American foreign policy lost that distinctive purpose. During the first decade of the twenty-first century, after the September 11, 2001, terrorist attacks, U.S. foreign policy once again had a transcendent purpose—fighting terrorism. Although terrorism remains a threat, countering it ceased to be the singular focus of U.S. foreign policy after its withdrawal from Afghanistan and Iraq. Since then, immigration, human rights, the environment, access to scarce resources, an expansionist Russia, and many other issues compete for attention in our increasingly global society.

The existence of competing, and sometimes contradictory, interests makes the creation of a grand strategy more important than it has ever been. As Bowie and Immerman argued, grand strategies do not provide answers to the specific questions that arise during a presidential administration; they establish long-term priorities that ensure consistency in how the United States answers those questions when they do arise. When prepared thoughtfully, they can also provide a blueprint for action by future presidents. As we have seen, after undertaking an extensive study, Eisenhower made some changes to the Cold War policies pursued by Truman. These changes, however, were adjustments to the approach, not the overall strategy. Eisenhower and every subsequent president, Republican or Democrat, remained committed to containment. This consistency helped to win the Cold War. For the United States to ensure its own security and maintain the credibility necessary to hold a leadership role in the world, our two political parties must define their common interests and work together to promote them abroad.

5

Indochina and the Domino Theory

At his press conference on April 7, 1954, Eisenhower was asked to comment "on the strategic importance of Indochina to the free world." His response articulated what came to be known as the "domino theory"—which was used as a rationale for U.S. intervention throughout the remainder of the Cold War. He explained how the domino theory worked like this:

> You have a row of dominoes set up—you knock over the first one, and what will happen to the last one is the certainty that it will go over very quickly. So, you could have [the] beginning of a disintegration that would have the most profound influences. . . . The loss of Indochina, of Burma, of Thailand . . . and Indonesia . . . you are talking really about millions and millions and millions of people. . . . [Then] it moves in to threaten Australia and New Zealand. So, the possible consequences of the loss are just incalculable to the free world.[1]

Despite Eisenhower's warnings, his administration did not intervene to prevent the loss of Indochina. The devastating consequences of U.S. intervention in Southeast Asia in the 1960s has led historians to near consensus that nonintervention in the 1950s was the correct course. What historians fail to agree on, however, is whether this was the course that Eisenhower chose, or whether he would have preferred to intervene and was prevented from doing so by Congress and America's allies. While events were still unfolding, *Washington Post* editorialist and Eisenhower critic Chalmers Roberts claimed that Eisenhower wanted to intervene but was prevented from doing so by congressional leaders. Roberts even identified April 3, 1954, the day that Secretary of State John Foster Dulles met with congressional leaders about the possibility of intervention, as "the day we didn't go to war."[2]

Few historians have shared Roberts's interpretation.[3] Early revisionists argued that Eisenhower did not want to intervene and had already decided against it by the time Dulles met with congressional leaders.[4] Later revisionists argued that Eisenhower erected conditions as a barrier against intervention, knowing that there was little likelihood that these conditions could be satisfied in time for the United States to intervene.[5] A third school of thought, however, argues that Eisenhower was neither determined to intervene nor was he adamantly against doing so. These historians argue that Eisenhower's conditions were not meant as a barrier to intervention but as a means of allowing for it only under the right circumstances. They believe that Eisenhower would have intervened "if conditions warranted it and if proper arrangements could be made."[6]

Congress did not prevent Eisenhower from intervening in the French-Indochina War, nor did Eisenhower ever make a definitive decision not to intervene. Eisenhower wanted to prevent the Indochina "domino" from falling, but as we shall see, he was not willing to do it at any cost. The conditions he set for American intervention sought balance—"a course between two extremes, one . . . would be unattainable, and the other unacceptable."[7] In his 1967 memoir *At Ease*, Eisenhower wrote that "unless circumstances and responsibility demanded an instant judgement, I learned to reserve mine until the last proper moment."[8] In this case, reserving judgment until the last possible moment avoided near certain disaster. His successors would not be so prudent.

The United States did not go to war in Vietnam during the Eisenhower presidency, but during the next three presidential administrations, more than fifty-eight thousand Americans died fighting there. Eisenhower's cautious approach to the Indochina crisis is a valuable lesson for our time. Throughout the spring and summer of 1954, Eisenhower insisted that several conditions be met before he was willing to intervene in the French-Indochina War. These conditions included the participation of a broad coalition of allies, the support of Congress, and submission of the conflict to the UN Security Council. Satisfying these conditions before engaging in armed conflict does not assure victory, but comparing Eisenhower's approach with that of later wartime presidents suggests that doing so creates a greater chance for success.

A War for Empire or a War against Communism?

During World War II, Japan occupied the French colonies of Indochina—Vietnam, Laos, and Cambodia. After Japan's defeat, a communist-led movement known as the Viet Minh declared Vietnamese independence. France's war with the Viet Minh was, on the one hand, a colonial war—an attempt to regain control over its former territory. On the other hand, it was a war against communism—an attempt to contain its spread like the war the United States would later fight in Korea. Although France had granted Vietnam, Laos, and Cambodia limited autonomy as Associated States within the French Union in 1949, the colonial aspect of the French-Indochina War represented a significant barrier to American participation.

Eisenhower's first use of the domino metaphor probably came in a March 1951 diary entry while he was in Paris serving as SACEUR. "The French have a knotty problem on that one," he wrote. "If they quit and Indochina falls to the Commies, it is easily possible that [all of] Southeast Asia and Indonesia will go, soon to be followed by India. That prospect makes the whole problem one of interest to us all." Although he hoped the French would prevail, he had his doubts even then. "I'm convinced that no military victory is possible in that kind of theater," he wrote. "Even if Indochina were completely cleared of Communists, right across the border is China with inexhaustible manpower."[9]

Less than two years after confiding to his diary that military victory was not possible in Vietnam, Eisenhower became president of the United States. In his inaugural address he defined the French-Indochina War as part of the global struggle in which "freedom is pitted against slavery; lightness against the dark." The faith of the free world, he said, "confers a common dignity upon the French soldier who dies in Indo-China, the British soldier killed in Malaya, the American life given in Korea."[10] In his State of the Union address the following month, he continued to link Indochina and other areas of U.S. interest in East Asia, claiming that the war in Korea was part of the "same calculated assault that the aggressor is simultaneously pressing in Indochina and Malaya, and the strategic situation that manifestly embraces the island of Formosa and the Chinese Nationalist forces there."[11]

Just six days after the inauguration, Secretary of State Dulles made a nationally televised speech on the foreign policy challenges faced by the new administration. Criticized by the *New York Times* for its "off-cuff" imprecision, Dulles's speech noted the importance of Indochina in the global struggle against communism.[12] "The Soviet Russians are making a drive to get Japan, not only through what they are doing . . . in Korea, but also through what they are doing in Indo-China. If they could get this peninsula of Indo-China," he warned, plus "Siam, Burma, Malaya, they would have what is called the rice bowl of Asia. . . . And you can see that if the Soviet Union had control of the rice bowl of Asia that would be another weapon which would tend to expand their control into Japan and into India."[13]

Although Dulles spent relatively little time on Indochina in his televised speech, two months later, after a meeting with Eisenhower, Defense Secretary Charles Wilson, Treasury Secretary George Humphrey, and Director of Mutual Security Harold Stassen, he wrote that it had "probably" become the "top priority in foreign policy." It was, he wrote, "in some ways more important than Korea because the consequences of loss there could not be localized, but would spread throughout Asia and Europe." The group had agreed that the United States would have to "step up considerably" its aid to France "if there was a plan that promised real success." China, however, would have to be deterred, "so they would not send their forces openly into Vietnam as they had done in Korea."[14]

Eisenhower had the opportunity to judge for himself whether such a plan was in place just two days later. On March 26, Eisenhower, Dulles, and several others met with a visiting delegation from France aboard the presidential yacht *Williamsburg*, as it cruised the Potomac to Mount Vernon and back. Included among the French dignitaries were Prime Minister René Mayer, Foreign Minister Georges Bidault, and Minister to the Associated States Jean Letourneau. Eisenhower sought assurances that France was committed to the defeat of communism in Indochina. He said that the United States was "very sympathetic" regarding the French problem in Indochina and was "interested in hearing of any French program" for its solution. "Knowledge of such a program was necessary to the United States so that it could see where and how it could be of assistance."[15]

When pressed for his plan to defeat the Viet Minh, Letourneau had said that "it is not a question of *winning* the war"; the goal was "to maintain a position of strength from which an honorable settlement could be negotiated," much like the United States was doing in Korea. In any event, he added, "victory was probably unattainable because of the likelihood that the Chinese would intervene in Indochina to prevent such an outcome, just as they had done in Korea."[16] Eisenhower later shared his doubts about the French commitment in Indochina with the NSC. Only two developments could save the situation, he said. The first was "a firm official statement by France as to the future independence of the Associated States when the internal conflict was over." The second was the appointment of a competent military commander. "Most of the French Generals sent out to Indochina," he said, "were a poor lot."[17] Despite his reservations, Eisenhower told Congress that in the coming year he proposed to make "substantial additional resources available to assist the French and the Associated States in their military efforts to defeat the communist Viet Minh aggression."[18]

The Navarre Plan

Later that same month, General Henri Navarre assumed command of the French forces in Indochina. Navarre, a decorated veteran of both world wars, spoke confidently of victory. "We will take the offensive," he declared, and "give back to our troops the mobility and aggressiveness they have sometimes lacked." This attitude pleased Eisenhower but put Navarre at odds with his superiors who reminded him that his primary mission was "not to destroy the Viet Minh or win an outright victory, but merely to create the conditions for an 'honorable' exit from the struggle."[19]

The JCS sent General John "Iron Mike" O'Daniel, also a veteran of both world wars—and Korea—to assess Navarre's strategy. O'Daniel was initially encouraged by the Navarre Plan. Navarre sought to "retake the initiative immediately" by carrying out local offensives in the summer of 1953. Then, beginning in September, he would lay the groundwork for a major battle that would take place in the fall and winter of 1953–54. By attacking the flanks and rear of the enemy he hoped to forestall a Viet Minh attack in the Red River Delta region where France still held the capital of Hanoi and the port of Haiphong. O'Daniel believed that Navarre was "honest and trustworthy" and would do everything possible to carry out his "aggressive" plan. O'Daniel concluded that if Navarre could get the support he needed from Paris, "he will do much toward bringing the war here to a successful conclusion."[20]

On July 3, France invited the Associated States of Vietnam, Laos, and Cambodia to begin talks to finalize their independence. Secretary Dulles used this invitation as a way of rejecting criticism that the war was a colonial one. "The pretext, until now, has been that the Associated States of Indochina were mere colonies and that the Communist war was designed to promote 'independence' rather than to expand by violence the Soviet camp," he told the UN General Assembly in September. "It is no longer possible to support such a pretext. . . . The communist-dominated armies in Indochina have no shadow of a claim to be regarded as champions of an independence movement."[21]

So, by the summer of 1953, the two developments that Eisenhower had said were necessary for France to "save the situation" had now come to pass—at least nominally. Adding to American optimism was the selection of Joseph Laniel as French prime minister in June. He and Foreign Minister Georges Bidault pledged an early and victorious conclusion to the war and called Navarre to Paris for consultations. Laniel accepted Navarre's plan and promised him: "I shall not make the same mistakes as my predecessors."[22] By the end of July, Laniel had put a price tag on the Navarre Plan. France would request an additional $400 million from the United States. This was on top of the $1.3 billion the United States had already planned to give France for the Indochina war.

On September 4, the day before the NSC met to begin consideration of this request, Eisenhower spoke to the National Governors' Conference in Seattle and, in a preview of the domino theory, prepared them for what he considered a necessary expense. Whether or not the war had begun as a colonial undertaking no longer mattered, he said. What did matter was that American security was being threatened by the expanding communist empire. He began with the question he assumed was on their minds: "Why is it" that we are we so concerned with the distant southeast corner of Asia? If Indochina fell to communism, he explained, several things would happen right away: Burma, Malaya, and possibly India would fall. And if the free world lost all of that, he asked, how would it hold Indonesia? "Somewhere along the line," he warned, communist expansion must be stopped. "That is what the French are doing. So, when the United States votes $400 million to help that war, we are not voting for a giveaway program. We are voting for the cheapest way that we can to prevent the occurrence of something that would be of the most terrible significance for the United States."[23]

At the August 6 meeting of the NSC, the State Department presented the French request for an additional $400 million for calendar year 1954 as a near emergency situation. For the last seven years, France had been spending $1.2 billion a year on the war in Indochina and had little to show for it but 148,000 casualties. The Viet Minh held the strategic initiative, and aid to the Viet Minh from Communist China was increasing—a trend that was expected to accelerate with the Korean Armistice. Not surprisingly, the war had become very unpopular in France, and there were increasing demands for withdrawal. Furthermore, the cost of the war, in both money and manpower, had made France unable to meet its commitments to NATO, which was of paramount importance to the United States.

There were signs, however, that the French request came at an important turning point. "The Laniel government," the State Department argued, "is almost certainly the *last* French government which would undertake to continue the war in Indo-China. If it fails, it will almost certainly be succeeded by a government committed to seek a settlement on terms dangerous to the security of the U.S. and the Free World." Based on these considerations, the State Department recommended that the additional $400 million to France be approved.[24] The NSC trimmed the figure slightly and approved $385 million in additional funds.[25]

Dien Bien Phu

In late November, five battalions of French paratroopers jumped from American transport planes into Dien Bien Phu, a remote valley near the Laotian border in extreme northwest Vietnam. The paratroopers established a base there from which they hoped to strike the supply lines of Viet Minh troops on their way to Laos.

The mountains and jungle that surrounded the valley prevented the overland movement of men and supplies, making it dependent on its airfield for survival and, therefore, a difficult location from which to conduct offensive operations. Despite Dien Bien Phu's drawbacks, Navarre believed it was impossible for the Viet Minh to place heavy artillery and antiaircraft guns in the mountains surrounding it. On December 3, he gave the order to hold the position at all costs. Three days later, Viet Minh General Vo Nguyen Giap decided to concentrate his forces around Dien Bien Phu.[26] The stage had been set for a major confrontation.

By January 8 the situation at Dien Bien Phu was bad enough that the NSC spent most of its meeting discussing the possibility of American intervention. DCI Allen Dulles reported that the French garrison was surrounded and outnumbered approximately three to one, but it was unclear whether the Viet Minh would launch an attack. Admiral Radford, now chair of the JCS, said that the Viet Minh may be able to take Dien Bien Phu if they launched an all-out attack and were willing to take heavy losses, but he did not believe they would do so because it would prevent them from carrying out their objectives in Laos. Allen Dulles added that the only reason for a Viet Minh attack was the political and psychological damage it would do to the French war effort.

Robert Cutler then turned the discussion to the question of U.S. involvement. Eisenhower asked why the French were unwilling to allow the Associated States to take their case to the UN, which might lead to the formation of an international coalition such as the one that had fought in Korea. The question raised the important issue of whether France saw Indochina as a colonial war or part of the international struggle against communism. Foster Dulles responded that the French feared UN involvement because of the precedent it would set for their other colonies. In the absence of a coalition, Eisenhower said that he "simply could not imagine putting ground forces anywhere in Southeast Asia." Regarding the United States replacing the French in Indochina, he was even more vehement. "I cannot tell you, how bitterly opposed I am to such a course of action. This war in Indochina would absorb our troops by divisions!"

Later in the meeting, Cutler pursued the question further. What would we do, he asked, "if the French turn to us and request the participation of U.S. forces?" Radford responded that the United States "should do everything possible to forestall a French defeat at Dien Bien Phu." This included, in his opinion, sending an aircraft carrier. He argued that the situation was serious because, contrary to French expectations, the Viet Minh had succeeded in placing heavy artillery and antiaircraft weapons on the high ground surrounding the French garrison. Radford believed American pilots could take them out. Secretary Humphrey opposed direct involvement. He said he "appreciated how serious the loss of Dien Bien Phu could be," but "it could not be . . . bad enough to involve the United States in combat in Indochina."

Eisenhower, who had spoken so adamantly earlier in the meeting, slipped into the role of mediator. He seemed to be looking for a position somewhere between Radford and Humphrey. To Radford he said it was "certainly going to be necessary" to get American planes involved, but "obviously, we couldn't just fly them into combat off the carrier." Then he reminded Humphrey that "no one was more anxious" than he was to keep Americans out of the jungles of Vietnam, but we could not "forget our vital interests" there. Radford then began to speculate: "If we could put one squadron of U.S. planes over Dien Bien Phu for as little as one afternoon, it might save the situation. Weren't the stakes worth it?" The president, for a moment, seemed to go along. "A little group of fine and adventurous pilots," he mused, "we should give these pilots U.S. planes without insignia and let them go." It could be arranged, Radford said. But then the president came back to reality. The responsible council members should study what additional steps could be taken to assist the French, he said, and make concrete proposals at a future council meeting.[27]

The Search for a Response

By the following week's NSC meeting, the planning board had completed work on a draft of "United States Objectives and Courses of Action with Respect to Southeast Asia" for the council's consideration. The document defined the Indochina war as one in which the "Communist and non-Communist worlds clearly confront one another on the field of battle." The loss of Indochina, in addition to its impact on South and Southeast Asia, would have "serious repercussions on the U.S. and free world interests in Europe and elsewhere." The "most urgent threat" to a free world victory in this war came from the "strong possibility" that the situation could deteriorate due to a "weakening of the resolve of France and the Associated States of Indochina to oppose the Viet Minh." If American aid continued, the document predicted, French forces were "not in danger of being militarily defeated by the Viet Minh unless there is a large-scale Chinese Communist intervention." Such an intervention was not expected unless the United States were to engage in combat. After approval by the NSC and Eisenhower, the draft became NSC 5405.[28]

Eisenhower's earlier request for concrete proposals resulted in two further developments. First, he established a "special committee," consisting of Undersecretary of State Walter Bedell Smith, Deputy Secretary of Defense Roger Keyes, Special Assistant

C. D. Jackson, Allen Dulles, and Radford, to report directly to the president on the "Southeast Asian problem" and produce a plan of action. Second, the JCS, in consultation with the CIA, undertook a study on how the United States might "assist in achieving the success of the Navarre Plan." Eisenhower was disappointed that despite the urgency of the situation, neither group had developed a proposal by the time of the next NSC meeting. Indochina, he said, "must not be allowed to go by default."[29]

At its first meeting, the special committee, rather than looking at the big picture as Eisenhower had intended, spent much of its time considering a French request for additional assistance. Specifically, they requested forty-seven B-26s and four hundred personnel trained to maintain them. Eisenhower approved the committee's recommendation to provide only twenty-two B-26s and two hundred maintenance personnel.[30] The French request for maintenance personnel set off alarm bells for some. Consequently, Eisenhower began to field additional questions on the matter at his weekly press conferences. When asked on February 3 about the presence of American military personnel in Indochina, he explained that they were engaged in "training and technical" activities but there were no "fighting units." Impatiently, he added "that is all there is to say on the subject."[31]

Some members of Congress were also concerned. In a letter to Defense Secretary Wilson, Senator John Stennis (D-MS) feared a slippery slope. "First we send them planes, then we send them men. . . . We are going to war, inch by inch."[32] When asked about Stennis's concerns at his next press conference, Eisenhower replied: "no one could be more bitterly opposed to ever getting the United States involved in a hot war in that region than I am; consequently, every move I authorize is calculated . . . to make certain that that does not happen." In response to a follow-up question, Eisenhower said he could "not conceive of a greater tragedy for America" than to get involved in a war in Indochina. America's role was to help the Vietnamese and the French resist the "encroachment of communism."[33] Stennis, however, continued to criticize the presence of American support personnel in Indochina, warning that it put the United States "in danger of becoming involved in World War III." Asked for comment, Eisenhower insisted that the United States would only go to war as a "result of the constitutional process," which was in the hands of Congress. "Let us have that clear," he added, "that is the answer."[34]

During his trip to Berlin for a four-power conference with the foreign ministers of Britain, France, and the Soviet Union, Secretary Dulles wrote Eisenhower that he planned to urge Bidault to "ignore any suggestion of negotiation over Indochina." Negotiations, he warned, were "slippery ground" and would "lead to further deterioration of morale in Indochina and France."[35] Above all, Dulles hoped to avoid a five-power conference, which would bring China into the discussions. Ultimately, Dulles had to give in. His fellow foreign ministers supported such a move, and Dulles feared that if he vetoed it, the Laniel government would fall and be replaced by a new government that would abandon Indochina. While disappointed, Dulles did not expect that France would push too hard for a negotiated settlement as long there was not a "military disaster in Indochina." The parties agreed to schedule the five-power conference in Geneva, Switzerland, beginning in late April.[36]

The Situation Worsens

On the afternoon of March 13, the anticipated attack on Dien Bien Phu began with a Viet Minh artillery bombardment that the French had not believed possible. "We are all surprised and ask ourselves how the Viets have been able to find so many guns capable of producing an artillery fire of such power," wrote a French Foreign Legionnaire. "Shells rained down on us without stopping, like a hailstorm on a fall evening. Bunker after bunker, trench after trench, collapsed, burying under them men and weapons."[37] Colonel Charles Piroth, the French artillery commander, could not silence the onslaught. When the bombardment turned to the airstrip, the isolated post's lifeline, French planes took off to avoid being destroyed on the ground. It was then that well-camouflaged Viet Minh antiaircraft batteries opened fire from the hills just beyond the runway, establishing air superiority without a single plane. As night fell, Viet Minh infantry attacked the French position known as Beatrice. The Viet Minh took tremendous casualties but overwhelmed the position in an hour's time.

The next day Viet Minh artillery rendered the airstrip unusable, and that night the French position known as Gabrielle came under attack from Viet Minh infantry. The Algerian forces defending Gabrielle were outnumbered eight to one but held off wave after wave before succumbing. That night Colonel Piroth told a fellow officer, "We're done for. . . . We're heading for a massacre, and it's my fault." Returning to his quarters, he held a grenade in his only hand—he had lost an arm in World War II—and pulled the pin with his teeth, taking his own life.[38] In the first two days of fighting both sides took heavy losses. Approximately 1,350 French Union forces died defending Beatrice and Gabrielle. Viet Minh losses are less clear but have been estimated at approximately double those of the French.

When the NSC met on March 18, the extent of the devastation was not yet apparent. After giving a casualty report, Allen Dulles said that the French were outnumbered two-to-one. Although he believed the outcome was "impossible to predict," he ventured that the French had a "fifty-fifty chance of holding out." Eisenhower was somewhat critical of the French effort, saying it was difficult for him to understand why Navarre had been so optimistic, but he did not think that being outnumbered two-to-one was as bad as it sounded, "in view of the fact that they [the French] were fighting from prepared and heavily fortified positions." Secretary Dulles confirmed that this was the biggest commitment that the Viet Minh had made so far and believed that "the whole operation was obviously a Vietminh preparation for the Geneva Conference." He said that he had warned the French foreign minister that if Indochina were put on the agenda for the five-power conference in Geneva, "it would be the signal for violent Vietminh attacks. . . . This was precisely what had happened."[39]

What had been unclear at the March 18 NSC meeting became increasingly so over the next few days. On March 20, Eisenhower held a ninety-minute "off the record" meeting at the White House with his senior national security team, Foster Dulles, Allen Dulles, Wilson, and Radford. The same group, minus Radford, met again the next day for another off-the-record meeting. No evidence of these meetings, other than notations in the White House daily appointments book, have been found, but James Hagerty's diary indicates that their subject was Indochina.[40] Radford likely missed the second meeting because he was with his counterpart, Chairman of the French Chiefs of Staff General Paul Ely, who had stopped in Washington for talks on his way home from Vietnam. It was Ely, more than anyone, who convinced American policymakers of the desperate situation in Dien Bien Phu and Indochina in general.

In several meetings with top-level policymakers while in Washington, General Ely indicated that although the present French government was determined to defeat the communists, the French people were weary of the war in Indochina. Ely shared Secretary

Dulles's belief that the Viet Minh assault on Dien Bien Phu was "undoubtedly for the purpose of achieving a major *political* victory."[41] The military value of Dien Bien Phu was not great enough to justify the sacrifices necessary for the Viet Minh to take it. They were attempting to do so only to influence French public opinion and to achieve "a position of strength from which to negotiate at Geneva."[42] When Secretary Dulles discussed Ely's visit with the president, Eisenhower reiterated that the United States could not get involved in the fighting unless the political preconditions for a successful outcome were in place. "He did not, however, wholly exclude the possibility of a single strike, if it were almost certain this would produce decisive results."[43]

By the time that the NSC met on March 25, its members were more pessimistic about the chances of a French military victory. Eisenhower, who had become increasingly critical of French strategy, proclaimed that the current situation was "sufficient indication that the population of Vietnam did not wish to be free from Communist domination." In a similarly pessimistic vein, Secretary Dulles said that what they were witnessing was "the collapse or evaporation of France as a great power." The question that remained was "Who should fill the void? . . . Would it be the Communists, or must it be the U.S.?" Finding the answer to that question occupied the council for the remainder of the meeting. Cutler pointed out that NSC 5405 had not contemplated the withdrawal of France. Consequently, the council instructed the planning board to consider what actions the United States would take in Southeast Asia if France withdrew. Eisenhower made clear that the planning board should consider the possibility of deploying American ground troops.[44]

Admiral Radford had one final day with General Ely following the NSC meeting. What transpired between them on March 26 remains unclear and has been the subject of much speculation. Ely was anxious to know what specific actions the United States was willing to take to relieve the desperate situation at Dien Bien Phu. Both men were aware of a plan—code-named Operation Vulture—that had been created by U.S. and French personnel in Saigon. The plan involved nighttime attacks on Viet Minh positions surrounding Dien Bien Phu by U.S. carrier-based aircraft and B-29s based in the Philippines. Radford said that 350 planes could be over Dien Bien Phu with two days' notice. Ely later claimed that Radford strongly supported the plan and said he could get Eisenhower's approval. Radford, on the other hand, claimed that he had only meant that the plan could be enacted within two days if it was approved. It may have been a simple matter of miscommunication. No translators were present and neither man was fluent in the other's language. As historian Fredrik Logevall has pointed out, however, both men wanted to implement Operation Vulture. While Ely may have heard what he wanted to hear, Radford likely conveyed the impression that he wanted to convey.[45] Several days later Radford called a meeting of the JCS to pose a question: Should the JCS recommend to the secretary of defense and the president that an offer be made to the French to render assistance at Dien Bien Phu with U.S. naval and air forces? The three chiefs of staff and the commandant of the Marine Corps all voted "no." Only Radford, the chairman, voted "yes."[46]

Setting Conditions

While making contingency plans, Eisenhower wanted to line up support from Congress, American allies, and the American public. "Congress would have to be in on any move," Eisenhower said, and "this might be the moment to begin to explore with the Congress what support could be anticipated in the event that it seemed desirable to intervene in Indochina." Eisenhower also wanted the UN involved. Although he knew France was opposed to UN involvement, he "did not see how the United States or other free world nations could go full out in support of the Associated States without UN approval and assistance." The president also raised the question of what other nations might be willing to partici-pate. "Australia, New Zealand, the Philippines, Formosa, the free nations of Southeast Asia, the British, and the French," he sug-gested. "That was enough, wasn't it?"[47] Finally, on March 29, Sec-retary Dulles made a speech, preapproved by the president, titled "The Threat of a Red Asia" to the Overseas Press Club of America. The *New York Times* called it the beginning of "a campaign to tell the United States public clearly and dramatically what is at stake in Indo-China." Communist domination of Asia, he warned, "was a possibility that should not be passively accepted, but should be met by united action."[48]

In anticipation of Secretary Dulles's meeting with congres-sional leaders, Eisenhower met briefly with Dulles, Wilson, and Radford on April 2. Dulles had drafted a possible congressional resolution on Indochina. It authorized the president "to employ the Naval and Air Forces of the United States to assist the forces which are resisting aggression in Southeast Asia."[49] It would expire on June 30, 1955. Eisenhower said that the draft reflected what he believed was desirable but thought that the meeting should be used to "develop the thinking of the congressional leaders" rather than presenting them with a resolution drafted by the adminis-tration. Dulles agreed and said that, personally, he thought of a resolution as more of a deterrent—one that would give the United States a strong position from which to put together a coalition of nations that would prevent the spread of communism in the area. Radford, Dulles believed, saw the resolution as the immediate authority to launch a strike to save Dien Bien Phu. Radford said that had been true, but he now believed that it may be too late to save Dien Bien Phu, the fate of which could be determined in "a matter of hours."[50]

The next day, Secretary Dulles and Radford met at the State Department with congressional leaders from both parties. After Radford gave an extensive briefing on the situation in Indochina, focusing on Dien Bien Phu, Dulles said that he thought the "president should have congressional backing so that he could use air and sea power in the area if he felt it necessary in the interest of national security." Senate majority leader William Knowland (R-CA) initially gave his approval, but after further discussion, the congressional leaders unanimously agreed that there should be no congressional action until the administration had "obtained commitments of a political and material nature from our allies." Dulles and Radford both pointed out that the president was not contemplating the use of ground forces, but the senators and congressmen were undeterred. "Once the flag was committed," they said, "the use of land forces would inevitably follow."[51] Chalmers Roberts, a journalist for the *Washington Post*, would later refer to April 3, 1954, as "the day we didn't go to war."

Roberts's characterization was an exaggeration, but the legislative leaders' meeting did represent a turning point. From then on, Secretary Dulles's efforts were devoted primarily to building a coalition of nations willing to intervene with the United States. On the following evening the president held an off-the-record meeting in the residence at the White House. According to White House Chief of Staff Sherman Adams, Eisenhower "agreed with Dulles and Radford to send American forces to Indochina under certain strict conditions." The first of those conditions was that it be a joint action to include Britain, Australia, New Zealand, and if possible, the Philippines and Thailand "so that the forces would have Asiatic [*sic*] representation." Second, the French would have to continue to fight and "bear the full responsibility until the war was over." Finally, the independence of Vietnam, Laos, and Cambodia must be guaranteed.[52]

Late that same night Secretary Dulles received a cable from the U.S. ambassador to France, Douglas Dillon, who had been summoned to a late-night meeting in Paris with Prime Minister Laniel and Foreign Minister Bidault. They told Dillon that "immediate armed intervention of U.S. carrier aircraft at Dien Bien Phu is now necessary to save the situation." They based their request on General Ely's report that Radford had given his assurance that if the French requested such an intervention, he would "do his best" to overcome opposition to it.[53] Eisenhower, in a phone conversation with Dulles the next day, turned down the request. "Such a move is impossible," he said. "In the absence of some kind of arrangement getting support of Congress, [it] would be completely unconstitutional and indefensible. . . . We cannot engage in active war."[54]

Reading the minutes of the NSC meeting on April 6, it is clear that events had overtaken the usual procedures of the council. The meeting began with an intelligence briefing. The situation at Dien Bien Phu was grim. The French had sufficient food to last for three days and ammunition to last for four or five. The airstrip was unusable, and it had become very difficult to drop supplies by parachute due to the closeness of the enemy's perimeter and the accuracy of their antiaircraft fire. Meanwhile, twenty thousand troops were on their way to replace Viet Minh losses. Cutler, unaware of Secretary Dulles's meeting with congressional leaders, then posed the question that the planning board had prepared for the meeting: Should the United States "intervene with armed forces in Indochina in the event that there was no other means of saving the area from Communist control"? Dulles told the council about his meeting and the three conditions that Eisenhower had subsequently outlined for any U.S. intervention. He concluded by saying, "We should, therefore, place all our efforts on trying to organize a regional grouping for the defense of Southeast Asia prior to the opening of the Geneva Conference."

Eisenhower's position is difficult to ascertain during this meeting. In his earlier discussions with Secretary Dulles and Radford he had set a very high bar for U.S. participation in the war, but he was easily provoked by those who suggested that the United States should accept France's fate. He dismissed Harold Stassen's prescient suggestion that the United States should accept the loss of northern Vietnam and focus instead on saving the south. And he "spoke sharply" to Humphrey when the treasury secretary suggested that the United States was trying to police "all the governments of the world." When Humphrey persisted, Eisenhower said that "Indochina was the first in a row of dominoes. If it fell, its neighbors would shortly thereafter fall with it, and where did the process end? . . . We cannot afford to let Moscow gain another bit of territory. Dien Bien Phu itself may be just such a critical point."[55] The president's comments anticipated those he would make in his press conference the following day, quoted at the beginning of this chapter.

Secretary Dulles spent most of his remaining time before departing for the Geneva Conference trying to put together a coalition of nations to contain communism in Southeast Asia. His efforts began with a trip to London where he attempted to persuade Prime Minister Winston Churchill and Foreign Secretary Anthony Eden to join the United States in a coalition to prevent the loss of Indochina. Dulles's arrival was preceded by a letter from the president to Churchill that played on his wartime colleague's appreciation for the lessons of history. "We failed to halt Hirohito, Mussolini, and Hitler by not acting in unity and in time. That marked the beginning of many years of stark tragedy and peril. May it not be that our nations have learned something from that lesson?"[56] Churchill and Eden were unmoved by Eisenhower's appeal and Dulles's attempts to persuade them. They did not share Eisenhower's belief in the domino theory, and they feared that escalation would risk the intervention of China and the onset of World War III. They believed it best to wait and see what could be achieved at the Geneva Conference.[57]

Dulles's trip to Paris was similarly unproductive. Just days before, Prime Minister Laniel had asked the United States to launch a carrier-based airstrike to save Dien Bien Phu and put France in a better bargaining position at Geneva, but this did not mean that France was interested in an international coalition. "France must have an opportunity to negotiate an honorable peace," Foreign Minister Bidault said. "If Geneva fails, collective security is a possibility, but nothing can be done before Geneva which would allow it to be said or thought that anything had been decided beforehand about what was to be done if Geneva failed."[58]

Dulles had one last chance before the Geneva Conference began—a meeting with Bidault and Eden in Paris beginning on April 22. By this time Bidault had altered his position. The situation in Dien Bien Phu, he believed, remained so "hopeless" that only a "massive" air strike by the United States could save it. Although he had been against an international coalition, he would support one now if that was what it would take for the United States to act. If Dien Bien Phu fell, however, he did not think France would have any further interest in a coalition. In that case, France would get out of Indochina entirely.[59] Dulles was encouraged by Bidault's willingness to consider united action but was troubled that Bidault was placing such great importance on Dien Bien Phu. "The situation here is tragic," he wrote to Eisenhower the following evening. "France is almost visibly collapsing under our eyes," and "Dien Bien Phu has become a symbol out of all proportion to its military significance."[60] Dulles attempted to shame Laniel into keeping up the fight. "Many people in the world," Dulles told the French prime minister, believed that France "could no longer be counted among the great powers." The way that France reacted to the fall of Dien Bien Phu, he said, would have "a tremendous influence on world opinion," and he hoped that France would "show that she still had the spirit of a great power."[61]

Dulles explained that the United States could not launch the kind of air strike that Bidault was asking for without congressional approval—and approval would require participation of the United Kingdom. Eden expressed "grave doubts that Britain would cooperate in any active fighting to save Indochina," but agreed to return to London to meet with Churchill.[62] Ultimately, neither the British nor French governments would agree to the conditions for U.S. involvement. France wanted a U.S. airstrike to improve its bargaining position at Geneva without the complications and long-term commitments that internationalizing the war would create. Britain feared that if it intervened with the United States then China would get involved, risking World War III. Both countries were prepared to take their chances at Geneva. Their responses also betrayed vestiges of colonial thinking. France feared that internationalizing the war on American terms, which meant granting full sovereignty to the Associated States, would set a bad precedent for its North African colonies. Churchill, when pressed on the issue, "repeatedly referred to the loss of India" and made the point that "since the British people were willing to let India go, they would not be interested in holding Indochina for France."[63] It seems that neither European ally could see the war in Indochina solely as a war against communist aggression, as the United States preferred to see it.

The Geneva Conference

The Geneva Conference began on April 26, 1954. The United States entered the conference, as Walter Bedell Smith pointed out, "with a lesser degree of common understanding with its allies than it had entered any previous international conference."[64] Asked at his April 29 press conference about American objectives in Geneva, Eisenhower displayed his pessimism. He said that the United States was "steering a course between two extremes, one of which, I would say, would be unattainable, and the other unacceptable." The unacceptable would be to let the anticommunist forces in Southeast Asia "crumble and disappear"; the unattainable would be to arrive at a "completely satisfactory solution."[65] Pessimism spilled over into the NSC meeting later that day. "A brief interval of silence" followed Radford's summary of the bleak situation at Dien Bien Phu, where he said the French were taking 150 casualties a day. In the past, Radford had offered the invincibility of American airpower as the answer to the most desperate situations, but he did not do so on this day. It was left to Stassen to make an attempt. It would be "impossible to let the communists take over Indochina and then try to save the rest of the world from a similar fate," he argued. "This was the time and place to take our stand." Eisenhower's response conveys the tremendous responsibilities of the presidency. He had already made the point that "if the United States went into Indochina alone it would mean a general war with China and perhaps with the USSR, which the

United States would have to prosecute separated from its allies." In his reply to Stassen, the president said that "before he could bring himself to make such a decision, he would want to ask himself and all his wisest advisors whether the right decision was not rather to launch a world war. If our allies were going to fall away in any case, it might be better for the United States to leap over the smaller obstacles and hit the biggest one with all the power we had." The tenor of the discussion that followed these remarks demonstrates that Eisenhower was not engaging in hyperbole. He had expressed the alternatives as he saw them.[66]

Later that same day, the NSC Planning Board discussed the potential use of nuclear weapons (which they referred to as "new weapons") in Indochina. The board came up with several questions that could be discussed at a future NSC meeting: "Should [the] decision be made now as to U.S. intention to use 'new weapons'? . . . Would one 'new weapon' dropped on Vietminh troop concentrations in reserve behind DBP be decisive? . . . Could one 'new weapon' be loaned to France for this purpose?" The board concluded that the "use of a 'new weapon' in Vietnam would tend to deter Chinese aggression . . . and that failure to use the 'new weapon' in Vietnam would tend to increase [the] chance of Chinese aggression." It is interesting to note that this discussion, which took place just two months after the first test of a deployable H-Bomb, made no mention of the type of nuclear weapon being considered. Robert Cutler had the opportunity to discuss these questions with Eisenhower and Vice President Nixon the following morning. Eisenhower did not believe that a "new weapon" could be used effectively in the jungles surrounding Dien Bien Phu. He did think that the United States "might *consider* saying to the French that we had never yet given them any 'new weapons' and if they wanted some *now* for possible use, we might give them a few."[67] Eisenhower and Dulles would later conclude that the use of atomic bombs on an Asian country for the second time in a decade would cause "very serious problems" for the United States and was not a realistic option.[68]

Dien Bien Phu fell to the Viet Minh on May 7, just one day before the Geneva Conference turned its attention to Indochina. Its collapse freed the Viet Minh for offensive action in the Tonkin Delta, putting the capital of Hanoi and the port of Haiphong at risk. The Eisenhower administration's main fear was that defeat at Dien Bien Phu would destroy what remained of the French will to fight. At the NSC meeting on May 8, the administration agreed on its position at the Geneva Conference. The United States would not associate itself with any proposal for a cease-fire before an acceptable armistice agreement had been reached. During the armistice negotiations, France should continue to oppose the Viet Minh "with all the means at their disposal." The United States would continue its aid to France and its efforts to create a coalition of nations to prevent further communist expansion in Southeast Asia.[69]

A few days later, Dulles communicated the conditions that would have to be met before Eisenhower would be willing to ask Congress for the authority to intervene in Indochina: (1) U.S. participation would have to be formally requested by France and the Associated States. (2) Thailand, Philippines, Australia, New Zealand, and the United Kingdom would have to receive similar requests. (3) The matter would have to be presented to the UN by one of the Associated States or Thailand. (4) France would have to grant the Associated States complete independence including the right to leave the French Union. (5) France would have to continue fighting in Indochina—U.S. forces would supplement those of France, not replace them, and U.S. forces would be principally naval and air. (6) An agreement would have to be reached on the command structure for participating nations and on the training of indigenous forces.[70]

Since Britain had rejected the possibility of united action in Indochina until after the Geneva Conference, Dulles focused on Australia and New Zealand. If these two British Commonwealth nations would participate, then perhaps the United States could proceed without Britain itself. On June 4, the Australian government declined to participate, preferring instead that a diplomatic settlement be concluded at Geneva. New Zealand soon followed suit. With its last real hope of building a coalition dashed and the situation in Indochina getting worse by the day, the U.S. attitude toward a negotiated settlement softened. "France would have to accept whatever terms they would get if they were to obtain a cease-fire," Dulles told the Australian ambassador.[71]

On June 12, the Laniel government lost a vote of no confidence, becoming the final casualty of Dien Bien Phu. On June 18, Pierre Mendès France was elected prime minister. Mendès France pledged to resign if he were unable to obtain a cease-fire in Indochina on reasonable terms by July 20. Meanwhile, believing there was no longer a chance that an agreement could be reached that the United States would be willing to sign, the U.S. delegation took on the role of "observers." Dulles told the NSC that he "thought it best to let the French get out of Indochina entirely and then try to rebuild from the foundations."[72] As his self-imposed deadline grew near, Mendès France requested that the United States send Dulles or Smith back to Geneva. He was able to convince a reluctant Dulles that communist participants at the conference would interpret the American absence as a rift in the Western alliance and would try to exploit it. Not wanting to strain relations with Britain and France further, Dulles conceded, and Eisenhower agreed to send Smith back.[73] "Your role at the conference," Dulles told Smith, "will be that of the representative of a nation friendly to the non-communist states . . . which desires to assist . . . in arriving at a just settlement. You will not, however, go beyond this role."[74]

A few hours past Mendès France's deadline, in the early morning hours of July 21, the conference completed the Geneva Accords on Indochina. They called for a cease-fire that would be monitored by an international control commission consisting of Poland, India, and Canada. France was required to evacuate the Tonkin Delta region and withdraw south of the seventeenth parallel, where Vietnam was to be temporarily partitioned. A three-mile-wide demilitarized zone was established on either side of the seventeenth parallel. Free movement of people between the two sides was allowed for three hundred days. Neither side was allowed to join a military alliance or seek military reinforcements. A general election would be held in June 1956 to unify the country. Separate agreements were signed with Laos and Cambodia granting their independence from France.

Bedell Smith did not sign the Geneva Accords but made a declaration stating that the United States "takes note" of the agreement and "will refrain from the threat or use of force to disturb them." The statement also said that the United States would view the renewal of aggression in violation of the agreement "with grave concern."[75] In his own statement later in the day, Eisenhower said that the United States was not "a party to or bound by the decisions taken by the conference" but hoped that they would "lead to the establishment of peace."[76] Despite the noncommittal nature of its public response, the United States was not entirely displeased with the outcome at Geneva. The biggest disappointment was the loss of the Tonkin Delta region, which included the capital city of Hanoi and the port city of Haiphong. The Eisenhower administration considered this region the key to the security of Southeast Asia. However, given the fact that the Viet Minh had dealt France a humiliating defeat at Dien Bien Phu and had two powerful friends on its side in Geneva—China and the USSR—the Western powers had done well to keep as much of Vietnam out of communist hands as they did. The United States would now, for better or worse, dedicate itself to the goal of maintaining a viable noncommunist state in South Vietnam.

Chalmers Roberts had referred to April 3, 1954, as "the day we didn't go to war." In doing so he gave the congressional leaders who met with Foster Dulles on that day credit for keeping the United States out of war by requiring the participation of a coalition of nations, preferably including the United Kingdom, before they would give the Eisenhower administration the authority to intervene in Indochina. This version gives the congressional leaders too much credit for preventing U.S. intervention. Before this meeting, Eisenhower was already determined to assemble a coalition of nations that would include not only Britain, but regional powers like Australia and New Zealand, and Asian nations like the Philippines and Thailand.

Another requirement that Eisenhower maintained throughout the months that he considered intervention was that France must grant independence and national self-determination to the Associated States of Indochina. Eisenhower believed this was the only way to impress upon the world that the war was not an effort by France to reestablish its colonial domination over the region but an attempt to stop the spread of communism. More importantly, an unequivocal grant of independence was the only way to deny the Viet Minh the source of their greatest hold over the Vietnamese people—that they were fighting a nationalist war against a colonial oppressor.[77] As Foster Dulles said two days after the Geneva agreement, "One of the lessons of Geneva was that resistance to communism needs popular support, and that in turn means that people should feel that they are defending their own national institutions."[78]

Arguing that it was Eisenhower, rather than Congress, who kept the United States out of war is not to argue that he was determined to keep the United States out. Eisenhower's national security team went to great lengths to satisfy his conditions; if they had been successful, it is likely that the United States would have intervened. But Eisenhower was unwilling to do so otherwise. "No Western Power," he wrote to SACEUR Alfred Gruenther, "can go to Asia militarily, except as one of a concert of powers, which must include Asiatic [*sic*] peoples. To contemplate anything else is to lay ourselves open to the charge of imperialism and colonialism or—at the very least—objectionable paternalism."[79] Eisenhower's policy in Southeast Asia was an attempt to find balance between the "unattainable" and the "unacceptable." Although the settlement in Geneva leaned toward the unacceptable, it bought Eisenhower time during which he would attempt to prevent the domino from falling.

The United States did not go to war in Vietnam during the Eisenhower presidency. This fact takes on added significance because during the next three presidential administrations, more than fifty-eight thousand Americans died fighting there. It is tempting to conclude that this alone makes Eisenhower's cautious approach to the Indochina crisis a valuable lesson for our time. Doing so, however, would be an oversimplification. The partition of Vietnam gave Eisenhower the opportunity to turn South Vietnam into a bulwark against communism, one that he hoped would prevent subsequent dominoes from falling.

By providing substantial monetary and military support for the corrupt regime of President Ngo Dinh Diem and participating in the circumvention of the unification election stipulated by the Geneva Accords, however, the Eisenhower administration contributed to the crises that Presidents John Kennedy and Lyndon Johnson later confronted.

In addition to independence for the Associated States and the participation of a broad coalition that included both regional and European allies, there were several other conditions Eisenhower insisted on before he was willing to intervene in the French-Indochina War. These included congressional support and submission of the conflict to the UN Security Council. Although a Security Council resolution could not be counted on because of the likelihood of a Soviet veto, submitting the conflict to the UN would have required the articulation of a clear rationale and achievable objectives for the conflict. Although public opinion was not a major consideration, Eisenhower also began preparing the American people for the possibility of war with public statements about the domino theory. One might speculate that, if he had insisted upon the same conditions, Johnson would have decided against Americanizing the Vietnam War in 1965. Johnson did secure congressional support in the form of the Gulf of Tonkin Resolution, and his administration ultimately convinced five other nations to participate, including four that were proposed by Eisenhower in 1954: Australia, New Zealand, Thailand, and the Philippines. Johnson, however, was never able to successfully articulate a clear rationale or achievable objectives. This cost him the support of a broader coalition and the American people.

Despite the lack of an easy lesson to be learned from Eisenhower's decision not to intervene in the French-Indochina War, the example he set by insisting that difficult conditions be met before committing American troops to battle remains relevant to our time. More recent examples are worth considering. In 1990, Iraq, under the leadership of Saddam Hussein, invaded and occupied Kuwait, its neighbor to the south. Fearing for the safety of Saudi Arabia and two-thirds of the world's petroleum reserves, President George H. W. Bush sought and received the support of the UN Security Council, the U.S. Congress, and the majority of the American people for military action in the Persian Gulf. The United States then led a coalition of thirty-five nations that in less than seven months, liberated Kuwait and assured the sovereignty of Saudi Arabia. Although it received its share of criticism, Operation Desert Storm was widely hailed as a model for post–Cold War conflict.

In 2003, the United States went to war in Iraq for the second time in a generation. In the aftermath of the September 11, 2001, terrorist attacks, the United States had launched a "war on terror," and President George W. Bush was determined to remove Saddam Hussein, who remained in power. Believing that Hussein's government possessed weapons of mass destruction (WMD) and had ties to al-Qaeda, George W. Bush launched a preemptive strike against Iraq. Like his father, he convinced Congress to authorize force. He also put together a small "coalition of the willing" that included the United Kingdom. He failed, however, in his attempt to win support of the UN and key allies such as Germany, France, and Canada. A slim majority of Americans supported the invasion just before it occurred in March. That majority grew during the major combat phase of the war, but by the fall of 2003, unforeseen complications and the failure to find WMDs caused support to drop. It remained low, and the war dragged on for another eight years. Satisfying a set of conditions before engaging in armed conflict does not assure victory, but comparing the experiences of George H. W. Bush with those of Lyndon Johnson and George W. Bush suggests that conditions like those Eisenhower set for intervention in the French-Indochina War create a greater chance for success.

6

Dealing with McCarthyism

On May 31, 1954, an audience of 1,800 sat in the main ballroom of the Waldorf-Astoria in New York City for Eisenhower's speech; another 400 gathered in a nearby room to watch the president on closed-circuit television. The occasion was the bicentennial of Columbia University, which Eisenhower had served as president from 1948 to 1953. The theme of the celebration, "Man's Right to Knowledge and the Free Use Thereof" was well suited for Eisenhower to publicly denounce McCarthyism, something many of his supporters had been encouraging him to do for nearly two years. Engaging the theme of the event, Eisenhower said, "We have too often seen education perverted into an instrument for the use and support of tyranny." In the preceding decades, he said, threats to the American way of life from fascism and communism, along with the dangers of nuclear war, had sown fear.

> Amid such alarms and uncertainties, doubters begin to lose faith in themselves, in their country, in their convictions. They begin to fear other people's ideas—every new idea. They begin to talk about censoring the sources and the communication of ideas. They forget that truth is the bulwark of freedom, as suppression of truth is the weapon of dictatorship. . . . Whenever, and for whatever alleged reason, people attempt to crush ideas, to mask their convictions,

to view every neighbor as a possible enemy, to seek some kind of divining rod by which to test for conformity, a free society is in danger.... Here in America we are descended in blood and in spirit from revolutionaries and rebels—men and women who dared to dissent from accepted doctrine. As their heirs, may we never confuse honest dissent with disloyal subversion.... Our dedication to truth and freedom, at home and abroad, does not require—cannot tolerate—fear, threat, hysteria, and intimidation.[1]

That morning, when the president went over his speech with his press secretary James Hagerty, he said that he did not expect much in the way of applause, given that the audience would consist primarily of academics.[2] He must have been pleasantly surprised when his oration was interrupted twenty times by applause. The most enthusiastic response came when he proclaimed that "through knowledge and understanding, we will drive from the temple of freedom all who seek to establish over us thought control—whether they be agents of a foreign state or demagogues thirsty for personal power and public notice."[3] According to the *New York Times*, this line was followed by thirty seconds of applause interspersed with shouts of "hooray!" Eisenhower had not mentioned Senator Joseph McCarthy by name, and when asked if the president had been referring to the senator, Hagerty replied "I am not going to try to interpret the president's remarks." The *New York Times* reported, however, that other, unnamed, administration sources replied, "Who else?" in response to the same question. In any event, the subject of the references was not lost on his audience.[4] With the Army-McCarthy hearings reaching their climax in Washington, Eisenhower's Columbia bicentennial speech came at a critical moment.

Early historians of the Eisenhower presidency were highly critical of his handling of McCarthy. One historian argued that "lacking strong leadership on the issue, the [Eisenhower] administration vacillated between opposition and appeasement of McCarthy."[5] That began to change in the 1980s. Fred Greenstein, whose book *The Hidden-Hand Presidency* has come to define Eisenhower revisionism, devoted more than a quarter of the book to "The Joe McCarthy Case" as an example of the strengths and weaknesses of Eisenhower's style. Greenstein concludes that "though Eisenhower was far from being the only (or even the decisive) agent of McCarthy's political demise, upon taking office he quickly recognized the importance of defusing the senator. . . . Throughout, Eisenhower rejected courses of action urged upon him by some of his closest allies that . . . [he believed] would have perpetuated McCarthy's influence."[6] Despite the arguments of Greenstein and other revisionists, however, Eisenhower's refusal to take on the senator directly is still one of the most criticized aspects of his presidency.[7]

Eisenhower sought balance in his approach to McCarthy. He refused to engage McCarthy in the kind of head-to-head confrontation many of his supporters desired. Eisenhower believed that such a confrontation would have further divided the Republican Party, putting the administration's legislative agenda at risk. He also believed that a confrontation with the president would increase McCarthy's notoriety, giving him exactly the kind of attention that he desired. Finally, Eisenhower refused to engage in "personalities," lowering himself and the presidency to McCarthy's level.[8] On the other hand, doing nothing, or embracing the senator as many Republican legislative leaders would have preferred, was never an option. Instead, Eisenhower worked indirectly to help bring about McCarthy's demise.

Eisenhower had good reasons to be concerned about confronting McCarthy directly, but they are insufficient to defend him from his critics who argue that he should have done so. Eisenhower referred to McCarthy as a demagogue. Demagogues claim to represent the interests of the common man against those of entrenched elites; they attain political power by appealing to the fears and prejudices of their followers. McCarthy was a particularly dangerous demagogue, one who used his power to destroy the lives and careers of those who stood in his way. As a popular president, Eisenhower had the power to take McCarthy on sooner and more directly. He also had the reputation to survive whatever reckless accusation the senator might have made against him. By working behind the scenes, Eisenhower contributed to McCarthy's demise, but his indirect approach failed to set a suitable example for dealing with demagogues.

The George Marshall Controversy

Elected to the U.S. Senate by the voters of Wisconsin in 1946, McCarthy was not well known outside his home state prior to 1950. The often-told story, perhaps more legend than fact, is that on January 7, 1950, Senator McCarthy had dinner at the Colony Restaurant in Washington, DC, with three friends, supporters, and fellow Catholics: Father Edmund Walsh, dean of the Georgetown University School of Foreign Relations, Charles Kraus, a professor of political science at Georgetown, and William Roberts, a Washington attorney. The objective that evening was to think of an issue that would give life to McCarthy's reelection campaign. It was Father Walsh who suggested the idea of communists in government, an idea that McCarthy jumped at.[9]

Politicizing the subject of communists in government was not a new idea. Richard Nixon, for example, had invigorated his own career with his investigation of Alger Hiss while a member of the House Committee on Un-American Activities (HUAC). But it would be McCarthy who gave his name to the anticommunist crusade of the 1950s. Just over a month after the dinner meeting, in a Lincoln Day speech to a women's Republican club in Wheeling, West Virginia, McCarthy said, "While I cannot take the time to name all of the men in the State Department who have been named as members of the Communist Party . . . I have here in my hand a list of 205 . . . that were known to the Secretary of State and who nevertheless are still working and shaping the policy of the State Department."[10] This unfounded accusation, and those that followed, propelled McCarthy to national prominence and defined the remainder of his political career.

Eisenhower's first encounter with McCarthy would not come until 1952. The roots of that encounter, however, go back to June 14, 1951. On that day, in a speech from the floor of the U.S. Senate, McCarthy charged that Secretary of Defense George Marshall was the key figure in "a conspiracy so immense, an infamy so black, as to dwarf any in the history of man." This conspiracy was one "to diminish the United States in world affairs, to weaken us militarily, to confuse our spirit with talk of surrender in the Far East and to impair our will to resist evil." President Truman was not a "conscious party to the great conspiracy," he said, because he "is only dimly aware of what is going on." In his speech, McCarthy identified six policies supported by Marshall and pursued by the United States that he claimed were consistent with policies advocated by the Soviet Union.[11] Marshall had been army chief of staff during World War II; and later, as secretary of state, he had initiated the European Recovery Program, better known as the Marshall Plan. Such a charge against a man who had devoted his professional life to the security of the United States was truly shocking.

As the Republican nominee for president in the fall of 1952, Eisenhower was expected to support all Republican candidates for office. This included McCarthy, who was up for reelection. Despite this, Eisenhower later recalled, he was determined to give "no appearance of aligning my views with his" and told his campaign staff to make no plans to visit Wisconsin. When he later discovered that he had been booked on a whistle-stop tour of the state, it "occasioned the sharpest flareup I can recall between my staff and I during the entire campaign."[12] On the morning that Eisenhower's campaign train entered the state, Wisconsin governor Walter Kohler and Senator McCarthy came aboard. In a conversation witnessed by Sherman Adams, Eisenhower's campaign manager, Eisenhower said to McCarthy that at their first stop in Green Bay "I'm going to say that I disagree with you." McCarthy replied, "If you say that, you'll be booed." Eisenhower shrugged his shoulders and said, "I've been booed before, and being booed doesn't bother me." In his brief remarks from the back of the train in Green Bay, with McCarthy and Kohler standing nearby, Eisenhower said that although he was concerned about domestic communism and would take appropriate action to eliminate it wherever it existed, he would not use methods that were un-American to do so. There were no boos from the sizable crowd that had greeted him.[13]

More important, however, was what Eisenhower said in his speech later that night in Milwaukee. Or, more precisely, what he did not say in his speech that night. Several weeks earlier, when it became clear that Eisenhower would have to visit Wisconsin, Emmet Hughes, one of his speech writers, suggested that the Milwaukee speech include a tribute to his friend and mentor George Marshall. Eisenhower liked the idea, and a paragraph was inserted that said:

> The right to question a man's judgement carries with it no automatic right to question his honor. With respect to one case I shall

be quite specific. I know that charges of disloyalty have in the past been levelled against George Marshall. . . . I was privileged through-out the years of World War II to know General Marshall person-ally. . . . I know him as a man and a soldier, to be dedicated with singular selflessness and the profoundest patriotism to the service of America.[14]

Before delivering the speech, however, Eisenhower approved the deletion of the specific reference to Marshall. Eisenhower later explained that in addition to Governor Kohler's objections, his staff was nearly unanimous in their opposition to referencing Marshall. They believed that because Eisenhower had defended Marshall on previous occasions, the only reason to do so in Milwaukee would be to antagonize McCarthy in his home state, something they believed would do more harm than good.[15] Unfortunately for Eisenhower, advance copies of the speech had been distributed to the press before his decision to delete the Marshall reference. This created the impression that Eisenhower had capitulated to McCarthy. The decision not to defend Marshall while on stage with McCarthy remains one of the most persistent criticisms of Eisenhower.

Eisenhower Develops a McCarthy Strategy

Eisenhower's next encounter with McCarthy came less than two weeks after his inauguration. On February 5, Eisenhower nominated Charles "Chip" Bohlen to serve as ambassador to the Soviet Union. McCarthy was determined to prevent Senate con-firmation of Bohlen because he had been an adviser to President Franklin Roosevelt during the 1945 Big Three conference at Yalta where Roosevelt had allegedly abandoned Eastern Europe to communism. Although the Senate Foreign Relations Committee had unanimously approved Bohlen's nomination, McCarthy led a fight against him on the Senate floor. "We find that his entire history is one of complete, wholehearted, 100 percent cooperation with the Acheson-Hiss-Truman regime," McCarthy said, referring to Dean Acheson, President Truman's secretary of state, and Alger Hiss, subject of the 1948 HUAC investigation led by Richard Nixon.[16]

Eisenhower sent Vice President Nixon to talk to Senator McCarthy. Nixon had begun to serve as intermediary between the president and conservatives in Congress. Eisenhower's moderate views and his desire to remain above the political fray, not to mention his inexperience in the world of politics, made such an intermediary necessary; and Nixon's credentials with conservatives made him an excellent choice. Nixon, however, was unsuccessful in preventing a floor fight over Bohlen.[17] Eisenhower stayed loyal to his nominee and Bohlen was ultimately confirmed, but Eisenhower was disturbed that eleven of the thirteen Senators who voted against Bohlen's confirmation were Republicans. "There were only two or three that surprised me by their vote," Eisenhower remarked; "the others are the most stubborn and essentially small-minded examples of the extreme isolationist group in the party."[18]

Despite McCarthy's reckless tactics, Eisenhower refused to denounce him publicly for several reasons. One was political. In the words of Vice President Richard Nixon, "Most Republicans in the House and Senate were then still strongly pro-McCarthy and wanted Eisenhower to embrace him, while the predominantly liberal White House staff members opposed McCarthy and wanted Eisenhower to repudiate him," but the president "was reluctant to plunge into a bitter personal and partisan wrangle, aware that if he repudiated McCarthy or tried to discipline him, the Republican

Party would split right down the middle in Congress and in the country."[19] The president's assessment was more nuanced: "There is a certain reactionary fringe of the Republican Party that hates and despises everything for which I stand. . . . In many cases, you will find that McCarthy's voting record does not align him very precisely with that group. However, the members of that gang are so anxious to seize on every possible embarrassment for the administration that they support him. . . . Old Guardism and McCarthyism become synonymous in the public mind—this is not necessarily the case at all."[20]

The second reason Eisenhower refused to denounce McCarthy was his belief that the best way to neutralize him was to ignore him. "I really believe that nothing will be so effective in combating his particular kind of troublemaking as to ignore him. This he cannot stand."[21] Eisenhower maintained that McCarthy fed off publicity. "Nothing would probably please him more than to get the publicity that would be generated by public repudiation by the President," he wrote to General Mills chairman Harry Bullis.[22] For this reason Eisenhower was angry at the attention given to McCarthy by the national news media. To Bill Robinson of the *New York Herald Tribune* he complained: "No one has been more insistent and vociferous in urging me to challenge McCarthy than have the people who built him up, namely, writers, editors, and publishers."[23]

The last reason was of a more personal nature. In letters to friends who encouraged him to get tough with McCarthy, Eisenhower explained his guiding principles on matters of "personality." To Kansas businessman Paul Helms he explained that from experience, "I developed a practice which, so far as I know, I have never violated. That practice is to avoid public mention of any name *unless it can be done with favorable intent and connotation*; reserve all criticism for private conference, speak only good in public."[24] To Paul Reed, chairman of the board of General Electric, he stated his belief that "the only effective answer to unjust and unfair attack is a constant repetition of truth. . . . To attempt to answer in terms of personal criticism is to place yourself in the hands of the attacker."[25] To his friend Swede Hazlett, he wrote, "I was interested in a statement of yours in which you express your satisfaction that 'at last you are ready to crack down on McCarthy.' . . . I disagree completely with the 'crack down' theory. I believe in the positive approach."[26] For Eisenhower these were not mere tropes. The transcripts of his press conferences, particularly on days when reporters were asking him about McCarthy, demonstrate that he truly lived by these principles.

The next battle between McCarthy and the Eisenhower administration, in late 1953, might have been avoided if Attorney General Herbert Brownell had not been overeager to establish the administration's own anticommunist credentials. In a speech on November 6, he made a startling allegation against former president Harry Truman. In early 1946, Truman had appointed Harry Dexter White to the position of executive director of the International Monetary Fund. Truman had done so, Brownell alleged, even though the FBI had provided him with evidence that White had transmitted classified information to agents of the Soviet Union.[27]

Former president Truman defended himself from these accusations in a nationally televised speech on November 16. More memorable than the defense of his actions, however, was the counteraccusation he made:

> It is now evident that the present administration has fully embraced, for political advantage, McCarthyism. . . . It is the corruption

of truth, the abandonment of the due process of law. It is the use of the big lie and the unfounded accusation against any citizen in the name of Americanism or security. It is the rise to power of the demagogue who lives on untruth; it is the spreading of fear and the destruction of faith in every level of our society.[28]

McCarthy demanded equal time from the networks to respond to President Truman. Much of his response was dedicated to condemning the Truman administration and its legacy, but he also issued a warning of sorts to the Eisenhower administration. The Republican Party, he said, had not created the situation, but it was now responsible for handling it. So far, McCarthy alleged, it was doing so no better than Truman had. With no irony intended, he concluded with a quote from Abraham Lincoln: "If this nation is to be destroyed, it will be destroyed from within."[29] For McCarthy, this criticism was rather mild, but C. D. Jackson believed that a line had been crossed.[30] When James Reston of the *New York Times* reported that Jackson believed McCarthy had "declared war on Eisenhower," it caused a stir in the White House. The resulting discussion provides a good example of Eisenhower's approach to dealing with McCarthy.[31]

Following the appearance of Reston's article, White House Chief of Staff Sherman Adams reminded the staff that they should not comment on McCarthy. White House legislative liaison Jerry Persons agreed, arguing that such talk would make it more difficult to get Eisenhower's legislative program through the Senate, where he believed that McCarthy controlled the votes of six other senators. Admitting that the "declaration of war" quote had been his, Jackson argued that "appeasing McCarthy in order to save his seven votes for this year's legislative program was poor tactics, poor strategy . . . and poor arithmetic, and that unless the president stepped up to bat on this one soon, the Republicans would have neither a program . . . nor [a] 1956." Jackson believed that Eisenhower should issue a strongly worded response to "face up to this declaration of war."[32]

Jackson began working on just such a response but believed he was being shut out of the conversation by those who sought accommodation with McCarthy. In a remarkable meeting with Eisenhower, Jackson and the others worked out their differences. In his diary Jackson recalled: "I pitched in as strongly as I could by telling him [Eisenhower] that so long as Taft was alive he might have been able to get out of the responsibility of leading the party, but now he could no longer get out of it." Eisenhower, he said, "twisted and squirmed" as he spoke. He "read my text with great irritation, slammed it back at me and said he would not refer to McCarthy personally—'I will not get into the gutter with that guy.'"[33]

According to Jackson, the meeting became more productive at that point with everyone, including the president, working on the statement. Later that day, at the president's press conference, he made the following statement: "In all that we do to combat subversion, it is imperative that we protect the basic rights of loyal American citizens. I am determined to protect those rights to the limit of the powers of the office with which I have been entrusted by the American people."[34] Compared to Jackson's desire that the administration reciprocate McCarthy's "declaration of war," the president's statement was relatively mild, but Jackson was satisfied.[35]

The Peress Case

When Republicans took over control of the Senate in 1953, McCarthy was passed over for the chairmanship of the Internal

Security Committee, which went to William Jenner of Indiana, one of his closest allies. Instead, McCarthy was given the chairmanship of the Committee on Government Operations. Although it was not considered a prestigious appointment, Government Operations had a Permanent Subcommittee on Investigations. McCarthy took the chair of this subcommittee for himself and turned it into the Senate's chief communist-hunting committee. It became known as the "McCarthy Committee."

Shortly after the blowup over the White case, McCarthy began an investigation into the case of Irving Peress, an army dentist at Camp Kilmer, New Jersey. Peress was drafted in October 1952 and commissioned as a captain in the army reserves. When filling out a loyalty form, Peress refused to answer questions relating to membership in subversive organizations, claiming "federal constitutional privilege." Army Intelligence ran a check on Peress and found "sufficient evidence of subversive and disloyal tendencies to warrant his removal." In the meantime, Peress was called to active duty and assigned to Fort Lewis, Washington, in preparation for deployment to Korea. This overseas deployment was subsequently cancelled, however, and Peress returned to Camp Kilmer in March 1953. It took three months for the file recommending his removal to catch up with Peress and another two months for the army to take any action. Asked to reply to another, more detailed, loyalty form, Peress refused to answer all but the most basic questions about himself, again claiming federal constitutional privilege. Army Intelligence received the form in September 1953.[36]

While Army Intelligence was analyzing his loyalty form, Peress applied for promotion. Active-duty medical professionals were eligible for promotion to a rank that would provide a salary roughly equivalent to what they had made as civilians. Although Peress's request for promotion arrived at army headquarters with a cover letter from Camp Kilmer recommending that the request be denied, it was inexplicably approved. In July 1953, Camp Kilmer came under the command of Brigadier General Ralph Zwicker, a highly decorated veteran of World War II. Zwicker was briefed on the Peress case three months later, and on October 21 he wrote a memo to General Withers Burress, commanding officer of the First Army, requesting that Peress be immediately relieved of duty. Despite the plea for immediacy, another month went by before Burress was informed and the army took action. On November 18, the Army Personnel Board, believing that it did not have the grounds to court-martial Peress, decided to take the most expedient route of granting him an honorable discharge. Peress was notified on January 18, 1954, and his discharge was scheduled for March 31, 1954.[37]

McCarthy learned of the Peress case in December 1953. On January 4, Roy Cohn, McCarthy's chief counsel, called Secretary of the Army Robert Stevens to ask about it. Stevens called Cohn back a few days later and said that the army was aware of the situation and that Peress was being discharged. On January 27, despite the army's assurances that the case had been dealt with, Peress was called to testify before McCarthy's committee. Peress appeared before the committee on Saturday, January 30. McCarthy, assuming that Peress was a communist, asked him questions about his activities. Peress declined to answer, taking the Fifth Amendment. McCarthy was also very interested in why Peress's deployment to Korea had been cancelled, how he had gotten promoted, and why he was being given an honorable discharge. A badly shaken Peress met with General Zwicker the following Monday morning and requested that his discharge from the army take place immediately. Zwicker was happy to accommodate his request, and Peress was given an honorable discharge the following afternoon.[38]

On Thursday, February 18, both Peress and Zwicker were called to testify before McCarthy's committee. Peress, now a civilian, refused to answer most questions, and it was Zwicker's testimony that made the bigger impact. Zwicker appeared without counsel and without adequate preparation. An impasse was reached when McCarthy asked, "Do you think, general, that anyone who is responsible for giving an honorable discharge to a man who has been named under oath as a member of the Communist conspiracy should himself be removed from the military?" After an unsuccessful attempt to dismiss the question as hypothetical, Zwicker responded, "That is not a question for me to decide, Senator." McCarthy ordered Zwicker to answer the question. "You will answer that question, unless you take the Fifth Amendment," he said. "I do not care how long we stay here, you are going to answer it." Zwicker then asked for a clarification of the question. "I mean exactly what I asked you, general, nothing else," McCarthy responded, "and anyone with the brains of a five-year-old child can understand that question." Zwicker finally responded that he did not believe that someone responsible for giving an alleged communist an honorable discharge should necessarily be removed from the military. McCarthy's response was over the top, even for him: "Then, general, you should be removed from any command. Any man who has been given the honor of being promoted to general and who says 'I will protect another general who protects Communists' is not fit to wear that uniform, general. I think it is a tremendous disgrace to the Army. . . . You will be back here, general."[39]

Zwicker's report of the incident quickly went up the chain of command to Secretary of the Army Robert Stevens. Stevens called Senator McCarthy to inform him that he would not allow Zwicker to testify again. After contacting other members of the committee, he released a statement to the press stating that "the prestige and morale of our Armed Forces are too important to the security of the nation to have them weakened by unfair attacks on our officer corps." Therefore, he had ordered Zwicker not to appear before McCarthy's committee again. He did, however, express his willingness to testify himself if asked to do so.[40]

By the time Stevens released his statement to the press, the White House had already begun its behind-the-scenes activities that would lead to McCarthy's downfall. On January 21, Attorney General Herbert Brownell hosted a meeting in his office. Among those present were Brownell, Sherman Adams, Deputy Attorney General William Rogers, who had arranged the meeting, U.S. Ambassador to the United Nations Henry Cabot Lodge, and Army Counsel John Adams. Except for John Adams, these men were among President Eisenhower's closest advisers.[41] The purpose of the meeting was to discuss McCarthy's threat to subpoena members of the army's Loyalty and Security Appeals Board as part of his ongoing investigation of Fort Monmouth, New Jersey. An executive order issued by President Truman in 1948 preventing such testimony was still in force, but Brownell and Rogers were doing the groundwork for Eisenhower to issue a more robust assertion of executive privilege if it became necessary.

After discussing this threat, the meeting turned to a different topic. John Adams described how Roy Cohn was putting intense pressure on the army to obtain special treatment for his friend and former member of the subcommittee staff, David Schine, who had been drafted. Cohn's campaign was taking place even as the subcommittee was investigating Fort Monmouth. Those present immediately saw how potentially damaging this information was to McCarthy, and Sherman Adams encouraged John

Adams to compile a detailed chronological narrative of what had taken place.[42]

On Tuesday, February 23, Secretary Stevens and John Adams attended a meeting with Vice President Nixon and Senate Republicans to plan for Stevens's appearance before the McCarthy subcommittee. Seeing how unprepared Stevens was for a confrontation with McCarthy, Nixon recommended an informal meeting between the two men. Nixon and the others present recommended that Stevens promise to cooperate with McCarthy if McCarthy promised to treat army witnesses with respect. The meeting was held at lunchtime the following day in the office of Senator Everett Dirksen (R-IL). Besides McCarthy, Stevens, and Dirksen, Senator Karl Mundt (R-SD), a member of the subcommittee, would also be present. Because of the menu, the meeting became known as the "Chicken Luncheon."[43] From the point of view of Stevens, it was more of an ambush. When he arrived at what was supposed to be a secret meeting, he found the hallway crowded with reporters. The senators proceeded to gang up on Stevens, and after a two-hour meeting the reporters were presented with a "Memorandum of Understanding" that stated that Stevens would "give the subcommittee the names of everyone involved in the promotion and honorable discharge of Peress, and such individuals will be available to appear before the subcommittee." No mention was made of army personnel being treated with respect.[44]

Eisenhower had been away from Washington and heard about the Chicken Luncheon after it had taken place. He was upset with the result of the meeting, and although he still refused to confront McCarthy directly, he initiated his own behind-the-scenes activities that would eventually contribute to the senator's demise. Eisenhower summoned Dirksen to his office and told him that the White House was drafting a new memorandum of understanding to be issued that day and requested his help getting the committee Republicans on board. Dirksen took the new agreement, drafted by Hagerty, to the Capitol, but McCarthy refused to sign. Undeterred, Eisenhower told Hagerty to prepare a statement for Stevens to read that evening at the White House.[45] At 6:15, in Hagerty's office, Stevens read the statement. "I shall never accede to the abuse of Army personnel under any circumstances, including committee hearings," he said. "I shall never accede to them being browbeaten or humiliated. I do not intend them to be deprived of counsel when the matter under consideration is one of essential interest to me as Secretary, as was the case with General Zwicker."[46]

On March 3, Eisenhower held his first press conference since Zwicker's appearance before McCarthy's committee. An expectant press turned out in larger than usual numbers. After a few opening remarks, the president said, "I want to make a few comments about the Peress case" and began reading from a prepared statement. He admitted that the army had made "serious errors" in the Peress case, but said he was confident that it was "correcting its procedures" and would "avoid such mistakes in the future." With that out of the way, he went on to say that no member of the executive branch was expected to "submit to any kind of personal humiliation when testifying" before a congressional committee. "In opposing communism," he continued, "we are defeating ourselves if either by design or through carelessness we use methods that do not conform to the American sense of justice and fair play." As he went on with his statement it became clear that the president was taking McCarthy's assault on the army personally. "I spent many years in the Army," he said, a fact known to everyone in the room. "In all that time, I never saw any individual of the Army fail to render due and complete respect to every member of Congress with whom duty brought him in contact. In all that time, I never saw any member of the Congress guilty of disrespect toward the public servants who were appearing before him." He made clear that he expected this tradition to continue:

> Except where the interests of the Nation demand otherwise, every governmental employee in the executive branch, whether civilian or in the Armed Forces, is expected to respond cheerfully and completely to the requests of the Congress and its several committees. In doing so it is, of course, assumed that they will be accorded the same respect and courtesy that I require that they show to the members of the legislative body. . . . I expect the Republican membership of the Congress to assume the primary responsibility in this respect.

He concluded with a reminder to Congress. "There are problems facing this nation of vital importance. . . . I regard it as unfortunate when we are diverted from these grave problems—one of which is vigilance against any kind of internal subversion—through disregard of the standards of fair play recognized by the American people." After finishing his prepared statement, Eisenhower indulged in what can only be considered wishful thinking: "And that is my last word on any subject . . . related to that particular matter."[47]

By Eisenhower's standards, it was a strongly worded statement, but many of the 256 reporters who attended the press conference felt let down. They had anticipated—even hoped—that the president would condemn McCarthy and his actions, engaging him by name for the first time. A disappointed William Lawrence of the *New York Times* reported that the president had opened his press conference with a "moderately critical statement about the 'disregard for standards of fair play.'"[48]

McCarthy was among those expecting a tougher response from Eisenhower. He had prepared a statement and scheduled his own press conference immediately following the president's. By the time he read Eisenhower's remarks he had little time to soften his statement. "If a stupid, arrogant, or witless man in a position of power appears before our committee and is found aiding the Communist Party, he will be exposed," McCarthy said, apparently referring to Zwicker. He claimed he was being attacked because he had brought to light "the cold unpleasant facts about a Fifth Amendment Communist Army officer who was promoted, given special immunity from duty outside the United States and finally given an honorable discharge with the full knowledge of all concerned that he was a member of the Communist party.... It now appears that he was a sacred cow of certain Army brass."[49]

Taking note of President Eisenhower's moderate statement and McCarthy's harsh reply was 1952 Democratic presidential nominee Adlai Stevenson. Referring to McCarthy during a televised speech in Miami, Florida, on March 6, Stevenson asked his Democratic audience, "Why . . . have the demagogues triumphed so often?" The answer, he said, was "inescapable." A small group within the party had "persuaded the president that McCarthyism is the best Republican formula for political success." Invoking Abraham Lincoln, he warned that "a political party divided against itself, half McCarthy and half Eisenhower, cannot produce national unity; cannot govern with confidence and purpose."[50]

McCarthy quickly asked the television networks for airtime to respond to Stevenson's "personal attack" on him, but Eisenhower took steps to prevent that from happening. Eisenhower asked Leonard Hall, chairman of the Republican National Committee, to make a request for time to respond to Stevenson's speech, saying that the party would choose a spokesperson. The question of who should reply to Stevenson, according to Vice President Richard Nixon, was discussed at length during a legislative leaders meeting.

Nixon was Eisenhower's choice. Looking straight at Nixon, he said, "I think we probably ought to use Dick more than we have been. He can sometimes take positions which are more political than it would be expected I take. The difficulty with the McCarthy problem is that anybody who takes it on runs the risk of being called a pink. Dick has experience in the field, and therefore he would not be subject to criticism."[51]

Although Nixon's speech was intended as a response to Adlai Stevenson, at Eisenhower's urging, he took a few shots at McCarthy as well. The most quoted line was vintage Nixon: "I have heard people say, 'Afterall, we are dealing with a bunch of rats. What we ought to do is go out and shoot them.' Well, I agree they are a bunch of rats. But remember this. When you go out to shoot rats, you have to shoot straight, because when you shoot wildly, it not only means that the rats may get away more easily . . . but you might hit someone else who is trying to shoot rats, too."[52]

It had been a tough week for McCarthy. Earlier in the week Senator Ralph Flanders (R-VT) had verbally attacked him on the floor of the Senate. "To what party does he belong?" Flanders asked of McCarthy. "It does not seem that his Republican label can be stuck on very tightly, when by intention or through ignorance he is doing his best to shatter that party whose label he wears. . . . What is his party affiliation? One must conclude that his is a one-man party, and that its name is McCarthyism, a title which he has proudly accepted." He went on to mock McCarthy's pursuit of Irving Peress. "He dons his warpaint. He goes into his war dance. He emits his war whoops. He goes forth to battle and proudly returns with the scalp of a pink Army dentist."[53]

On Thursday, March 11, John Adams distributed his narrative on the Schine case to members of McCarthy's subcommittee. From there it found its way to the press. It detailed the pressure applied by McCarthy, Cohn, and the subcommittee staff to obtain special treatment for Schine. It included attempts to secure a commission for Schine, attempts to get him assigned to New York so that he could continue his work on the committee staff, suggestions that his period of basic training be shortened, and numerous demands for special privileges such as weeknight and weekend passes and relief from unpleasant duties.[54] As the McCarthy Committee was in the midst of investigating Fort Monmouth, these efforts created the impression that the committee might ease up on its investigation in return for special treatment of Schine.

Despite McCarthy's direct involvement in the campaign on behalf of Schine, the primary focus was on Cohn, whose profanity-laced phone calls accounted for most of the forty-four items in Adams's narrative.[55] McCarthy might have been able to avoid further scrutiny by firing Cohn, but he refused to do so. "There is only one man the communists hate more than Roy Cohn," McCarthy said. "That's [FBI Director] J. Edgar Hoover." Instead, McCarthy counterattacked. He claimed that it was the army, not his committee staff, that was guilty of "blackmail." The army was holding Schine "hostage" in an attempt to prevent his committee from exposing communists in their ranks. To support his claim, McCarthy produced eleven documents that no other members of the subcommittee had seen before. One of the documents was allegedly a report on a meeting attended by Stevens, McCarthy, and Cohn, among others. It claimed that Stevens had said that if McCarthy brought out everything it had on the army he would be forced to resign. "Mr. Stevens asked that we hold up our public hearings on the Army," it said. "He suggested that we go after the Navy, Air Force and Defense Department instead."[56]

The charges and countercharges between the army and McCarthy made clear that a congressional investigation would have to take place. Less clear was how the Senate's Permanent Subcommittee on Investigations could proceed against its own chairman. When asked about the possibility of McCarthy presiding over the investigation, Eisenhower weighed in: "If a man is a party to a dispute, directly or indirectly, he does not sit in judgement on his own case."[57] After some talk of turning the investigation over to the Armed Services Committee, the Permanent Subcommittee on Investigations ultimately decided to handle it. McCarthy would step down as chair during the hearings but would retain the right to cross-examine witnesses and vote on matters of procedure. Karl Mundt assumed the chair, and Ray Jenkins, an attorney from Tennessee, replaced Cohn as special counsel for the subcommittee. Joseph Welch, a trial lawyer from Boston, replaced John Adams as special counsel for the army.[58]

According to historian David Oshinsky, the Army-McCarthy hearings were supposed to focus on two distinct questions: Did McCarthy, Cohn, and members of the subcommittee staff exert improper pressure on the army to get preferential treatment for Schine; or did Stevens, Adams, and the army use blackmail and bribery to stop the subcommittee's investigation of the army? The issues, however, were more complex than that. They included the integrity of the Armed Forces, the constitutional separation of powers, the moral responsibilities of federal workers, and the future of McCarthy. In addition, "They pitted Republican against Republican, the President against Congress, and the subcommittee against their chairman."[59]

The Army-McCarthy Hearings

The Army-McCarthy hearings began on April 22, 1954, nearly six weeks after the account of the pressure campaign by McCarthy and Cohn on behalf of Schine became public. Chairman Mundt predicted that they would last a week. Americans had never seen McCarthy in action before his subcommittee, and it did not take long for the network television broadcasts of the hearings to become a national obsession. Many Republicans began to fear that McCarthy's behavior was doing a disservice to the party. On May 11, Dirksen presented a plan that would shorten the hearings and get them off television by taking them into executive session.[60] The other Republicans on the committee were enthusiastic, but Mundt needed consent from all the principals, and Stevens objected. On the day the subcommittee voted on Dirksen's plan, Eisenhower called Secretary Wilson and told him not to put any pressure on Stevens to go along.[61] Without Stevens's consent, the televised hearings, and the damage they were doing to McCarthy, would continue.

During his testimony on May 12, John Adams made a crucial mistake. He volunteered information about the meeting on January 21 during which Sherman Adams had suggested he prepare a written record of all the McCarthy committee's requests related to Schine.[62] Jenkins did not realize the importance of this testimony at the time but later recalled John Adams to question him further about the meeting. Welch objected, citing an order that had been issued by President Truman prohibiting officials from testifying about high-level discussions in the executive branch. The committee members were not satisfied with this claim of executive privilege as it had come from a previous administration. Welch knew that if John Adams testified about the meeting it would not be long before Sherman Adams, Brownell, Rogers, and Lodge, who were also present, would all be called to testify. He therefore asked to delay Adams's appearance, giving him time to investigate the matter.[63]

The White House was already prepared for the likelihood that executive branch officials would be called to testify about meetings at the White House.[64] Earlier in the year, Eisenhower had asked the Justice Department to prepare a memorandum on executive privilege.[65] He told Republican legislative leaders he would not allow his advisers, many of whom had been at the January 21 meeting, to testify: "Any man who testifies as to the advice he gave me won't be working for me that night."[66] By that time, Eisenhower had already sent the Justice Department memo to Wilson along with a letter directing him not to allow his employees to testify. At the hearing John Adams read the letter to the committee from the witness chair.

> Because it is essential to efficient and effective administration that employees of the executive branch be in a position to be completely candid in advising with each other on official matters, and because it is not in the public interest that any of their conversations or communications, or any documents or reproductions, concerning such advice be disclosed, you will instruct employees of your department that in all of their appearances before the subcommittee of the Senate Committee on Operations regarding the inquiry now before it, they are not to testify to any such conversations or communications or to produce any such documents or reproductions.[67]

In response to questions from the press Eisenhower held firm, saying he had "no intention whatsoever of relaxing or rescinding the order." He said that he had issued the order "because I saw an investigation going where it appeared that there was going to be a long side track established and go into a relationship between the president and his advisers that had no possible connection with this investigation."[68] McCarthy's passive-aggressive response reflected a desire to avoid a head-to-head confrontation with the

president: "I don't believe that this is the result of President Eisenhower's own personal thinking. I am sure that if he knew what this
was all about, he would not sign [such] an order."[69] He also seemed
genuinely nonplussed. "For the first time since I got into this fight
to expose communists, I'm sort of at a loss to know what course
to take. I think the White House made a great mistake. What we'll
do I don't know."[70]

McCarthy was right to be concerned. His method of investigating communists in government required a steady flow of
documents and information from those throughout the executive
branch who were sympathetic to his cause. Democratic members
of the subcommittee raised the question of whether McCarthy
himself could be indicted for possessing documents that had been
turned over to him in violation of the president's order. "If any
Administration wants to indict me for receiving and giving the
American people information about communism, they can just go
right ahead," McCarthy responded. His informants had taken oaths
"to defend their country against enemies—and certainly communists are enemies." These oaths were "over and above any presidential directive." McCarthy had already said enough to invoke a
presidential response, but he continued: "As far as I am concerned,
I would like to notify those 2,000,000 federal employees that I feel
it is their duty to give us any information which they have about ...
communism ... there is no loyalty to a superior officer which can
tower above and beyond their loyalty to their country."[71]

Eisenhower was enraged by McCarthy's assertion that federal
employees should defy his order. He called it "the most disloyal
act we have ever had by anyone in the government of the United
States." McCarthy, he said, "is trying deliberately to subvert the
people we have in government, people who are sworn to obey
the law, the constitution and their superior officers." McCarthy,

he said, was making "exactly the same plea of loyalty to him that Hitler made to the German people. Both tried to set up personal loyalty within the government while both were using the pretense of fighting communism."[72]

It was just a few days later that Eisenhower made his speech at the Columbia University bicentennial dinner. Eisenhower's assertion of executive privilege was a significant barrier to McCarthy's case against the army, and the senator's attempts to get around it further exposed his reckless and boorish behavior to a television audience. The low point for McCarthy came when he publicly smeared the reputation of Fred Fisher, a young lawyer at Welch's law firm, revealing that he had once belonged to the Lawyers Guild, which HUAC had accused of being the "legal bulwark of the Communist Party."[73] As a preface to Welch's defense of Fisher he said, "Until this moment, Senator, I think I never really gauged your cruelty or your recklessness." When McCarthy continued his attack, Welch famously interrupted: "Let us not assassinate this lad further, Senator. You have done enough. Have you no sense of decency, sir, at long last? Have you left no sense of decency?"[74] This is, perhaps, the best remembered criticism of McCarthy.

The McCarthy-Welch exchange took place on June 9. One week later, on June 17, the Army-McCarthy hearings ended inconclusively. What Mundt had hoped could be accomplished in one week had taken nearly two months. Before returning to Boston, Welch visited Eisenhower in the Oval Office. According to Hagerty, "The President congratulated Welch for a very fine job. Welch told the President that he thought that if the hearings had accomplished nothing else, the army had been able to keep McCarthy in front of the television sets for quite a while, long enough to permit the public to see how disgracefully he acted. He said he was sure this would be helpful in the long run. The President agreed with him on this."[75]

McCarthy's Censure

The following month, Senator Flanders submitted a resolution to censure Joseph McCarthy: "Resolved, that the conduct of the junior senator from Wisconsin is unbecoming a member of the United States Senate, is contrary to senatorial traditions, and tends to bring the Senate into disrepute, and such conduct is hereby condemned."[76] The resolution was referred to a special committee selected by Vice President Nixon. It consisted of three Republicans and three Democrats and was chaired by Arthur Watkins (R-UT).

The committee began its meetings on August 31. Watkins was determined not to lose control the way that Mundt had done during the Army-McCarthy hearings. Television cameras were banned, and McCarthy himself would be kept in line. The committee considered five charges against McCarthy: contempt of the Senate or a senatorial committee; encouraging federal government employees to violate the law by providing him with classified materials; receipt or use of a confidential or classified document; abuse of Senate colleagues; and abuse of General Zwicker. On September 27, the committee recommended that McCarthy be censured on counts one and five. It dismissed the other three charges.[77]

Although McCarthy's popularity had dropped considerably, his censure was a topic that the Senate had no desire to take up just six weeks before the election. Instead, a special session was called for November 8, six days after the election. On day two of the session, Watkins introduced the committee's resolution recommending that McCarthy be censured on two counts. McCarthy's response was defiant:

I would have the American people recognize, and contemplate in dread, the fact that the Communist party—a relatively small group of deadly conspirators—has now extended its tentacles to that most respected of American bodies, the United States Senate; that it has made a committee of the Senate its unwitting handmaiden. . . . I am not saying . . . that the Watkins Committee knowingly did the work of the Communist party. I am saying it was the victim of a Communist campaign; and having been victimized; it became the Communist party's involuntary agent.[78]

The censure vote took place on December 2. The charge of abuse of Zwicker was dropped from the resolution, not because senators approved of the way he had been treated, but because some feared that censure on such a charge would limit the Senate's power to conduct investigations. The final version of the censure resolution, therefore, condemned Senator McCarthy only for showing contempt to the Senate and its committees.[79] The final vote was 67–22. All forty-four Democrats and one Independent voted in favor of censure; the Republicans split evenly, twenty-two for and twenty-two against. Many of the Republicans who voted against censure were strong McCarthy supporters while others feared a weakening of Senate investigatory powers. Among those voting against censure were most of the Republican Senate leadership.[80]

On Saturday, December 4, at an informal meeting in the Oval Office, Eisenhower congratulated Watkins. Afterward, Hagerty walked Watkins out and told the press the president had congratulated the senator "for a fine job in handling his committee with dignity and respect."[81] This was widely reported in the next day's newspapers. The result of Eisenhower's brief meeting with Watkins was McCarthy's long-awaited break with the president. On December 7, McCarthy read a statement before a meeting of his subcommittee. In it he said that he believed he should "apologize to the American people" for an "unintentional deception." In 1952 he had campaigned for the president, promising that Eisenhower would "fight against communists in government." Unfortunately, he said, "in this I was mistaken."[82] When Hagerty informed Eisenhower of McCarthy's statement, he was unphased. "That's all right with me," he said. "I never had any use for him."[83]

The Senate resolution censuring McCarthy was, for the most part, symbolic. It did not unseat him. It did not even remove him as chair of the Government Operations Committee or its Permanent Subcommittee on Investigations, something seniority-conscious senators opposed. It merely condemned him for those actions found to be in contempt of the Senate and its committees. Coming when it did, however, just after the Republican Party had lost control of the Senate in the 1954 midterm elections, it did coincide with McCarthy's loss of his chairmanships. McCarthy wielded much less power and influence in the years after his censure, but he continued to serve in the Senate until his death in 1957 at the age of forty-eight.

Eisenhower sought balance in his approach to McCarthy. He refused to engage McCarthy in the kind of head-to-head confrontation many of his supporters desired; but doing nothing or embracing the senator, as many Republican legislative leaders would have preferred, was never an option. Instead, Eisenhower worked indirectly to help bring about McCarthy's demise. This approach satisfied no one at the time. He did enough to anger McCarthy and his supporters, but not enough to satisfy the senator's critics. Brownell, writing after much time for reflection, summed it up well: "I think he [Eisenhower] understood better than all of us what made McCarthy so powerful and threatening and how he could be cut down to size and eventually defeated. A direct and forceful response of the sort President Truman had attempted would be futile. It would only elevate McCarthy to the president's stature if not require the president to stoop to McCarthy's level. It would further give McCarthy the kind of forum and public attention necessary for his attacks. It would demean the presidency. And it would divide the nation."[84]

On June 21, 1955, Eisenhower met with his White House legislative team. Toward the end of the meeting, a Senate resolution sponsored by McCarthy came up. After a brief discussion of the resolution, Eisenhower closed the meeting by asking if the others had heard a gibe that was going around Washington: "It's no longer McCarthyism, it's McCarthywasm!"[85] One can easily forgive Eisenhower this uncharacteristic indulgence. By this time, McCarthy was no longer a problem requiring his daily attention. Eisenhower's indirect approach, particularly his assertion of executive privilege at a key moment in the Army-McCarthy hearings, had contributed to the senator's demise, but it was not primarily responsible for it. That is exactly how Eisenhower wanted it. He believed that McCarthy was the Senate's problem to deal with, and with some help from him, they had eventually done so. Ultimately, though, McCarthy was responsible for his own demise.

Eisenhower and Truman both referred to McCarthy as a demagogue. In the United States, this term had been most recently applied to Governor Huey Long who had become the virtual dictator of Louisiana in the 1930s. Demagogues are not defined by a particular ideology—McCarthy was a conservative Republican while Long was a liberal Democrat. What defines them are their methods. They position themselves as outsiders, fighting for the interests of common people against those of entrenched elites. Demagogues arouse passions by appealing to the fears and prejudices of their followers, exaggerating threats, disparaging their political enemies, and rejecting the established norms of political conduct. In his Columbia University bicentennial address, Eisenhower argued that truth is the best weapon with which to fight demagogues. Demagogues and their followers, however, are unconcerned with the veracity of their claims and are not persuaded by reason. Eisenhower avoided a direct confrontation with McCarthy, believing that it would demean him and the presidency while fueling the senator's popularity. He also feared that it would derail his legislative agenda. But demagogues must be stood up to. Truman stood up to McCarthy, but the senator easily dismissed him as an enabler of the communist conspiracy he claimed to be fighting. He could not have dismissed Eisenhower so easily. If Eisenhower believed that democracy was in danger, as he suggested in his Columbia University address, then an earlier and more direct approach was called for.

Donald Trump's presidency provides a contemporary example of the danger that demagogues pose to American democracy. During the 2016 presidential primaries, other Republican candidates were critical of Trump, but after his surprising victory, criticism from within the party fell mostly silent. As had been the case with McCarthy, some hoped that supporting him would advance their careers or their political agendas. Others feared opposing him would invite his fury and that of his followers. Although Democrats continued to criticize Trump, this only fueled his popularity. Trump's claim that the 2020 election was stolen, his associates' efforts to aid him in overturning the results of that election, and his supporters' attempt to disrupt the recording of the electoral college vote threatened the transfer of presidential power. The events of January 6, 2021, led some who had previously supported

Trump's claims to stand up to him. Fortunately, their actions came in time to prevent a constitutional crisis. As with McCarthy, however, those who had the ability to eliminate the threat he posed should have done so sooner, more directly, and without regard to their political future.

7

Brown v. Board *and the Little Rock Desegregation Crisis*

President Eisenhower had not planned to be at the White House on the morning of September 24, 1957. Earlier in the day he had returned to Washington from Newport, Rhode Island, where he had been taking a late summer working vacation. As he entered the Oval Office in a grey three-piece suit, the others in the room could see the grim determination on his face. In a national television and radio address, he was about to tell the American people that he had issued an executive order sending federal troops to Little Rock, Arkansas. After greeting his audience, the president put on his glasses and began to read from a carefully prepared text.

> I should like to speak to you about the serious situation that has arisen in Little Rock. To make this talk I have come to . . . the White House. I could have spoken to you from Rhode Island . . . but I felt that, in speaking from the house of Lincoln . . . my words would better convey the sadness I feel in the action I was compelled today to make and the firmness with which I intend to pursue this course until the orders of the federal court at Little Rock can be executed without unlawful interference. In that city, under the leadership of demagogic extremists, disorderly mobs have deliberately prevented the carrying out of proper orders from a federal court. . . . Whenever normal agencies prove inadequate to the task and it becomes

necessary for the Executive Branch of the federal government to use its powers and authority to uphold federal courts, the president's responsibility is inescapable. In accordance with that responsibility, I have today issued an executive order directing the use of troops under federal authority to aid in the execution of federal law at Little Rock, Arkansas.[1]

Just two months earlier, in response to a question about school desegregation, Eisenhower had said "I can't imagine any set of circumstances that would ever induce me to send Federal troops . . . into any area to enforce the orders of a Federal court, because I believe [the] common sense of America will never require it."[2] That assessment proved to be inaccurate. But how should we interpret Eisenhower's actions? Had his refusal to publicly endorse the Supreme Court's decision in *Brown v. Board of Education* emboldened southern segregationists? Had his lack of enthusiasm for school desegregation made him hesitant to intervene until a constitutional crisis required it? Or did Eisenhower's deployment of federal forces within the United States, a decisive act unprecedented in modern times, assure the ultimate success of school desegregation?

Early assessments of Eisenhower's leadership in civil rights were universally critical. The most prominent among them were written by authors who had close connections to President John Kennedy. Arthur Schlesinger Jr., special assistant to the late president, and Theodore Sorenson, a Kennedy speech writer, each wrote best-selling accounts of the Kennedy administration, published in 1965. Their admiration for Kennedy was clear, as was their belief that his leadership in the field of civil rights had led to the major legislative breakthroughs of the Johnson years. Although they did not specifically address the Eisenhower administration's work in the field, their portrayal of Kennedy made Eisenhower seem inactive by comparison.[3]

In 1977, their interpretation was backed up by a surprising source: Chief Justice of the United States Earl Warren, author of the *Brown v. Board* decision. Published posthumously, Warren's account was openly critical of Eisenhower, who had appointed him to the Supreme Court. Warren wrote that he "always believed that Eisenhower resented our decision in *Brown v. Board*." While "excited and racist-minded public officials and candidates for office proposed and enacted every obstacle they could devise to thwart the Court's decision" he wrote, "no word of support for the decision ever emanated from the White House." Warren believed that if Eisenhower had merely said, "it should be the duty of every good citizen to help rectify more than eighty years of wrongdoing by honoring that decision," the country would have been relieved "of many of the racial problems which have continued to plague us."[4]

The first historians who dealt with Eisenhower's civil rights record were greatly influenced by Warren's criticism of the president for his lack of public support of *Brown*. This led them to conclude that he intervened at Little Rock not out of any enthusiasm for school integration, but only because of the Arkansas governor's defiance of federal court orders.[5] Although historian Stephen Ambrose's biography of the president was overwhelmingly positive, he asserted that in the field of civil rights, Eisenhower had been a failure: "On one of the great moral issues of the day, the struggle to eliminate racial segregation from American life, he provided almost no leadership at all. His failure to speak out, to indicate personal approval of *Brown* . . . did incalculable harm to the civil-rights crusade and to America's image."[6] The publication of Ambrose's biography came just as historians were beginning to revise the historical interpretation of nearly every aspect of the Eisenhower presidency. Since Ambrose was a revisionist himself, his conclusions on Eisenhower's civil rights record were widely accepted.

It took another twenty years for this interpretation of Eisenhower's civil rights record to be challenged. In his book *A Matter of Justice*, historian David Nichols concluded that the "distortion" of Eisenhower's record in the field of civil rights was "no longer sustainable." Nichols provided numerous examples of Eisenhower's active engagement in civil rights and argued that public support for the *Brown* ruling would have made little difference in the face of southern resistance. If Eisenhower framed his action at Little Rock in terms of upholding court orders rather than enforcing integration, he argued, that was no different than Lincoln initially framing the Civil War in terms of preserving the union, rather than ending slavery.[7]

Politicians are often criticized for being "all talk and no action." In the case of Eisenhower's legacy in the field of civil rights, however, the opposite is true: Eisenhower's actions are recognized, but he is criticized for his reluctance to talk. Eisenhower's record in civil rights was impressive for a president in the 1950s. He desegregated the District of Columbia, completed the desegregation of the U.S. military, and his Justice Department proposed the Civil Rights Act of 1957 that, although flawed as a result of the compromises necessary to get it through Congress, was the first federal civil rights act passed since Reconstruction. Even when it comes to the desegregation of public schools it is difficult to criticize his actions. After the Supreme Court's decision in *Brown v. Board*, there was never any doubt that Eisenhower would enforce that decision as the law of the land. Just how far he was willing to go in this regard became clear when he sent federal troops to Little Rock, Arkansas, in 1957.

And when the Supreme Court placed implementation of *Brown v. Board* in the hands of the federal courts, Eisenhower appointed federal judges to southern circuit courts who would uphold the ruling. But, by refusing to publicly support the *Brown v. Board* decision, Eisenhower failed to provide the moral leadership the country needed on this divisive issue.

As he did in other areas, Eisenhower sought balance on the issue of public-school segregation: balance between the requirements of *Brown v. Board*, which outlawed public-school segregation, and the legacy of *Plessy v. Ferguson*, which had protected it for fifty years; balance between those who demanded an immediate end to public-school segregation and those who sought to delay the process indefinitely; balance between the responsibilities of the federal government and the rights of states. He failed to see, as his critics have pointed out, that segregation was not an issue that called for moderation.

Eisenhower's position on civil rights contributed to the early stages of a major political party realignment in the United States, an understanding of which remains important in our time. Although politics were not Eisenhower's primary consideration, there were political advantages to be gained from this approach, and future Republican presidential candidates would more consciously exploit them.

Brown v. Board

Eisenhower is often criticized for his refusal to state unambiguous support for the Supreme Court's decision in *Brown v. Board*, which ruled that separate public schools for whites and Blacks were "inherently unequal" and, therefore, a violation of the Fourteenth Amendment. This left many Americans with the impression, right or wrong, that he did not personally agree with it. A public statement in support of *Brown* would not have been likely to change the minds of hardened segregationists, but it might have dissuaded them from testing his resolve to enforce the decision. Furthermore, a statement of support from someone of Eisenhower's stature would have provided the nation with invaluable moral leadership on this divisive issue. In his memoirs, published more than ten years after the decision, Eisenhower said that he had agreed with the court on *Brown*.[8] Evidence from the time suggests otherwise, but if this was the case, he missed an important opportunity to provide that moral leadership.

Two fundamental beliefs shaped Eisenhower's policies on civil rights and contributed to his decision not to publicly endorse the Supreme Court's ruling in *Brown v. Board*. The first was that the role of the federal government should be limited to those areas where it had clear jurisdiction. This enabled Eisenhower to make significant progress in the desegregation of the District of Columbia, for example, but it allowed the southern states to perpetuate segregation within their own jurisdictions. The second of these fundamental beliefs was that people's feelings about race could not be changed through legislation or executive action. Speaking on civil rights in his first press conference as a presidential candidate, Eisenhower said, "I do not believe we can cure all the evils in men's hearts by law."[9] This belief, which suggested that only the passage of time could bring an end to racial discrimination, played into the hands of southern segregationists and alienated many African Americans.[10] The *Brown v. Board* decision challenged both of these beliefs. Not only was education an area in which the federal government had no clear jurisdiction, it was an area that segregationists felt very strongly about, and one in which law was unlikely to cure the evil in their hearts.

In June 1953, after ordering a second round of arguments in the *Brown v. Board* case, the Supreme Court invited Attorney General Herbert Brownell to file an *amicus curiae*, or "friend of the court," brief stating the administration's position on whether segregated public schools were in violation of the Fourteenth Amendment. Brownell believed that segregation by race in public schools was unconstitutional, and he was eager to share this opinion with the court. Eisenhower initially resisted the Supreme Court's invitation to file an *amicus curiae* brief, considering it a breach of the separation of powers. In a memo to Brownell, Eisenhower stated his opposition to the request: "The court cannot possibly . . . delegate its responsibility and it would be futile for the Attorney General to attempt to sit as a court and reach a conclusion as to the true meaning of the Fourteenth Amendment."[11] The president did not realize that it was common for the Supreme Court to request such *amicus curiae* briefs. In fact, the Truman administration had already filed one on *Brown v. Board* taking a strong stand against the constitutionality of segregated public schools. Brownell convinced Eisenhower that such a brief would have to be filed, but the president was never entirely comfortable with the idea.

Governor James Byrnes of South Carolina wrote to the president to try to influence the administration's response to the court. Eisenhower was already concerned about how the executive branch would enforce a ruling that segregated public schools were unconstitutional. Byrnes predicted that such a ruling would result in the southern states virtually shutting down their public-school systems and giving state funds to private schools for whites only. Byrnes's letter made a lasting impression on the president, reinforcing his belief that the White House should stay out of the controversial issue. In Eisenhower's response to Byrnes, he disassociated himself from the *amicus curiae* brief that Brownell would file on behalf of the administration. "It became clear to me that the questions asked of the Attorney General by the Supreme Court demanded answers that could be determined only by lawyers and historians," Eisenhower responded. "Consequently, I have been compelled to turn over to the Attorney General and his associates full responsibility in the matter. He and I agreed that his brief would reflect the conviction of the Department of Justice as to the *legal aspects* of the case. . . . It is clear that the Attorney General has to act according to his own conviction and understanding."[12]

Eisenhower's desire to keep the federal government out of public-school desegregation was thwarted by the Supreme Court's ruling on May 17, 1954. It declared that "in the field of public education, the doctrine of 'separate but equal' has no place," thereby denying segregated schools protection under the court's 1896 decision in *Plessy v. Ferguson.*[13] *Brown v. Board* had made public-school desegregation the law of the land, and Eisenhower, sworn by his presidential oath to uphold that law, could not long refuse to play a role. The most controversial position Eisenhower took in the field of civil rights, perhaps the most controversial position he took in any field during his presidency, was his refusal to endorse the *Brown* decision. He said nothing publicly about it until asked at his press conference on May 19. His carefully prepared response was brief: "The Supreme Court has spoken and I am sworn to uphold the constitutional processes in this country; and I will obey."[14]

Eisenhower may have also been considering the political implications. In 1952 he had been the first Republican presidential candidate to make significant inroads into the South, winning the electoral votes of four southern and three border states.[15] Most of his supporters in the South had been "Eisenhower Democrats" who voted for him because of his popularity as a war hero, not because of his party affiliation. Some of Eisenhower's political advisers believed that if he came out strongly in favor of the Supreme Court's ruling in *Brown v. Board*, he might win some additional votes from Blacks and liberals in the North who were in favor of desegregation. Others argued that these converts would not make up for the white southern votes he would lose if he took such a stand.[16]

After the *Brown v. Board* decision, the White House was deluged with letters from white southerners expressing concern and resentment over the decision. Many blamed Eisenhower personally. Rather than writing off such sentiments as reactionary or obstructionist, Eisenhower was troubled that white southerners might consider *Brown v. Board* a Republican or, worse, an Eisenhower administration decision. At the May 19 press conference, Eisenhower was asked whether he was concerned about losing southern supporters since the court's decision had come "under the Republican administration." He responded, "The Supreme Court, as I understand it, is not under any administration."[17] Although he had little patience for those who talked of nullification or noncompliance with the court's decision, he empathized with white southerners who were apprehensive about school desegregation. Most of Eisenhower's closest friends were southerners, and he had spent much of his life on segregated army posts. He did not wish to criminalize people who had until now, by virtue of the *Plessy v. Ferguson* decision, been within the law. Because of this, Eisenhower hoped that the court would adopt a policy of gradualism in its implementation of *Brown*.

It is difficult to reconcile Eisenhower's desire to keep the federal government out of the desegregation of public schools with his appointment of Chief Justice Earl Warren who wrote the unanimous decision in *Brown v. Board*. When Chief Justice Fred Vinson died in September 1953, the *Brown* case was already before the

Supreme Court. Eisenhower understood that his appointment to replace Vinson would play an important role in its decision on the case. Eisenhower was also aware that Warren was progressive on the issue of race relations and, as governor of California, had supported fair employment legislation for Blacks.[18] Defending his choice of Warren to his more conservative brother Edgar, who had called the appointment "a tragedy," Eisenhower wrote, "To my mind he is a statesman. . . . a man of national stature . . . of unimpeachable integrity, of middle-of-the-road views, and with a splendid record."[19]

Some historians have claimed that Eisenhower later regretted his appointment of Warren, calling it "the biggest mistake of his presidency," but there is no record of this.[20] Brownell, Eisenhower's closest adviser on judicial matters, said that Eisenhower never made such a comment to him and doubted that he would have made it to others, stating that it did not reflect the president's views and would have been "uncharacteristic." Brownell did admit the possibility that Eisenhower may have made the remark in an "off-hand" way, perhaps when dealing with someone who hoped that Eisenhower regretted the choice.[21]

In the year between the court's May 1954 decision and May 1955 when it announced how the verdict would be implemented, Eisenhower went on record as favoring a gradual implementation of school desegregation. In a presidential statement read to the delegates present at the annual meeting of the National Association for the Advancement of Colored People (NAACP) in June 1954, Eisenhower said: "We must have patience without compromise of principle. We must have understanding without disregard for differences of opinion which actually exist. We must have continued social progress, calmly but persistently made."[22] Eisenhower hoped that the court would adopt such a stand as well. In an October letter to Swede Hazlett, he wrote: "The segregation issue will, I think, become acute or tend to die out according to the character of the procedure orders that the Court will probably issue this winter. My own guess is this—they will be very moderate and secure a maximum of initiative to local courts."[23]

Once again, the Supreme Court invited the attorney general to file a brief stating the administration's opinion on the implementation of school desegregation. This time there is no record of Eisenhower considering such a request an abdication of the court's powers. In fact, he personally edited Brownell's draft to make sure that it reflected his opinion that the decision should be implemented gradually.[24] At a press conference on November 23, 1954, the day before Brownell filed his brief, Eisenhower hinted at what it contained. The president referred to "great practical problems" and "deep-seated emotions" in the South and said he hoped that the court would "take into consideration these great emotional strains" and "try to devise a way where, under some form of decentralized process, we can bring this about."[25]

The brief filed by Brownell the next day reflected Eisenhower's preference for a gradual, decentralized implementation of the court's decision that would consider circumstances unique to local situations. The brief recommended that the federal court system serve as the overseer of the desegregation process. Local school boards should develop and implement programs under the supervision of the federal district court that served the affected school district. The brief also recommended that school districts be required to submit a plan within ninety days of the court's ruling.[26]

On May 31, 1955, in a ruling known as *Brown v. Board II*, the Supreme Court announced its decision on the implementation of public-school desegregation. The court placed primary responsibility for developing desegregation plans with the local school boards. The district courts would have jurisdiction and were directed to consider local factors when judging implementation plans. The school boards, however, were to make a "prompt and reasonable start" and proceed "with all deliberate speed." The burden of justifying delays was to be borne by the local authorities.[27]

Although the Supreme Court had adopted the decentralized, gradual approach to desegregation that the administration had recommended in Brownell's brief, Eisenhower was still not entirely pleased with the outcome. In future years, when civil unrest in the South forced a presidential response, Eisenhower would often blame the troubles on the Supreme Court. To his secretary Ann Whitman, Eisenhower said that "the troubles brought about by the Supreme Court decision are the most important problem facing the government, domestically, today." When Whitman asked what alternative course the court might have adopted, the president responded: "Perhaps they could have demanded that segregation be eliminated in graduate schools, later in colleges, later in high schools, as a means of overcoming the passionate and inbred attitudes" that had developed over generations.[28] To Hazlett, Eisenhower complained: "No single event has so disturbed the domestic scene in many years as did the Supreme Court's decision of 1954 in the school desegregation case." This decision and other subsequent ones, he said, "have interpreted the Constitution in such fashion as to put heavier responsibilities than before on the federal government in the matter of assuring to each citizen his guaranteed constitutional rights."[29] These comments, however, were made only in private to trusted friends and associates.

In public, Eisenhower never criticized *Brown v. Board*, but he also refused to endorse it. He urged his cabinet members, when speaking on the issue, to stress the need for "calmness, sanity, and reason," hoping that they might pacify the racial tension that had been growing in the South since the *Brown v. Board* verdict.[30] He also expressed his disappointment in the fact that southern authorities were devoting their energy to acts of defiance rather than developing plans to comply with the court's decision.[31] Eisenhower also realized, in the wake of the decision, the importance of appointing federal judges who had not publicly opposed the ruling and would faithfully uphold it. Particularly important were the judges he appointed to the fourth and fifth circuit appeals courts. Eisenhower's first Supreme Court appointment after the *Brown* decision was of great symbolic importance. John Marshall Harlan II was the son of the lone dissenting justice in the *Plessy v. Ferguson* case upholding racial segregation. Occasionally, southern senators would appeal directly to Eisenhower to change his appointments for posts in their states, even offering legislative support if he would nominate candidates who were unsupportive of civil rights. According to the attorney general, Eisenhower never failed to support one of his nominees in such a situation.[32]

In 1956 and 1957 the Eisenhower administration dedicated itself to the passage of a civil rights act that would enforce the right of southern Blacks to vote. There were several reasons for the emphasis on voting: first, the administration wished to shift emphasis away from the explosive issue of desegregated schools; second, Eisenhower believed that if Blacks had the right to vote, they could more readily achieve their other civil rights without the federal government having to step in; and finally, Republicans were anxious to tap into the southern Black vote. The result of this effort was the Civil Rights Act of 1957. The legislation created a bipartisan commission to investigate the problem of Blacks being denied the right to vote because of their race, created the Civil

Rights Division and a new assistant attorney general for civil rights in the Department of Justice, and allowed federal prosecutors to charge those who interfered with the right to vote with contempt of court. A Senate amendment guaranteed those charged with federal contempt the right to a jury trial. Although this amendment greatly weakened the act, it was still a significant step forward—the first federal civil rights legislation since Reconstruction.

Little Rock Central High School

In May 1955 the U.S. Federal Court for the Eastern District of Arkansas accepted the desegregation plan submitted by the Little Rock Board of Education. The plan would begin with the integration of Little Rock Central High School in the fall of 1957, achieving full integration of all Little Rock public schools by 1963. It greatly divided the Little Rock community. On the opening day of the fall term, Governor Orval Faubus, claiming that it was necessary to maintain the peace, called out the National Guard to prevent Blacks from entering the school. By stepping in to prevent the Little Rock Board of Education from complying with a federal court order, Faubus initiated the federal-state confrontation over school desegregation that Eisenhower had sought to avoid since the Supreme Court's 1954 decision.

In response to Faubus's defiance of a court order, Federal District Judge Ronald Davies requested that the Justice Department begin collecting information concerning those individuals, including the governor, who were preventing the desegregation of Central High. This ended Eisenhower's hope that the crisis could be defused without the direct involvement of the executive branch. In response to the governor's plea to the president for understanding and cooperation, Eisenhower insisted that he would support and defend the Constitution by all legal means at his command. He added that he expected Faubus to cooperate fully with the Justice Department's investigation.[33]

Despite Eisenhower's terse reply to Faubus, he was still seeking a way to defuse the situation before a direct confrontation became necessary. U.S. Congressman Brooks Hays, who represented the Arkansas district that included Little Rock, suggested a meeting between Faubus and the president. Sherman Adams was convinced that Faubus had realized that he had made a mistake and was looking for a way out of the situation. He told Eisenhower that he thought such a meeting was a good idea. Faubus, he said, was not really a segregationist since his son went to an integrated college—he just thought that desegregation should proceed more slowly. Brownell was against such a meeting, taking the hard line that Faubus had violated a federal court order and should be forced to comply. Eisenhower rejected Brownell's position saying that it failed to take into consideration the situation in the South. The Justice Department, he said, should make clear that it only wanted to ensure the National Guard was not being used to prevent a court order from being carried out: "By no means does the Federal government want to interfere with the governor's responsibilities." Adams's argument for a meeting appealed to Eisenhower's philosophy of gradualism, moderation, and balance, and he agreed to meet with Faubus if the governor would request the meeting and state in his request that he would be "guided by federal court orders."[34]

On September 11, Faubus submitted such a request, and Adams set up a September 14 meeting at the Naval Station in Newport, Rhode Island, where the president was vacationing.[35] Eisenhower and Faubus were alone for twenty minutes. By Eisenhower's account, Faubus went to great lengths to tell the president that he was a law-abiding citizen and that he recognized the supremacy of federal law. Eisenhower sensed that Faubus wanted to resolve the situation. He later recalled suggesting to the governor that he "go home and not necessarily withdraw his National Guard troops, but just change their orders.... Tell the Guard to continue to preserve order but to allow the Negro children to attend Central High School." Eisenhower also warned that in any "trial of strength between the President and a Governor ... there could only be one outcome—that is, the State would lose." He added that he "did not want to see any governor humiliated." When Faubus left, Eisenhower was under the impression that the governor had agreed that he would change the National Guard's orders immediately upon returning home.[36]

Before returning home, Faubus spoke to the press. He said that he and the president had had a "friendly and constructive" discussion, and that he had "assured the president of my desire to cooperate with him in carrying out the duties resting upon both of us." He added that "I must harmonize my actions under the constitution of Arkansas with the requirements of the Constitution of the United States." In regard to desegregation, he said, "I have never expressed any personal opinion regarding the Supreme Court decision of 1954. ... That is not relevant. That decision is the law of the land and must be obeyed." He added that "in so doing, it is my responsibility to protect the people from violence in any form." When asked whether he intended to remove the National Guard troops from Central High before classes on Monday morning, he said that decision would have to wait until he returned to Arkansas.[37]

Faubus then returned home and, after consulting with his political advisers, decided not to remove the National Guard or change its orders. When Eisenhower heard of this, he was furious.

He telephoned Brownell in Washington and said, "You were right, Faubus broke his word." The president, however, was still reluctant to use the military to force compliance with the court's orders out of fear that Faubus would shut down the public-school system, as Byrnes had warned, and that other southern states would follow suit. Brownell began to fear they would have no other choice and told the president that he would begin conferring with the secretary of the army in case such a move proved necessary.[38]

On September 20, Faubus failed to appear in federal court as ordered, prompting Judge Davies to issue an order forbidding Faubus or the Arkansas National Guard from interfering with his previous order to integrate Central High. That evening Faubus withdrew the National Guard, suggesting the possibility that the crisis might end without the direct confrontation that Eisenhower hoped to avoid. Eisenhower's statement the next day reflected his relief that the situation seemed to be coming to an end. He asked the people of Little Rock to "preserve and respect the law— whether or not they personally agree with it," and to "vigorously oppose any violence by extremists."[39]

Federal Intervention

Eisenhower's hope that removing the National Guard would end the crisis was in vain. Faubus's prediction of imminent violence, which he had used as justification for calling out the National Guard in the first place, had become a self-fulfilling prophesy. Encouraged by Faubus's defiance of the courts, groups such as the White Citizens Council had whipped segregationists into a frenzy. On the morning of September 23, a crowd of several thousand converged on Central High to protest the admission of Black students.[40] At 3:44 p.m. central time, Woodrow Wilson

Mann, the mayor of Little Rock, sent Eisenhower a telegram. Local law enforcement had been unable to control the mob, and the "Little Rock Nine" had to be removed from the grounds for their own safety.[41] The "mob," he said, had been "no spontaneous assembly. It was agitated, aroused, and assembled by a concerted plan of action." One of the "principal agitators," Mann informed the president, was Jimmy Karam, "a political and social intimate of Governor Faubus," which suggested that the governor was at least aware of the plan.[42]

That afternoon, Hagerty released a presidential statement. Eisenhower wanted to "make several things clear in connection with the disgraceful occurrences" in Little Rock. Orders of the court, the statement read, "cannot be flouted with impunity by any individual or mob of extremists." The president said that he was willing to "use the full power of the United States including whatever force may be necessary to prevent any obstruction of . . . the orders of the federal court." He still hoped that the "American sense of justice and fair play" would prevail, however, and lamented that it would be a "sad day" for the country "if school children can safely attend their classes only under the protection of armed guards."[43]

The statement was followed up by an executive proclamation: "Obstruction of Justice in the State of Arkansas." The proclamation stated that "certain persons in the state of Arkansas, individually and in unlawful assemblages . . . have willfully obstructed the enforcement of orders of the United States District Court." This obstruction of justice, it said, "constitutes a denial of the equal protection of the laws secured by the Constitution." The president, it concluded, commands "all persons engaged in such obstruction of justice to cease and desist . . . and to disperse." The proclamation cited Title 10 of the U.S. Code. Section 332 of Title 10 allows the president to use the armed forces of the United States "as he considers necessary" to enforce federal law or suppress unlawful obstructions to it.[44] It is the same law that George Washington had used to suppress the Whiskey Rebellion in 1794.

The next day the situation worsened. Mann sent Eisenhower a telegram at 9:06 a.m. central time that said: "The immediate need for federal troops is urgent. The mob is much larger in numbers at 8 am than at any time yesterday. . . . Situation is out of control and police cannot disperse the mob."[45] The second telegram from Mayor Mann prompted a swift response from Eisenhower. It was now clear to him that there was no way of avoiding the use of federal troops. Tentative plans to use National Guardsmen from other parts of the state were abandoned in favor of using regular army troops. Eisenhower federalized all the Arkansas National Guard, and by the end of the day one thousand paratroopers from the 101st Airborne Division, many of them Korean War veterans, arrived from Fort Campbell, Kentucky.[46] In another important step, Eisenhower decided to leave Newport and return to Washington. Eisenhower had, up to this point, resisted returning to Washington for two reasons. First, he thought that "to rush back to Washington every time an incident of serious character arose would be a confession that a change of scenery is truly a 'vacation' for the President and is not merely a change of his working locale." Second, he did "not want to exaggerate the significance of the admittedly serious situation in Arkansas. I do not want to give a picture of a cabinet in constant session, of fretting and worrying about the actions of a misguided governor who, in my opinion, has been motivated entirely by what he believes to be political advantage in a particular locality."[47]

The stated purpose for Eisenhower's return to Washington was to deliver a national television and radio address to the American people to explain the federal government's response to the recent events in Little Rock. In the address, quoted at the beginning of this chapter, Eisenhower explained that a "mob" in Little Rock, "under the leadership of demagogic extremists," had deliberately prevented the carrying out of federal court orders to admit Black children to Central High. Local authorities, he said, had been unable to control the mob, making it necessary for the executive branch of the federal government to become involved. The president's responsibility being "inescapable," he had ordered the use of federal troops. These troops, he said, "are not being used to relieve local and state authorities of their primary duty to preserve the peace and order of the community. Nor are the troops there for the purpose of taking over the responsibility of the School Board and the other responsible local officials in running Central High School." The troops were only there "for the purpose of preventing interference with the orders of the Court."

On this occasion, Eisenhower chose not to state support for the Supreme Court's decision in *Brown v. Board*, but merely to say that it should be obeyed because it was the law. "It is important that the reasons for my action be understood by all our citizens," Eisenhower said. "As you know, the Supreme Court of the United States has decided that separate public educational facilities for the races are inherently unequal and therefore compulsory school segregation laws are unconstitutional. Our personal opinions about the decision have no bearing on the matter of enforcement; the responsibility and authority of the Supreme Court to interpret the Constitution are very clear."[48] Eisenhower was acting on his constitutional obligation to enforce a federal court order. The nature of that order was, at least in terms of this obligation, irrelevant. It is worth noting, however, that on the day Eisenhower became aware of the situation in Little Rock, he had, for the first time, endorsed the *Brown* decision. "The Supreme Court in its decision of '54," he said at his September 3 press conference before leaving for Newport, "pointed out the emotional difficulties that would be encountered by Negroes if given equal but separate schools, and I think probably their reasoning was correct, at least I have no quarrel with it."[49] Surprisingly, given Eisenhower's past reluctance to offer even a qualified endorsement such as this, his comments were not major news.[50]

The president's address made every effort to direct blame away from the people of Little Rock, pointing out that many of the agitators had been brought in from outside the community. Although Eisenhower did not mention Governor Faubus by name, it was clear that the president considered him to be one of the "demagogic extremists." In a telegram to Senator Richard Russell (D-GA) released four days later, Eisenhower's opinion of Faubus's role became more explicit: "Had the police powers of the State of Arkansas been utilized not to frustrate the orders of the Court but to support them, the ensuing violence and open disrespect for the law and the Federal Judiciary would never have occurred," Eisenhower wrote. "As a matter of fact, had the integration of Central High School been permitted to take place without the intervention of the National Guard, there is little doubt that the process would have gone along quite smoothly and quietly as it had in other Arkansas communities."[51]

Contrary to Eisenhower's earlier statement that any direct confrontation between federal and state power would inevitably result in a federal victory, the situation in Little Rock remained a standoff. Black children were admitted to Central High, but only because federal troops remained on the premises to keep the peace. Eisenhower refused to remove federal troops until Faubus agreed that he would not obstruct court orders and would maintain order in Little Rock so that those orders could be carried out.

Faubus would only agree that he personally would not obstruct court orders; he refused to offer assurances that he would not allow others to do so.[52]

On October 14, one-half of the army troops were withdrawn and four-fifths of the National Guard were defederalized. On November 27, the last of the 101st Airborne left Little Rock, and the remaining federalized National Guard took over control of the school area. These guardsmen would remain until school let out in May 1958.[53] This was not the end of the standoff. In September 1958, Faubus, using powers given to him by the Arkansas State Legislature, closed the four public high schools in Little Rock. This was the outcome Eisenhower had feared all along. In June 1959 the federal court ordered that the schools reopen for the fall 1959 term. When school began, local law enforcement authorities were successful in dispersing a small crowd, and three Black students enrolled without further incident.[54] Sending federal troops to Little Rock was anything but moderate—many whites in the South saw it as nothing less than an act of war. But even during this decisive action, there were those who were disappointed in what they believed to be Eisenhower's lack of leadership on the issue. Less than a month after the president ordered the 101st Airborne to Little Rock, Frederick Morrow, the first African American to hold an executive position in the White House, wrote in his diary: "Of late I dread going to the office. The letters and phone calls are from irate friends and citizens who are fed up with the president's moderate stand on civil rights. They accuse him of refusing to assume the moral leadership of the country."[55] Emmet Hughes, a speech writer for Eisenhower but also one of his harshest critics, believed that the president's actions in Little Rock had little to do with civil rights. "Eisenhower kept affirming his resolve to maintain respect for the law. . . . But he refused, with equal tenacity, even to hint that he personally respected the *worth* of the law." Eisenhower, he wrote, "was never more decisive than when he held to a steely resolve *not* to do something that he sincerely believed wrong in itself or alien to his office."[56]

Politicians are often criticized for being "all talk and no action." In the field of civil rights, however, Eisenhower is accused of being all action and no talk. His actions were commendable. He desegregated the District of Columbia, completed the desegregation of the U.S. military, signed the first civil rights legislation since Reconstruction, and after the Supreme Court's decision in *Brown v. Board*, appointed federal judges to southern districts who would uphold the ruling. Finally, when Arkansas governor Orval Faubus violated a federal court order by interfering with a public-school desegregation plan, Eisenhower sent federal troops to Little Rock. By refusing to state his unambiguous support for the Supreme Court's decision in *Brown v. Board*, however, he left many Americans with the impression that he did not personally agree with it. In his memoirs, published more than ten years after the decision, Eisenhower wrote:

> After the Supreme Court's 1954 ruling, I refused to say whether I either approved or disapproved of it. The court's judgement was law, I said, and I would abide by it. This determination was one of principle. I believed that if I should express, publicly, either approval or disapproval of a Supreme Court decision in one case, I would be obliged to do so in many, if not all cases. Inevitably I would eventually be drawn into a public statement of disagreement with some decision creating a suspicion that my vigor of enforcement would, in such cases, be in doubt. Moreover, to indulge in a practice of approving or criticizing Court decisions could tend to lower the dignity of government, and would in the long run, be hurtful. In this case I definitely agreed with the unanimous decision.[57]

This rationale, although logical, seems incongruous with his earlier statements. More consistent with his statements from the time is that Eisenhower refused to publicly endorse *Brown* based on two of his fundamental beliefs. The first was that the role of the federal government should be limited to those areas where it had clear jurisdiction. The second was that people's beliefs about race could not be changed through legislation or executive action. *Brown v. Board* challenged both of these beliefs. Not only was education an area in which the federal government had no clear jurisdiction, it was also an area that segregationists felt very strongly about, and one in which laws or, in this case, court orders were unlikely to alter their beliefs. Although a public statement in support of *Brown* would not have changed the minds of determined segregationists, it might have dissuaded them from testing his resolve to uphold the decision.

Eisenhower sought balance on the issue of public-school segregation: balance between the requirements of *Brown v. Board*, which outlawed public-school segregation, and the legacy of *Plessy v. Ferguson*, which had protected it for fifty years; balance between those who demanded an immediate end to public-school segregation and those who sought to delay the process indefinitely; balance between the responsibilities of the federal government and the rights of states. When explaining his political philosophy to Bradford Chynoweth in 1954, Eisenhower had said that "excluding the field of moral values, anything that affects or is proposed for masses of humans is wrong if the position it seeks is at either end of possible argument."[58] But Eisenhower failed to see segregation as a moral values issue. Thus, he was unable to provide the moral leadership the nation needed on this divisive issue in the years immediately following *Brown v. Board*.

Eisenhower's civil rights position contributed to the early stages of a major political party realignment in the United States, an understanding of which remains important for our time. As we have seen, Eisenhower believed that in most cases civil rights should be handled by the states and, therefore, sought to limit the role of the federal government. He also showed empathy for the views of white southerners. Although politics were not Eisenhower's primary consideration, there were political advantages to be gained from this approach, and future Republican presidential candidates would more consciously exploit them.

Richard Nixon, the Republican Party's presidential nominee in 1960, narrowly lost the election to John Kennedy, but like Eisenhower, he did well in the South. Kennedy, fearful of losing any more of the region's electoral votes, proceeded cautiously on civil rights. After Kennedy's untimely death, Lyndon Johnson, his southern vice president, took up the cause. In the 1964 presidential election, many white southern Democrats, uncomfortable with Johnson's support of the recently passed Civil Rights Act of 1964, voted for the Republican presidential candidate Senator Barry Goldwater (R-AZ) who had voted against the legislation, saying it violated states' rights. Although Goldwater lost to Johnson in a landslide, the 1964 election demonstrated that the Democratic Party could no longer take the South's electoral votes for granted.

In the late 1960s, Republican strategists began more actively courting the white southern vote by pursuing what came to be known as the "southern strategy."[59] Recognizing that straightforward opposition to civil rights was unpopular in the North, Republicans appealed to white southerners by positioning themselves as the party of states' rights. Later, when some in the civil rights movement abandoned their commitment to nonviolence, Republicans began to emphasize "law and order." The Republican

Party's pursuit of the southern strategy throughout the 1970s and 1980s contributed to its emergence as the dominant party in the region by the end of the twentieth century. In 2005, the chairman of the Republican National Committee, hoping to court Black voters, formally apologized for the party's use of the southern strategy.[60] This apology notwithstanding, some within the party have continued to pursue it.[61]

The southern strategy, while making the Republican Party dominant in the South, secured the Black vote for the Democratic Party. Democratic candidates in the years since have been guilty of taking this vote for granted.[62] Given their own shameful history in the South, this is a mistake Democrats should avoid. Clearly both parties have been guilty of exploiting race for political gain.

8

Sputnik and the Race for Space

On January 7, 1958, in a speech prior to the opening of the second session of the Eighty-Fifth Congress, Senate majority leader Lyndon Johnson (D-TX) told his party caucus that during the intersession recess an "urgent race" had begun. This race, he claimed, was more important than the race to develop ballistic missiles— it was the race to control outer space. It was imperative that the United States win this race, he explained, because the winners would become the "masters of infinity" with "total control over the earth." Johnson argued that the Eisenhower administration had not placed the "evaluation of the importance of control of outer space" in the hands of those most qualified. Rather, he said, the decisions were made "within the framework of the government's annual budget." This approach, he said, had "appeared and reappeared as the prime limitation upon our scientific advancement."[1]

The "urgent race" Johnson referred to had begun on October 4, 1957, when the Soviet Union successfully placed Sputnik, the first artificial satellite, into earth orbit. Sputnik was a 184-pound, polished metal sphere twenty-two inches in diameter. It was equipped with four external antennas and a radio transmitter that emitted signals at two frequencies that could easily be picked up by receivers on earth. It travelled 18,000 miles per hour, orbiting the earth every ninety minutes on an elliptical orbit with a perigee (nearest point) of 143 miles above sea level, and an apogee (farthest point) of 584 miles above sea level. The launch was not completely unexpected. Both the United States and the Soviet Union had promised to launch satellites during the International Geophysical Year (IGY) that lasted from July 1957 to December 1958. The American public, however, had assumed that the United States would be the first to do so. The Soviet launch, therefore, led to a panic in the United States that was fueled by politicians, like Johnson, and media critics who claimed that the United States had fallen behind in the race for space. Although Johnson's speech suggests otherwise, the primary concern was not the achievement of a position that would afford the Soviet Union "control over the earth." Paramount for most was the belief that if a Soviet R-7 rocket could place a satellite in orbit, then it could also deliver a nuclear warhead to a target in the United States.

In the months following Sputnik, mainstream newspapers and periodicals criticized Eisenhower for allowing the Soviet Union to beat the United States in the race to orbit a satellite and for allowing a "missile gap" that threatened American security. Critics interpreted his attempts to play down the importance of the launch as proof of his complacency and lack of leadership. Historians have been kinder to Eisenhower. Recognizing that the United States was not appreciably behind the Soviet Union in missile development, they have validated his refusal to take drastic action in the period following Sputnik. Where historians continue to criticize Eisenhower is his failure to recognize the psychological impact of Sputnik, and his inability to convince Americans to trust in his judgment. This interpretation is best represented by historian Robert Divine in his book *The Sputnik Challenge*. "The passage of time has confirmed the wisdom of [Eisenhower's] response,"

Divine argued. "His refusal to support hasty or extreme measures in the wake of *Sputnik* proved fully justified." Despite this, Divine criticized Eisenhower's leadership during the crisis: "Eisenhower, for all his prudence and restraint, failed to meet one of the crucial tests of presidential leadership: convincing the American people that all was well in the world."[2]

More recently, historian Yanek Mieczkowski challenged the commonly accepted thesis that the Soviet launch of Sputnik caused an outbreak of mass hysteria in the United States. "The vast majority of Americans did not panic after *Sputnik*," he argues, "nor did the satellite generate any deep fear among the populace." The crisis, he claims, was generated by "elite voices," primarily politicians and members of the news media. Some may have sincerely believed there was a crisis—that America's security was at risk. Others recognized that Sputnik had made Eisenhower politically vulnerable, "and they pounced." The defense industry and the scientific community also participated, seeing an increased opportunity for government research grants.[3]

Eisenhower had never considered the U.S. satellite program to be in a race with the Soviet Union, and the reaction to Sputnik by the news media, scientific community, and Congress caught him off guard. His response to Sputnik was an attempt to find balance between their demands, which he considered to be an overreaction, and staying the course, in which he had great confidence. Ultimately, he agreed to increase defense spending to a level he believed was unnecessary and expand the federal government's role in education, something with which he was uncomfortable. In both cases, however, he had succeeded in scaling back the proposals of those who wished to do considerably more.

Eisenhower's desire to balance the nation's need for both military security and economic prosperity remains relevant in our time. Current budget deficits make it clear that we are spending more than we have. Evidence also suggests that we are spending more than necessary to ensure our nation's security and, depending on one's political point of view, neglecting other areas in need of attention.

Initial Reactions to Sputnik

President Eisenhower was at his farm in Gettysburg, Pennsylvania, when he received news of Sputnik's launch from his press secretary James Hagerty late in the day on Friday, October 4. Hagerty, fielding questions from the press, said that the United States had "never thought of our [space satellite] program as one which was in a race with the Soviets," and that the launch would have no effect on the timetable of the U.S. program, which planned to launch a smaller satellite in the spring of 1958. "Ours is geared to the International Geophysical Year," he said, "and is proceeding satisfactorily in accordance with its scientific objectives." After consulting with White House Chief of Staff Sherman Adams the next morning, Eisenhower released a brief statement that Hagerty read to the press. "The launching of the Soviet Satellite is, of course, of great scientific interest," he said. "It should contribute much to scientific knowledge that all countries are seeking to gain for the world during the International Geophysical Year." When asked if the statement meant that the satellite had "no defense or security significance," he replied that he was sticking with "scientific interest."[4]

The congressional reaction was led by Senator Stuart Symington (D-MO), who interpreted Sputnik very differently than the president. "The recently announced launching of an earth satellite," Symington said in a statement from Kansas City, "is but more proof of growing Communist superiority in the all-important missile field." The senator left no doubt that he blamed Eisenhower's fiscal conservatism for the failure of the United States to lead the world in satellite and missile technology. "At the same time" that the Soviet Union was achieving its superiority, Symington claimed that "for fiscal reasons" the United States was continuing "to cut back and slow down its own missile program." He ended his statement with a call for the Senate Armed Services Committee to open an investigation, "because the future of the United States may well be at stake."[5]

Sputnik's launch had been scheduled to coincide with an IGY conference in Washington, DC, and many of America's top scientists had the awkward experience of learning about it while attending a reception for the event at the Soviet embassy. While the scientists mingled over drinks, word spread through the crowd that the New York Times had received a Radio Moscow report of the launch. Despite their disappointment, they magnanimously congratulated their Soviet colleagues for the accomplishment. Not all scientists were so magnanimous. When Richard Witkin of the New York Times asked "high-ranking scientists" whether the United States could have launched a satellite before the Soviet Union "if money had not been held back and time wasted," many, he reported, had answered "yes."[6] One scientist who believed this was Wernher von Braun, director of the Army Ballistic Missile Agency (ABMA). On the day of the launch, he was giving newly appointed Secretary of Defense Neil McElroy a tour of Redstone Arsenal, near Huntsville, Alabama. Upon hearing of the launch von Braun exploded. "For God's sake turn us loose and let us do something," he said to the secretary. "We can put up a satellite in sixty days, Mr. McElroy! Just give us a green light and sixty days!"[7]

Back in Washington on Tuesday morning, Eisenhower asked Deputy Secretary of Defense Donald Quarles about the published claims that the army could have put a satellite into orbit several months before the Soviet Union. Quarles said that "there was no doubt that the Redstone, had it been used, could have orbited a satellite a year or more ago." Taking the position that he would adhere to at the next day's press conference, Eisenhower recalled that "timing was never given too much importance in our own program."[8] The army's claim was legitimate. On September 20, 1956, ABMA launched the first Jupiter-C missile, based on the Redstone rocket, from Cape Canaveral, Florida. It landed in the ocean 3,350 miles from the launch pad—a distance record. It had reached an altitude of 682 miles—also a record. At this altitude it could have launched a satellite. In fact, prior to launch, an eager von Braun had been warned *not* to put a satellite in the nose cone.[9]

Later that day, Eisenhower met with Detlev Bronk, president of the National Academy of Sciences, to go over a statement that he planned to release prior to his press conference the next day. "His intent," Eisenhower said, "was not to belittle the Russian accomplishment. He would like, however, to allay hysteria and alarm." Bronk approved of the statement with one or two minor changes. Adams asked Bronk if he thought there was "anything in this achievement to alter our research and development program." Bronk said there was not and that "we cannot constantly change our program with every action by the Russians." He said that "if the president were asked if the scientists had been given adequate responsibility and opportunity to develop a satellite, he should say that they had been."[10]

The press release the next day explained that in October 1954, the Eisenhower administration had decided to institute a scientific satellite program as part of the U.S. contribution to the IGY. The scientific aspects of the program were assigned to the National Science Foundation (NSF) and the U.S. Committee for the IGY, while the Department of Defense would supply the rocketry needed to place the satellite in orbit. Defense awarded this project to the Naval Research Laboratory (NRL). Because the NRL was not involved in ballistic missile research, its work on Vanguard, as the NRL satellite program was called, would serve two purposes. First, in keeping with the IGY's mission, all data from the project could be shared with scientists throughout the world. Second, it would prevent any interference with the ongoing army and air force military missile programs. Eisenhower emphasized that Vanguard was never given the top priority that missile research enjoyed and, therefore, the "speed of progress in the satellite project cannot be taken as an index of progress in ballistic missile work." The statement ended with a reminder that "our satellite program has never been conducted as a race with other nations."[11] Nor could it have been. The big drawback of Vanguard was that it was an entirely new rocket and would not be ready before 1958.

The president's carefully worded statement did not satisfy the 245 reporters who had assembled that day, and his responses did little to calm the hysteria to which many in the news media, not to mention the political and scientific communities, had succumbed. One week earlier, most of the questions at the presidential press conference had been about the ongoing Little Rock integration crisis, and Eisenhower had been praised for his handling of them. Faced with this new crisis, he stumbled a bit. The first question set the tone: "Russia has launched an earth satellite. They also claim to have had a successful firing of an intercontinental ballistic missile. . . . I ask you sir, what are we going to do about it?" Eisenhower's response did not say what he intended to do about it, instead he reviewed what had already been done, emphasizing that despite its growing cost, he had always given Project Vanguard whatever it had asked for. "There never has been one nickel asked for accelerating the program. Never has it been considered a race." Eisenhower was clearly sensitive to the claim that his fiscal austerity had cost the nation a chance to pull ahead in the race for space. Perhaps sensing that he was deflecting criticism, something that would have been uncharacteristic of him, another reporter asked, "Do you think that our scientists made a mistake in not recognizing that we were . . . in a race with Russia in launching this satellite, and not asking you for top priority and more money to speed up the program?" Clearly wishing to move on, his response was brief: "No, I don't."

Considering his determination to downplay the event, Eisenhower made some notable, and perhaps unintended, admissions. He said that scientists were "astonished" at Sputnik's weight. He volunteered that it was "probably true" that the Soviets had gained a political and psychological advantage throughout the world. And when asked if he was satisfied with U.S. progress in the missile field, he said "I wish we were further ahead and knew more." He also betrayed his frustration at times, something he tried not to do in public. He said that to him "there didn't seem to be a reason . . . to grow hysterical about it [Sputnik]." In response to one suggestion, he said, "Suddenly all America seems to become scientists" (that at least got him a laugh). Most quoted, however, was his response to a question that played to his strengths: "In light of the great faith which the American people have in your military knowledge and leadership, are you saying at this time that with the Russian Satellite whirling about the world, you are not more concerned nor overly concerned about our nation's security?" In its attempt to be precise, his response seemed equivocal: "Well, I have time and again emphasized my concern about the nation's security. . . . Now, so far as the satellite itself is concerned, that does not raise my apprehensions, not one iota."[12]

If Eisenhower had led with, and refused to stray from, his lack of concern, he might have been more convincing. Instead, he had buried the lede in a long press conference during which he did, at times, seem concerned. The next day's coverage of Eisenhower's press conference was not good. "We agree with Ike that the Russian *Sputnik* up there can't hurt us. It isn't armed, it apparently isn't likely to fall on us," said an editorial in the *New York Post.* "Despite his reassurances, the country remains uneasy. For the first time we know what it feels like to be a have-not nation. We have no *sput-niks*, and all the rationalizations of all our leaders . . . [do not] alter that fact. . . . We see poor planning, lack of imagination, underestimation of our adversary, faulty education, a lack of scientists. . . . We see a nation obsessed with material comforts, more adept at producing washing machines than *sputniks*."[13]

Crafting a Response

The October 10 meeting of the NSC was devoted almost entirely to the subject of earth satellites and the missiles that carry them. DCI Allen Dulles reviewed the world reaction to Sputnik. The Soviet Union was, he said, seeking to make the most of the satellite launch and the preceding test of an intercontinental ballistic missile (ICBM) for propaganda purposes. Although their efforts were aimed primarily at the Middle East and other areas of the developing world, an interview published the previous day in the *New York Times* made clear that they were aimed at the West as well. In it, Soviet premier Nikita Khrushchev said, "When we announced the successful testing of an intercontinental ballistic missile, some American statesmen did not believe us . . . now that we have successfully launched an earth satellite, only technically ignorant people can doubt this. The United States does not have an intercontinental ballistic missile; otherwise, it would have easily launched an earth satellite of its own. We can launch satellites because we have a carrier for them, namely the ballistic missile."[14]

The NSC held an extended discussion of the difference between the American and Soviet satellite programs. Quarles explained that the Soviet Union's satellite program had been integrated into its ICBM program from the beginning, and its prime objective was to be the first nation to orbit a satellite. Their success made clear that their abilities in the field of rocketry were greater than the United States had believed. The United States had separated its satellite and ICBM programs. Doing so necessitated a longer timeline, but it had allowed the United States to be "very open and aboveboard" about what it was doing, said Quarles, while "the Russians have not been." In addition, he said, the satellite that the United States would deploy would be more sophisticated and provide more useful data. Bronk added that he was "greatly concerned" that the United States "avoid getting our whole scientific community into a race to accomplish everything before the Russians do." The president concurred. He told those present that when they spoke to members of Congress or to the press "he could not imagine anything more important" than that they "stand firmly behind the existing earth satellite program which was, after all, adopted by the Council after due deliberation."[15]

What Eisenhower and the NSC did not yet know was that there was a connection between the tremendous power of the Soviet R-7 rocket and the lack of sophistication of Sputnik. Soviet scientists had not yet developed the ability to miniaturize their instruments or create lightweight metal alloys. Powerful rockets were necessary just to get their hardware off the ground. Soviet missile guidance systems also lagged behind those of the United States. So, the Soviets could launch a missile that would travel a great distance, but their nuclear warheads were not yet small enough to fit inside the nose cone, and they could not be sure that the missile would come down within range of its target.[16]

Eisenhower later reflected that "there were two problems created by the Soviet *Sputnik*." The first was a short-term one, "to find ways of affording perspective to our people and so relieve the current wave of near-hysteria." The second problem was long-term— "to take all feasible measures to accelerate missile and satellite programs."[17] It was with these problems in mind that he spoke to the Science Advisory Committee in the Office of Defense Mobilization (ODM). The meeting had been planned before Sputnik but took on a greater importance given the circumstances. Eisenhower told the group that "he would like to try to create a spirit—an attitude toward science similar to that held toward various kinds of athletics in his youth." He added that perhaps it was a good time to do so. "People are alarmed and thinking about science, and perhaps this alarm could be turned to a collective result." With this in mind he planned to make a series of speeches on science and national security. One member of the group, Nobel Prize–winning physicist Isidor Rabi, suggested the idea of naming a presidential science adviser—an idea that Eisenhower liked.[18]

On November 7, Eisenhower addressed the American people from the Oval Office. By this time, the Soviet Union had launched a second satellite, Sputnik II. The 1,121-pound satellite carried a dog named Laika and a limited life-support system. Its weight required a rocket with at least 500,000 pounds of thrust—enough to power an ICBM for a 5,000-mile flight. "I am going to lay the facts before you—the rough with the smooth," he said. "Some of these security facts are reassuring; others are not." He began with the reassuring—an impressive list of modern arms possessed by the United States. Then, not wanting to dismiss an "achievement of the first importance," he recognized the scientists responsible for Sputnik. But, he said, "Earth satellites, in themselves, have no direct present effect upon the nation's security," and "although the Soviets are quite likely ahead . . . of us in satellite development, as of today the over-all military strength of the free world is distinctly greater than that of the communist countries."[19]

Moving on to the promotion of science he had discussed with the science advisers, he said that one of the nation's greatest deficiencies was the failure "to give high enough priority to scientific education and to the place of science in our national life." Following through on Rabi's recommendation he said that he had created the position of special assistant to the president for science and technology to which he would appoint James Killian, president of the Massachusetts Institute of Technology. The Science Advisory Committee would also be moved from the ODM to the White House, becoming the Presidential Science Advisory Committee (PSAC).[20] After his appointment, Killian told the press that he saw his job "as a means to integrate American science in every proper way with national policy making."[21] Killian's appointment was not a hollow gesture. He attended meetings of the cabinet and the NSC and became one of Eisenhower's most trusted advisers.

Eisenhower also responded to some of the criticism he had endured since Sputnik. To prevent interservice rivalries from holding up ballistic missile development in the way his critics claimed it had held up satellite development, he was creating the position of guided missile director in the Department of Defense to administer all missile development without regard to branch of military service. In response to demands for a massive increase in defense spending, however, he was less accommodating. "We can have both a sound defense, and the sound economy on which it rests," he promised, "if we set our priorities and stick to them and if each of us is ready to carry his own share of the burden."[22]

In his follow-up speech the next week in Oklahoma City, Eisenhower said that he understood the fear that had gripped many Americans since the launch of Sputnik. "When such competence . . . is at the service of leaders who have so little regard for things human, and who command the power of an empire, there is danger ahead for free men everywhere," he said, referring to the Soviet Union. "That, my friends, is the reason why the American people have been so aroused about earth satellites." At the same time, he sought to assure Americans that despite what they were hearing from his critics in Congress and the press, they were safe. "The Soviets must be convinced that any attack on us and our allies would result, regardless to damage to us, in their own national destruction," he told the assembled crowd. "A principle deterrent to war is the retaliatory nuclear power of our Strategic Air Command and our Navy. . . . It will be some time before either we or the Soviet forces will have long-range missile capability equal to even a small fraction of the total destructive power of our present bomber force." Eisenhower assured the crowd that although maintaining and protecting the nuclear deterrent would be expensive, it would be done. "Our people," he said, "will not sacrifice security to worship a balanced budget." He would not, however, give in to demands that he spend more than what was necessary. "Over the long term a balanced budget is one indispensable aid in keeping our economy and therefore our total security, strong and sound."[23]

The speeches did not have the effect that Eisenhower had hoped. Reviews ranged from harsh criticism to lukewarm praise. A Gallup poll showed that his popularity had dropped from 79 percent in January 1957 to 57 percent in November 1957. With the Little Rock situation ongoing and the economy struggling, the drop cannot be attributed entirely to Sputnik, but it certainly did not help.[24] Eisenhower had planned to deliver a third speech in response to Sputnik in Cleveland later that month, but he was unable to do so. After lunch on Monday, November 25, Eisenhower complained of dizziness, then discovered he was having difficulty speaking. To his frustration, some words came out jumbled and others he could not remember at all. The president had suffered a mild stroke. The constant strain he had been under since the 1956 election campaign—and more recently by the concurrent Little Rock and Sputnik crises—had likely contributed to its onset. Within two days he had recovered his ability to speak and resisted any further restrictions on his activity. "If I cannot attend to my duties," he told Mamie Eisenhower, "I am simply going to give up this job. Now that is all there is to it."[25] Eisenhower did indeed attend to his duties. In fact, his secretary Ann Whitman said that in the days after his stroke he attended them with a new vigor, perhaps attempting to show that he still had it in him.

The Gaither Report

The winter of 1957–58 offered Eisenhower no break from the strain of his job. The period was defined primarily by debate over the defense budget. The terms of the debate were shaped not only by post-Sputnik political pressure, but by the unfortunate timing of the Gaither Report. The Gaither Committee, or more formally, the Office of Defense Mobilization Security Resources Panel, had been appointed by Eisenhower in April 1957 to study the Civil Defense Administration's proposal to spend $40 billion on blast and fallout shelters. Despite the president's request that the panel limit its study to passive defense measures that would protect the American people in the event of a nuclear attack, the Gaither

Committee undertook a much broader study that included active defense measures such as improving the nation's nuclear deterrent to prevent an attack. The committee submitted its report during the sensitive period following Sputnik when Eisenhower was attempting to calm fears and prevent Congress from overreacting with demands for massive increases in defense spending.

The Gaither Committee's brief but alarming report estimated that if current trends in defense spending continued, the USSR's annual military expenditures would be double those of the United States by the end of the 1960s. "The singleness of purpose with which they have pressed their military-centered industrial development," the report warned, "has led to spectacular progress." Most notable was the assumption that they had already surpassed the United States in ICBM development. Its conclusion was that "active defense programs now in being and programmed for the future will not give adequate assurance of protection to the civil population." To lessen American vulnerability to surprise nuclear attack, the Gaither Committee made several recommendations. These included the following: reducing the response time for the Strategic Air Command (SAC), the primary deterrent to such an attack; protecting SAC by dispersing aircraft and building blast shelters for its aircraft and personnel; increasing the planned initial numbers of Thor and Jupiter intermediate range ballistic missiles (IRBMs) from 60 to 240; increasing the planned initial numbers of Atlas and Titan ICBMs from 80 to 600; accelerating production of Polaris, the submarine-based IRBM; and creation of a nationwide system of fallout shelters. To implement the measures that the Gaither Committee considered of the highest value (everything mentioned here except for fallout shelters) would increase U.S. defense spending by $3–5 billion dollars per year for the next five years. This, the committee believed, would necessitate an increase in taxes and cuts in domestic spending such as highway construction. The final paragraph of the report was, no doubt, worded for its shock value. "By 1959, the USSR may be able to launch an attack with ICBMs carrying megaton warheads, against which SAC will be almost completely vulnerable under present programs. . . . If we fail to act at once, the risk, in our opinion, will be unacceptable."[26]

On November 7, the same day that he addressed the American people from the Oval Office, the NSC discussed the Gaither Committee report. If Eisenhower was angry that the Gaither Committee had exceeded its authority and put unnecessary pressure on him to increase spending, he did not show his anger to the council. He did tell them that despite the seriousness of the report, it was "essential that we neither become panicked nor allow ourselves to be complacent." Rather, he said, they should make an urgent "economic, psychological, and political survey" of what should be done—and do it. He even suggested that in this regard, perhaps Sputnik had been helpful. He added that he had received information that day indicating that "fear had pervaded the population of the United States," and that it was important that they not "appear frightened."

Eisenhower did not disagree with all the recommendations of the Gaither Committee, but it was clear that he believed that the increased spending that the report recommended would damage the economy on which American security was based. "Was the panel proposing to impose controls on the U.S. economy?" he asked, reminding the council that he had removed controls upon taking office, believing this would allow the economy to grow more rapidly. He commented that "if those present were a group sitting in the Kremlin, we would probably adopt the recommendations . . . *in toto*, regardless of the effect of such action on our people." But of course, he could not do that. "We have a big problem of molding public opinion as well as of avoiding extremes."[27] Eisenhower would later write that "the president, unlike a panel which concentrates on a single problem, must always strive to see the totality of the national and international situation. He must take into account conflicting purposes, responding to legitimate needs but assigning priorities and keeping costs within bounds."[28]

Historian David Snead has pointed out another flaw in the Gaither Report that certainly influenced Eisenhower's decisions about which of its recommendations to accept and which to dismiss. In making its recommendations, Snead wrote, the Gaither Committee "failed to evaluate the likelihood of the risks the Soviet Union might take to achieve its goals; therefore, it proposed major increases in defense spending that did not reflect the improbability of a Soviet attack."[29]

At the conclusion of the NSC meeting, Eisenhower said that it would be interesting to see how long the Gaither Report could be kept secret. Within a month the Gaither Committee report had leaked to the press, and in December the *Washington Post* published a summary of its findings. In his accompanying story, Chalmers Roberts said that the "Gaither Report portrays a United States in the gravest danger in its history."

> It pictures the nation moving in frightening course to the status of a second-class power. It shows an America exposed to an almost immediate threat from the missile bristling Soviet Union. It finds America's long-term prospect one of cataclysmic peril in the face of rocketing Soviet military might and of a powerful, growing Soviet economy and technology which will bring new political, propaganda, and psychological assaults on freedom all around the globe. Many of those who worked on the report . . . were appalled, even frightened, at what they discovered to be the state of the American military posture in comparison with that of the Soviet Union.[30]

Roberts's editorial missed the mark by a wide margin. His remarks, and the Gaither Committee's report, compared American missile development with what they *assumed* the Soviet Union had already done. Eisenhower was confident that their assumptions were incorrect. Since 1956, American U-2 planes had been making regular overflights of the Soviet Union. From an altitude of 70,000 feet, U-2 reconnaissance flights photographed a strip of Soviet territory 125 miles wide and 3,000 miles long. The images were clear enough to read a newspaper headline. From this intelligence data, Eisenhower knew that the Soviet Union was not as far along in its ICBM development as Sputnik had made it seem. They were still in the early stages of testing and had made no preparations for their deployment. Contrary to claims being made by his critics, the Soviets were no more than a few months ahead of the United States in ICBM development. The primary deterrent to World War III, America's nuclear arsenal and its current delivery system, the long-range B-52 bomber, were not in danger of surprise attack.

Allen Dulles advised Eisenhower that he should tell the American people that "the United States has the capability of photographing the Soviet Union from a very high altitude without interference." The idea of doing so must have been very attractive to Eisenhower. Such an admission would have silenced his critics and eased his burdens tremendously, but he refused to jeopardize the program by exposing it.[31] The closest he came was in a letter to Swede Hazlett. "You can understand that there are many things that I don't allude to publicly," he wrote during the month following Sputnik, "yet some of them would do much to allay the fears of our own people."[32]

Sputnik and the U-2 were tied together in another way as well. At his post-Sputnik press conference, Eisenhower had been asked whether satellites had "significance in surveillance of other countries." He had responded, "I wouldn't believe at this moment you have to fear the intelligence aspects of this."[33] In fact, it was the surveillance potential of satellites that interested Eisenhower the most. He had always been tentative about the use of the U-2, admitting that if he became aware of the Soviet Union overflying U.S. territory, he would consider it an act of war. If satellites could provide superior intelligence from low earth orbit, it would eliminate the need to violate Soviet airspace. The air force was already at work on WS-117L, a reconnaissance satellite to replace the U-2. The day before the press conference, Eisenhower had commented that the "Russians have in fact done us a good turn, unintentionally, in establishing the concept of freedom of international space."[34] No nation protested that Sputnik had violated their territory.

On the same day as Eisenhower's stroke, Lyndon Johnson opened Senate hearings on the U.S. satellite and missile programs. Johnson had arranged for his Defense Preparedness Subcommittee to hold the hearings rather than the full Senate Armed Services Committee as Symington had called for. With Johnson and Symington as leading candidates for the 1960 Democratic presidential nomination, this move was a bit of intraparty politics. Johnson wanted to take a more bipartisan approach to the hearings. This, he believed, would make both Symington, who wanted to blame Eisenhower, and Republicans, who wanted to blame Truman, look like they were playing politics with national security. If successful, it would also make him look presidential.[35]

Congressional critics claimed that Eisenhower had allowed interservice rivalries to interfere with the development of ballistic missiles. Eisenhower was sensitive to this criticism because he believed that competing missile projects had inflated the budget for weapons development. But with four ballistic missile systems making significant progress, and none of them hurting for need of additional funding, the criticism that development had been compromised was misplaced. The air force had two ICBM projects, Atlas and Titan. IRBMs, which, if deployed in Europe, would give the United States the ability to strike targets in the Soviet Union before ICBMs were available, were under development by the air force, which had Thor, and the army, which had Jupiter. All four of these missiles required highly volatile liquid fuel that needed to be stored at very low temperatures. This meant that they had to be fueled just before launch, which cut down response time significantly. To solve this problem, the air force was developing Minuteman, a solid-fueled ICBM. Solid-fueled missiles were ready to launch and could, therefore, be housed in protective silos. They had the added benefit of being much lighter. The navy was developing a solid-fueled IRBM called Polaris that could be launched from a specially designed, and very expensive, submarine.

Eisenhower found himself in a difficult position. He did not want to build too many first-generation, liquid-fueled missiles, knowing they would be obsolete when solid-fuel missiles became available. Nor did he want to overspend on solid-fuel missiles before the research had proven them viable. What he did want to do was end duplication and unnecessary spending by eliminating the less promising projects in the ICBM and IRBM categories. So Eisenhower's determination to "maintain a defense posture of unparalleled magnitude and yet do so without a breakdown of the economy" would not have disadvantaged ballistic missile research and development; but in a post-Sputnik America, he could not appear to be sacrificing security for the sake of a balanced budget.[36] In a letter to financier Frank Altschul, Eisenhower had commented at length regarding the difficulty of providing security without destroying what he was trying to defend.

You mention that security is more important than balanced bud-
gets. . . . The problem is not so simple as the statement implies. . . .
We must remember that we are defending a way of life. . . . That way
of life, over the long term, requires observance of sound fiscal policies . . . so that the system may continue to work primarily under
the impulse of private effort rather than by fiat of centralized government. Should we resort to anything resembling a garrison state,
then all that we are striving to defend would be weakened and, if
long subjected to this kind of control, could disappear.[37]

If the United States was behind the Soviet Union in missile development, it was not because Eisenhower had not given it high priority. As historian Yanek Mieczkowski has argued, post-Sputnik
claims by congressional Democrats and the Gaither Committee
that Eisenhower had allowed the Soviet Union to open a "missile
gap" between itself and the United States "ignored the emphasis
that he had placed on missile development and national security."[38]
Absent the setback in the unplanned race to orbit a satellite, U.S.
missile development made significant progress under Eisenhower.
In 1953, his first year in the White House, the United States had
spent $3 million on missiles. In 1957, the year of Sputnik, it spent
$1.4 billion. Wernher von Braun, designer of the German V-1 and
V-2 rockets used against Britain in World War II and now working on the U.S. Army's Jupiter missile, defended the president from
charges of not prioritizing missiles. "The United States had no ballistic missile program worth mentioning between 1945 and 1951.
Those six years, during which the Russians obviously laid the ground
work for their large rocket program, are irretrievably lost. . . . Our
present dilemma is not due to the fact that we are not working hard
enough now, but that we did not work hard enough during the first
six to ten years after the war."[39] Vice President Nixon was quick to
see the political benefits of this position—blame Truman.

Although Eisenhower emphasized to Defense Secretary McElroy and his science adviser James Killian that he did not want to spend money in response to public pressure, the defense budget increased approximately $2 billion as a result of Sputnik, the Gaither Report, and Democratic claims of a missile gap.[40] It is tempting to conclude that Eisenhower compromised his principles by agreeing to spend money that he did not believe was necessary for American security, but without revealing the existence of the U-2 intelligence it was really the best he could do. Given that the Gaither Report had recommended an additional $3–5 billion per year for defense, the $2 billion Eisenhower conceded to under intense pressure could be considered a victory. "I had made as strong a case for confidence and sane direction as I could," he later wrote. "I was hampered, of course, by the fact that I could not reveal secrets which in themselves would have reassured our people."[41]

Satellites, the NDEA, and NASA

In his first press conference following Sputnik's launch, Eisenhower had promised that the United States would put up a satellite in December 1957. That promise was ill-advised. On December 6, after several delays in the countdown, the press watched as Vanguard exploded on the launchpad. "Vanguard Rocket Burns on Beach; Failure to Launch Test Satellite Assailed as Blow to U.S. Prestige," proclaimed the *New York Times*.[42] Others were not so diplomatic, "Flopnik," "Kaputnik," and "Rearguard," were among the many attempts to derive humor from an embarrassing public failure. On January 28, 1958, after a ten-day delay, a second Vanguard launch was called off after a fuel leak was discovered fourteen seconds before liftoff. The administration was quick to point out that Vanguard did not use military rockets, so its failures had no bearing on the ballistic missile program. Earlier that month, however, Killian had recommended that although Vanguard should be allowed to attempt the launches that were already scheduled, the program should not be expanded. Any additional resources should be given to the army's Jupiter program, which he said should be supported and encouraged in their quest to launch a satellite.[43]

Finally, just after midnight on February 1, an army Jupiter-C (formerly known as the Redstone) missile put Explorer, America's first satellite, into space. "That's wonderful," Eisenhower said to Hagerty. "I surely feel a lot better now. . . . Let's not make too great a hullabaloo over this." Within eight weeks, the United States placed two additional satellites in orbit. On March 17, Vanguard finally succeeded. Although it was just six inches in diameter and weighed only three and a half pounds, its orbit was 2,500 miles above sea level, and it was expected to remain in orbit for two hundred years (it is still there!). On March 26, Explorer III went into orbit (Explorer II had failed to reach orbit on March 5). By the end of 1960, the United States had successfully launched thirty-one satellites, and sixteen were still in earth orbit. Sputnik had fallen out of orbit on January 4, 1958, burning up on reentry after ninety-two days in space. This left Sputnik II as the lone Soviet satellite in earth orbit.[44]

Later in life Eisenhower admitted that keeping the satellite program separate from missile development might have been a mistake. "It would have been easier, in hindsight," he wrote, "to have used the Redstone from the beginning." Former secretary of defense Charlie Wilson admitted the mistake almost immediately after the Sputnik launch. "Non-interfering with the high-priority ballistic missiles was certainly reasonable at the time," he wrote in a memo to the president, "even though it may appear questionable in retrospect."[45]

Following the launch of Sputnik, many Americans expressed the opinion that prosperity had made the United States overly materialistic and in turn complacent about things that really mattered. "The Roman Empire controlled the world because it had roads," Lyndon Johnson said. "The British Empire was dominant because it had ships. . . . Now the communists have established a foothold in space. It is not very reassuring to be told that next year we will put a better satellite into the air. Perhaps it will even have chrome trim and automatic windshield wipers."[46] Senator Styles Bridges (R-NH) echoed the theme. "The time has clearly come," he said, "to be less concerned with . . . the height of the tailfin on the car and to be more prepared to shed blood, sweat and tears if this country and the free world are to survive."[47] One area where Americans had become "soft" according to this point of view was education. Russians had beaten Americans into space because the United States had deemphasized science and mathematics. Eisenhower was reluctant to get the federal government involved in education, but he would have to compromise here just as he had with the defense budget.

Eisenhower's proposals for federal aid to alleviate the nationwide classroom shortage due to the postwar baby boom had been complicated in the two previous years by desegregation amendments, and the heightened tensions caused by the Little Rock crisis made it very unlikely that such a bill could be passed in 1958. Secretary of HEW Marion Folsom later recalled that the decision to shift the emphasis of the education program predated the launch of Sputnik. "We both felt it would be unlikely that we could get any classroom construction legislation through," Folsom wrote. "The President said, 'why can't we get up something to step up the teaching of mathematics and science and put that in?'"[48] By the time Folsom presented his plan to the Cabinet, Sputnik had been launched, giving added impetus to the program.[49] In fact, by this time, Eisenhower's main concern, as with defense spending, was to prevent Congress from going too far. "Some alarmed citizens," he later wrote, "were urging vastly increased spending and wholesale revision of our schools so as to turn nearly every student into a scientist or engineer as quickly as possible."[50]

The administration adopted Folsom's plan, and Eisenhower presented it to Congress on January 27, 1958. Folsom called it a "well rounded program ... preferable to the many radical proposals certain to be introduced in the next session."[51] For the NSF, the proposal recommended additional funds for the training of math and science teachers, additional funds to improve the content of science courses at all levels, an increase in graduate fellowships, and funds to allow the NSF to initiate new programs providing fellowships for secondary school science teachers, aspiring high school math and science teachers, and graduate teaching assistants. Other programs to be administered by the HEW included a program of ten thousand federal scholarships a year for four years for qualified high school graduates who lacked the financial resources to go to college, federal matching grants to the states to improve and expand the teaching of science and math, graduate fellowships for students to prepare for college teaching careers, federal matching grants to help universities to expand their graduate programs, and support for universities to expand and improve the teaching of modern foreign languages. Eisenhower emphasized: "This emergency program stems from national need, and its fruits will bear directly on national security. The method of accomplishment is sound: the keystone is state, local, and private effort; the federal role is to assist—not control or supplant—those efforts."[52] The proposed four-year program would cost $1.6 billion.[53]

The administration's bill, the National Defense Education Act (NDEA), made it through Congress relatively easily. The national attention generated by the news media over Sputnik made every member of Congress anxious to contribute to the U.S. effort to catch up with the Soviets in technology, and training more students in math and science seemed, to many, a good way to start. The main controversy regarding the bill was over Eisenhower's request for ten thousand federal scholarships a year for four years. The House passed an amendment stripping the bill of its scholarship provisions and placing the $120 million that would have financed them into a low-interest college loan fund.[54] Eisenhower, who was personally uncomfortable with the scholarships, was not disappointed when they were eliminated. The loans, Eisenhower believed, would "make an education available to the student while encouraging self-reliance."[55] Once the scholarship provision was eliminated, the NDEA passed the House easily. The Senate passed a version of the bill that included twenty-three thousand federal scholarships but accepted the House of Representatives' version in conference committee. Eisenhower signed the NDEA into law on September 2, 1958, noting that it would "do much to strengthen our American system of education so that it can meet the broad and increasing demands imposed upon it by considerations of basic national security."[56]

Meanwhile, in February 1958, congressional activity threatened to take the initiative for space policy away from the White House. Senators Albert Gore (D-TN) and Clinton Anderson (D-NM) introduced legislation to put all space programs under the Atomic Energy Commission (AEC), while Hubert Humphrey (D-MN) and Estes Kefauver (D-TN) introduced legislation to create a new Department of Science and Technology. Meanwhile, Lyndon Johnson created a new Senate Committee on Outer Space, which he would chair himself. In response, Secretary McElroy, to avoid the kind of interservice rivalries that many blamed for holding up missile research, placed all military space activities under the direction of the newly created Advanced Research Projects Agency (ARPA). The administration also announced that it was considering a separate civilian agency to direct nonmilitary space activity.[57]

On February 4, when the subject of a civilian space agency came up at a Republican congressional leaders' meeting, Eisenhower spoke in favor of leaving all space-related activity within the Defense Department. Citing the reconnaissance satellite as the primary example, Eisenhower said, "Our major interest in this for some years will be a defense one." Eisenhower showed little interest in space exploration, stating his objection to putting "unlimited funds into these costly ventures where there was nothing of value to the nation's security." When Senator William Knowland (R-CA), remembering the impact of Sputnik on world opinion, spoke in favor of a lunar probe, Eisenhower was unmoved. "I'd rather have a good Redstone than hit the moon," he said. "I don't think we have an enemy on the moon!" Even accounting for the possibility that Eisenhower had exaggerated his position to impress the congressional leaders, it was clear that he had reservations about the value of a civilian space agency.[58]

Later that day, Eisenhower announced that he had asked PSAC to make a recommendation regarding a new agency. Killian had been present at the Republican congressional leaders' meeting and knew Eisenhower's reservations, but he and the other members of PSAC strongly believed that "a separate agency largely centered about non-military activity" was important. Having ruled out the possibility of keeping the space program within the military, PSAC also considered the alternatives that had been proposed in Congress. They believed that the AEC's primary mission was too far removed from space policy, and they rejected the idea of creating an entirely new Department of Science and Technology—something Eisenhower was unlikely to support.[59]

Ultimately, PSAC decided that the National Advisory Committee for Aeronautics (NACA), an independent agency founded in 1915, was best suited to take on the task of directing civilian space programs. NACA had been created by President Woodrow Wilson in 1915 "to supervise and direct the scientific study of the problems of flight with a view to their practical solution."[60] NACA's history of cooperation with the military eased fears about the potential for unproductive competition between a civilian space agency and the Department of Defense. On March 5, Killian recommended to Eisenhower that all civilian space activity be placed under the direction of NACA, which would be reconstituted as the National Aeronautics and Space Administration (NASA). Eisenhower, who by now had warmed to the idea of a civilian space agency, responded positively. His lone reservation was that duplication of effort between NASA and ARPA would lead to wasteful spending. Killian explained that both agencies would have to bring their proposals to the president for approval, so Eisenhower would have the final word.[61] Eisenhower approved the recommendation and on April 2, 1958, sent a message to Congress proposing legislation to create NASA and give it jurisdiction over all civilian space programs.[62]

NASA was well received by Congress, which acted with remarkable speed. In June, the House and Senate each passed a bill creating NASA. The Senate version proposed the creation of a "Space Council" to advise the president on space policy. Killian told Johnson that Eisenhower opposed the idea of a Space Council, preferring an administrator who would report directly to him, but Johnson refused to eliminate it from the bill. On July 7, at the senator's request, Johnson and Eisenhower met at the White House. Eisenhower later told Killian that he had given in on the Space Council to speed passage of the bill. The nine-member Space Council, Johnson had explained, would be modeled on the NSC with the president as chair and seats for the secretaries of state and defense. Having overcome the president's objections, the conference committee included the Space Council in the final version of the bill, which the House and Senate each passed unanimously. On July 29, Eisenhower signed the bill creating NASA into law. Several days later he appointed Keith Glennan, president of Case Western Reserve University, NASA's first administrator.[63]

On November 8, one month after Sputnik and the Gaither Committee report, and three weeks before his stroke, Ike wrote a letter to his oldest brother Arthur. It was clear that the string of crises since his reelection was getting to him.

> This past year . . . seems to have been one of steadily mounting crises and pressures, culminating in the Little Rock situation at home and blows to our prestige by that and by the Russian scientific achievements in the past few weeks. When I wake up in the morning I sometimes wonder just what new problem can possibly be laid on my desk in the day to come; there always seems to be an even more complex one than I could have imagined.[64]

Sputnik had certainly taken a toll on Eisenhower, but by the spring of 1958 it seemed that he had weathered the worst of the storm. A public opinion survey conducted by Claude Robinson in the days following Sputnik and supplemented with additional data following the launch of the American satellite Explorer suggested that most Americans were not particularly concerned. Furthermore, most did not blame the president. Although 95 percent of Americans were aware of Sputnik, 40 percent had dismissed it without serious thought. After Sputnik, 80 percent thought the United States was "at least even" with the Soviet Union or would "catch up before long." As for the reasons the United States was behind in the development of missiles, 69 percent blamed science education, 67 percent believed the United States had become "complacent" about its national strength, 63 percent blamed interservice rivalries in the military, 61 percent believed that scientists did not get appropriate recognition, and 41 percent thought Congress (not Eisenhower) was too economy minded. Only 39 percent thought that Eisenhower had failed to provide the necessary leadership. Among those who did blame Eisenhower, political allegiance was a contributing factor—54 percent were Democrats and 33 percent were Republicans. Robinson concluded that Eisenhower's popularity, which had declined in the summer of 1957, had fallen no further as a result of Sputnik.[65]

In his response to Sputnik, Eisenhower attempted to find balance. He believed that the news media, scientific community, and Congress were overreacting, but he understood that staying the course would not be possible. His task was made more difficult by the Gaither Report and his unwillingness to divulge U-2 intelligence. Ultimately, he agreed to increase defense spending and expand the federal government's role in education, but in both cases, he had succeeded in scaling back the proposals of those who wished to do considerably more. Although he initially opposed the creation of a civilian space agency, he came to see the benefits of one and proposed NASA, which would prove its value in the decade to come.

Eisenhower's determination to prevent a dramatic increase in military spending in response to Sputnik is consistent with his desire to balance the needs of military security with those of economic prosperity. The Great Equation, as Eisenhower called it, is a topic that remains relevant in our time. There are many ways to compare military spending during the Eisenhower administration with our own. In 1960, Eisenhower's last full year in office, U.S. military spending was $47.35 billion. In 2020, it was $778.23 billion. After adjusting for inflation this is an increase of more than 80 percent. Well over half of that increase occurred during the ten-year period following September 11, 2001, during which the United States fought wars in Afghanistan and Iraq. Military spending as a percentage of GDP, however, has gone down. In 1960, U.S. military spending was 9 percent of GDP, while in 2020, it was 3.7 percent. This is not surprising since the GDP has gone up more than 500 percent since the Eisenhower administration.[66]

Perhaps a better way to determine whether the Great Equation is in balance is to ask the questions that Eisenhower would have asked. *Are we spending more than we have?* Based strictly on the budget deficit, yes. The 1960 budget, Eisenhower's last, was balanced. By contrast, in 2020 there was a budget deficit of $3.13 trillion.[67] *Are we spending more on defense than necessary?* If we compare the United States with other nations, it seems so. The United States spends more on defense than any other nation in the world—more than the next nine nations combined and nearly 40 percent of the world's total.[68] *Are we neglecting other necessary expenses?* The answer to this question is a subject of much debate. Because of the growth of mandatory spending, such as Social Security, Medicare, Medicaid, and interest on the federal debt, discretionary spending as a percentage of the federal budget is shrinking. In 2022, it was just over 30 percent. Defense spending accounted for almost half of that.[69] What remains is vigorously contested.

9

Eisenhower and the Farewell Address

On January 17, 1961, just three days before leaving office, President Eisenhower addressed the nation for the last time. Now a seventy-year-old man who had devoted his entire adult life to his country, few would have criticized him if he had simply said goodbye and wished the nation well. But those who tuned in to watch the televised speech heard far more than a sentimental leave-taking. Instead, Eisenhower's last presidential speech would be remembered primarily for its warning about what he called the military-industrial complex:

> This conjunction of an immense military establishment and a large arms industry is new in the American experience. The total influence—economic, political, even spiritual—is felt in every city, every statehouse, every office of the federal government. We recognize the imperative need for this development. Yet we must not fail to comprehend its grave implications. Our toil, resources and livelihood are all involved; so is the very structure of our society.
>
> In the councils of government, we must guard against the acquisition of unwarranted influence, whether sought or unsought, by the military-industrial complex. The potential for the disastrous rise of misplaced power exists and will persist.
>
> We must never let the weight of this combination endanger our liberties or democratic processes. We should take nothing for

granted. Only an alert and knowledgeable citizenry can compel the proper meshing of the huge industrial and military machinery of defense with our peaceful methods and goals, so that security and liberty may prosper together.[1]

Eisenhower's Farewell Address is the most enduring speech of his presidency, and historians have not tired of analyzing its content and debating the motives behind its warnings. As with other aspects of Eisenhower's presidency, critical early reviews of the speech gradually gave way to a more positive assessment. As time went by, historian Chester Pach wrote, "Eisenhower looked less like a befuddled or belated statesman and more like a prophet who foresaw vital and enduring issues of contemporary U.S. public policy."[2]

One of the most intriguing aspects of the speech is that on its surface, it seems to contradict his eight-year presidency. After all, Eisenhower presided over a peacetime military with a budget that was only slightly smaller than it had been when he took office during the Korean War, and a nuclear stockpile that was exponentially larger. This raises the question of when Eisenhower became concerned about it, and why he waited until his departure to draw attention to it. Historian James Ledbetter asked, "If the threat was as profound as he laid it out—'economic, political, even spiritual'—why did he wait until he was leaving office to warn the country?" Surveying the literature, he found a variety of answers. One argument is that Eisenhower was a hypocrite— one who publicly advocated views such as those in the Farewell Address to "placate particular audiences and manage the insecurity that arose from his administration's strategic reliance on nuclear weapons." An alternative is that Eisenhower was sincere: he genuinely held the views expressed in his farewell address, but over the years he had been "hemmed in" by advisers and members of Congress who did not share them, and by the Soviet Union, whose intransigence prevented him from acting on them. A third possibility is that Eisenhower's views changed over time. At the beginning of his administration, he accepted the New Look's reliance on nuclear deterrence, but he became increasingly uncomfortable with it as time went on. Finally, there are those who argue that Eisenhower was not opposed to the existence of a military-industrial complex as long as he—or someone equally capable of controlling it—was in command, but the inexperience of the incoming Kennedy administration caused him to issue the warning.[3] Eisenhower, according to this argument, was worried that Kennedy and Johnson, "trapped by their exaggerated claims about missile gaps," were likely to increase military spending to vindicate their past judgments.[4]

None of these arguments alone fully explains Eisenhower's Farewell Address. Eisenhower was sincere in his warning about the military-industrial complex—otherwise he could have left the White House without mentioning it at all—but, as we have seen, he was certainly not "hemmed in" by his advisers. It is also true that Eisenhower's views on maintaining a massive peacetime military had changed over the years. The change, however, was not a growing unease regarding U.S. reliance on nuclear weapons; he had always considered them a deterrent and repeatedly reminded the JCS that their purpose was to prevent war. What changed was his level of comfort regarding the cost of the U.S. arsenal. "During the years of my presidency, and especially the latter years," he wrote in *Waging Peace*, "I began to feel more and more uneasiness about the effect on the nation of tremendous peacetime military expenditures."[5] This was especially true after Sputnik when claims of a missile gap had forced Eisenhower to approve a defense budget that was larger than he believed was necessary. Eisenhower did fear that Kennedy was unprepared to resist the pressures of the military-industrial complex, but he had already felt those pressures himself to an uncomfortable degree.

Eisenhower's Farewell Address was not an attempt to deny responsibility for the birth of the military-industrial complex. Its creation was the unfortunate but predictable result of the conscious decision he had made to maintain a high, but sustainable, level of military spending due to the unprecedented demands of the Cold War. Nor was it a call for the military-industrial complex to be destroyed, although in later years some would choose to interpret it that way. Rather, it was a warning that future presidents and "an alert and knowledgeable citizenry" should "guard against the acquisition of unwarranted influence" by the military-industrial complex, lest it lead to "the disastrous rise of misplaced power." The key to understanding Eisenhower's Farewell Address, indeed the key to understanding his presidency, is balance. "Each proposal must be weighed in the light of a broader consideration: the need to maintain balance," he said in a mostly forgotten part of the speech. "Good judgment seeks balance and progress; lack of it eventually finds imbalance and frustration."

Eisenhower's Farewell Address was not particularly well received in 1961, but it is now considered the most important speech of his presidency. Its warning about the military-industrial complex was accepted as prophesy by those who opposed American involvement in the Vietnam War—a conflict Eisenhower had avoided—and remained popular with critics of military spending throughout the Cold War. More recently, references to the military-industrial complex surged as a result of the September 11, 2001, terrorist attacks and the subsequent wars in Afghanistan and Iraq.

The Idea for the Speech

Eisenhower was heavily involved in the writing of his speeches. At the end of his second term, his speech writers were Malcolm Moos and Ralph Williams. In a 1988 interview conducted by the Eisenhower Presidential Library, Williams provided insight into the process. Eisenhower liked to receive a full first draft of a speech before he began to think seriously about it. Once the first draft was complete, Williams said, the president would become "intensely involved." Before the speech was finished, an important speech would go through "ten to fifteen drafts"—each new draft beginning when the speech writers received Eisenhower's comments on the previous one. According to Williams, the president's comments were usually sent by messenger; it was unusual for Moos or himself to work directly with Eisenhower.[6] In his 1974 memoir, Milton Eisenhower explained the role that he played. "I nearly always rewrote the speech completely, giving it a normal progression in fact and thought and easily using the president's own phrases which were not different from my own." Only then, he said, did Eisenhower begin to mark it up. Milton believed that Moos was an "especially effective" speechwriter for his brother and that the help he gave on Moos's drafts was "fairly easy."[7] Williams explained that "draft by draft, it literally became his very own speech from the beginning to the end." Eisenhower "would edit—not only the textual and substantive material—but he would fiddle with words." By the time Eisenhower delivered the speech "it was, in every sense of the word, his speech." Eisenhower, he reiterated, "was not a man to let anybody put words in his mouth. If he said those words, he meant them."[8]

Records at his presidential library make clear that by May 1959, Eisenhower was considering the possibility of a farewell address.

At that time, he was thinking of giving the speech to a joint session of Congress. "There would be no profit in expressing, in such a setting, anything that was partisan in character," he wrote to Milton. "Rather I think the purpose would be to emphasize a few homely truths. . . . A collateral purpose would be, of course, merely to say an official 'goodbye.'"[9] Malcolm Moos recalled that about this same time, the president had said to him, "By the way, Malcolm, I want to have something to say when I leave here, and I want you to be thinking about it. . . . I'm not interested in capturing headlines, but I want to have a message and I want you to be thinking about it well in advance."[10] What, exactly, that message would be clearly had not been decided, but with his brother Milton and Moos involved it was unlikely to consist of "a few homely truths," and he must have known he would make headlines no matter what he said.

An inspiration for Eisenhower's Farewell Address was the one given by George Washington as his presidency was nearing an end. Eisenhower would never have presumed to compare himself to Washington, one of his boyhood heroes, but the similarities are unmistakable. Both men had spent most of their adult lives in the military, had become irrevocably associated with victory in a transformative war, had grudgingly agreed to enter politics, and served two terms as president. Now, like Washington, Eisenhower hoped to give the next generation of leaders the benefit of his experience. Washington's Farewell Address was certainly on the minds of Moos and Williams as they worked on Eisenhower's speech.[11] One line in particular stands out. Washington urged Americans to "avoid the necessity of those overgrown military establishments, which under any form of government are inauspicious to liberty, and which are to be regarded as particularly hostile to republican liberty."[12]

On October 31, 1960, Williams wrote to Moos with some ideas for the 1961 State of the Union address. One of those ideas was "the problem of militarism." Elaborating, Williams wrote that "for the first time in its history, the United States has a permanent war-based industry. . . . General officers retiring at an early age take positions in [a] war-based industrial complex shaping its decisions and guiding the direction of its tremendous thrust. . . . We must be very careful to ensure that the 'merchants of death' do not come to dictate national policy."[13] Moos was immediately taken by Williams's suggestion and asked him to develop the idea further. In an interview given to the Columbia Oral History Project in 1972, Moos noted three influences that made him particularly interested in the "war-based industrial complex" Williams had described. First, Eisenhower's naval attaché Pete Aurand often left copies of his aerospace journals in Moos's office, and Moos was "astounded" at the number of advertisements placed by companies in defense-related industries. Second, Moos, who had been on the faculty of Johns Hopkins University, had a former graduate student who was studying the growing number of retired military officers who were taking executive positions in the defense industry. And third, as a former academic, Moos was aware of the role that defense dollars played in scientific research undertaken by universities.[14] Eventually, Williams changed "war-based" to "military," believing that "military-industrial complex" more accurately described the situation.[15] In November, Moos gave Eisenhower a draft of the speech that included Williams's idea. The president responded enthusiastically: "I think you've got something here."[16]

Milton Eisenhower became heavily involved in December. After discussing the speech with his brother throughout the month, on December 30 Milton dictated a new opening to Ann Whitman, the president's secretary. He then added extensive handwritten comments to her typed draft. This document represents a major turning point in the speech's evolution. The new opening indicated that Eisenhower's farewell would not be a speech to Congress but a televised address directly to the American people. According to historian Delores Janiewski, Milton's "proximity to the president during this crucial phase in late December indicates that he actively participated in the decision."[17] Delivering his Farewell Address from the Oval Office not only changed the speech's audience, it also freed it from the formal expectations of the constitutionally mandated State of the Union. Eisenhower transmitted his State of the Union address, a summary of his administration's accomplishments, to Congress in writing on January 12.[18]

There are only seven drafts of the Farewell Address in the collection at the Eisenhower Presidential Library. Although other documents indicate that work started two months before, the earliest of these is dated January 6. According to Eisenhower's appointment schedule, he met with Milton and Moos together on that day. The president had two additional meetings with his brother on the sixth and then, on the seventh, Milton wrote extensive handwritten comments on the previous day's draft.[19] The president then met with Moos and Milton again on the tenth, and with his brother alone on the thirteenth. The final draft is dated January 16, the day before Eisenhower delivered it. These meetings suggest that the president and his brother were directly engaged in drafting the speech.[20] The seven drafts produced in this short span, however, show a nearly completed speech with only minor changes being made. According to Williams, it was very unusual that so few changes were made in the last seven drafts of such an important speech: "Apparently it was what he wanted to say because he made so few changes to it." Moos meeting directly with the president was also unusual, according to Williams.[21]

Crafting the Message

Although some critics considered Eisenhower's warnings about the growth of the military-industrial complex hypocritical, his concerns were not new. As army chief of staff, Eisenhower had fought the rapid demobilization of the U.S. military that took place following World War II. Believing that American weakness had encouraged communist aggression, Eisenhower refused to repeat that pattern after the end of the Korean War. The result was the largest peacetime military budget in American history. But the New Look was designed to provide sufficient security at a cost that was sustainable over the long term. Doing more, he believed, not only threatened the economic health of the country, it risked the very freedom the United States sought to defend. Soviet leaders wanted to "force upon America and the free world an unbearable security burden leading to an economic disaster," Eisenhower said in a May 1953 speech. "We live in an age of peril; we must think and plan and provide so as to live through this age in freedom— in ways that do not undermine our freedom even as we strive to defend it." Above all, the United States must not "imitate the methods of the dictator"; it must not devote itself to the "grim purposes of the garrison state."[22]

According to Harold Stassen, in December 1954, Eisenhower made his concerns about the growth of the defense industry and its close ties to the military a central point in a meeting with the secretary of defense and the JCS. At the time the army and navy chiefs were upset because their share of the defense budget had fallen due to the implementation of the New Look; but Eisenhower was determined not to give in to their demands for more. "Our national security will depend as much upon our economic strength as our military strength," Stassen later recalled the president saying, "and . . . our military establishment must take on some responsibility for our economic strength." This was "extremely important," Eisenhower said, shifting emphasis. "If the military and our industry leaders ever team up, they can dictate the whole country. And they will end up with too much power. And that will be bad. . . . There's a real danger of the military ganging up with powerful industrial leaders, and parceling out the contracts for weapons and research and all kinds of products and services. Bigness means lots of money to hand out—and that's dangerous, dangerous." He reemphasized these themes when he brought the meeting to a close. "I want you to know where I stand in my general philosophies of military doctrine, how closely it meshes with the economic policies of the country, and how we've got to keep the military and industry balanced and apart, so they don't team up for monopolies—and too much power."[23]

Despite the unprecedented size of the military budget, Eisenhower was under constant pressure to spend more. This was particularly true following Sputnik and the release of the Gaither Committee report. Ralph Williams recalled that during this period it was easy to see the military-industrial complex at work. Throughout his presidency, he said, Eisenhower had "suffered the slings and arrows of people who wanted more money for defense," but the post-Sputnik claims of a missile gap took the onslaught to a new level. The air force "had a tremendous network of help among the aerospace suppliers and the congressional people who benefitted— whose districts benefitted—from these [Defense] contracts." And because of Eisenhower's focus on the budget, "Democrats figured they had a live one: here was a miserly president pinching pennies at the expense of the nation's security." When it came time to suggest possibilities for the Farewell Address, the military-industrial complex "found a rather ready and willing receiver" in the president. Eisenhower's "sense of fair play had been outraged," and "he just wanted to set the record straight. . . . He could also envision the possibility of this thing getting out of control and inducing the government to do some very dumb and dangerous things at the behest of these people who had so much influence."[24]

James Killian, the president's science adviser, confirmed Eisenhower's concern during the post-Sputnik period over the influence of the defense industry. "Repeatedly, I saw Ike angered by the excesses, both in text and advertising, of the aerospace-electronics press, which advocated ever bigger and better weapons to meet an ever bigger and better Soviet threat they had conjured up," Killian wrote. He remembered the president saying, "We must avoid letting the munitions companies dictate the pattern of our organization."[25]

The military-industrial complex might have more accurately been termed the military-industrial-congressional complex since all three played an important role in the situation Eisenhower was describing. As Eisenhower explained in his memoir:

> The military services are rarely satisfied with the amounts allocated to them. . . . The makers of the expensive munitions of war, to be sure, like the profits they receive, and the greater the expenditures the more lucrative the profits. Under the spur of profit potential, powerful lobbies spring up to argue for even larger expenditures. And the web of special interest grows. Each community in which a manufacturing plant or a military installation is located profits from the money spent and the jobs created in the area. This fact, of course, constantly presses on the community's political representatives—congressmen, senators, and others—to maintain the facility at maximum strength. All of these forces . . . override the convictions of responsible officials.[26]

One can easily imagine the above paragraph in the Farewell Address itself, rather than in a presidential memoir published more than four years later. If Eisenhower or his speech writers did consider implicating Congress, or Democrats, in the growth of the military-industrial complex, there is no record of it in the existing drafts of the speech. However tempting it might have been to point fingers, doing so would have run counter to the tone that Eisenhower hoped to maintain with his speech. Communications scholar Charles Griffin has written that the president saw his farewell "as an opportunity to emulate the rhetorical precedent of his hero [George Washington] by striking back at his foes without compromising, indeed, while enhancing his stature as a man of principle."[27] Janiewski agrees; the speech did not use ideological labels, she said, because Eisenhower "chose to emphasize maturity and self-control as attributes of the statesman."[28]

There are other examples of a self-conscious attempt to soften the language of the speech in regard to the military-industrial complex. Milton Eisenhower's handwritten comments on December 30 added "an alert, knowledgeable, and dedicated citizenry" to the speech as a balance that could "compel the proper meshing of the huge machinery of our defenses with our peace-oriented economy so that liberty and security may both prosper." This insertion suggests that, although the military-industrial complex represented a threat, it was one that a healthy democracy could handle. In a later draft, Moos added the words "whether sought or unsought" following the warning to "guard against the acquisition of unwarranted influence" by the military-industrial complex. The change was made to avoid the suggestion that "they were deliberately trying to subvert our liberties."[29]

Early in the speech, Eisenhower said that the nation faced many threats, "new in kind or degree," but he would "mention two only." The first of these was the military-industrial complex. The second was a "revolution in the conduct of research." Because of the demands of the Cold War, "a steadily increasing share" of scientific research was being conducted "for, by, or at the direction of, the Federal government." Government needs and government grants, he feared, had become "a substitute for intellectual curiosity." The danger that the nation's scientists would be dominated by "federal employment, project allocations, and the power of money," he said, "was ever present." An "equal and opposite danger" was that public policy could become "the captive of a scientific-technological elite." It is easy to see that the advertisements in aerospace trade journals, mentioned by Moos and Killian, had an influence on this line of the speech. It was the task of the statesman, Eisenhower said, "to mold, to balance, and to integrate" these forces to fit the needs of a free society.

Forgotten Parts of the Speech

Eisenhower's warnings about the military-industrial complex and, to a lesser extent, the scientific-technological elite have been the exclusive focus of scholars who have studied the Farewell Address. They are also the parts of the speech that have remained in our national consciousness. But other aspects of the speech are no less relevant to our times. Some of them were likely overlooked because they seemed so commonplace at the time. Less than a minute into the speech, Eisenhower said: "Like every other citizen, I wish the new president, and all who will labor with him, Godspeed. I pray that the coming years will be blessed with peace and prosperity for all." Despite the fact that John Kennedy, a Democrat, had beaten Richard Nixon, Eisenhower's vice president, in a very close election, this line was likely written without a moment's thought or hesitation, and listeners surely forgot it just as quickly. The turmoil following the 2020 presidential election, however, reminds us that the peaceful transfer of power should not be taken for granted.

In the next sentence Eisenhower went on to say, "Our people expect their president and the Congress to find essential agreement on questions of great moment, the wise resolution of which will better shape the future of the nation." His administration and Congress, he said, had "cooperated well," avoided partisanship, and accomplished a great deal, and for this he offered his gratitude. The origin of these lines goes back to the early planning stages for the Farewell Address. In a May 1959 letter to his brother Milton, Eisenhower said that he was undecided about whether he should give "a so-called 'farewell' talk." The reason he had "been toying with the idea," he said, was because of his experience "working with a Congress controlled by the opposite political party." This experience made him eager to share his thoughts about the "responsibilities and duties of a government that must be responsive to the will of majorities, even when the decisions of those majorities create apparent paradoxes."[30] Divided government, which Eisenhower had to contend with for six years, has become more common in the years since his presidency. The extreme partisanship that now accompanies it has made many Americans less hopeful, and some Americans less desirous, that their president and Congress will find "essential agreement" whether or not the questions are of "great moment."

As a guide to understanding Eisenhower's presidency, one forgotten aspect of his Farewell Address stands out—his admonition to seek balance. The Sputnik crisis was likely the short-term inspiration for his comments on balance: "Crises there will continue to be," he said. "In meeting them, whether foreign or domestic, great or small, there is a recurring temptation to feel that some spectacular and costly action could become the miraculous solution to all current difficulties." Eisenhower mentioned two of the "miraculous" solutions he had fought off in the months following

Sputnik—"a huge increase in newer elements of our defense," and "a dramatic expansion in basic and applied research"—but he was using the line to set up a bigger point.

> Each proposal must be weighed in the light of a broader con-sideration: the need to maintain balance in and among national programs—balance between the private and the public economy, balance between cost and hoped for advantage—balance between the clearly necessary and the comfortably desirable; balance between our essential requirements as a nation and the duties imposed by the nation upon the individual; balance between action of the moment and the national welfare of the future. Good judgment seeks balance and progress; lack of it eventually finds imbalance and frustration.

Eisenhower later integrated the management of the military-industrial complex into his theme of balance. "It is the task of states-manship," he said, "to mold, to balance, and to integrate" the forces of the military-industrial complex "within the principles of our democratic system." But this section has wider applicability. Mov-ing on, he incorporated the most fundamental of his beliefs, fiscal responsibility, into his theme by admonishing his listeners to bal-ance their desires for today with their hopes for tomorrow: "We . . . must avoid the impulse to live for today only, plundering for our own ease and convenience, the precious resources of tomorrow. We cannot mortgage the material assets of our grandchildren without risking the loss also of their political and spiritual heri-tage. We want democracy to survive for all generations to come."

Reaction to the Speech

Given the fact that the Farewell Address is now remembered as the most important speech of Eisenhower's presidency, it may be surprising that immediate reaction to it was not generally positive.

The *Washington Post* reported the speech contained "little that was new." *Le Monde* (France) concurred, saying that it was "without originality." Some who praised the content of the speech did so in a backhanded way. *The Nation*, a progressive weekly, wrote that "nothing became Mr. Eisenhower's career in office like the leaving of it. . . . For eight years, Mr. Eisenhower has depressed his fellow Americans by a seeming inability to grasp the major problems of his era; but now in the closing days of his administration he spoke like the statesman and democratic leader we had so hungered for him to become."[31]

The next day, at his final press conference, Eisenhower was asked only one question specifically about his Farewell Address—it concerned the scientific-technological elite. In his response, Eisenhower elaborated on the danger of public policy becoming captive to a scientific-technological elite. "When you see almost every one of your magazines, no matter what they are advertising, has a picture of the Titan missile or the Atlas," he said, it causes "an insidious penetration of our own minds that the only thing this country is engaged in is in weaponry and missiles. . . . We just can't afford to do that. The reason we have them is to protect the great values in which we believe." It is interesting that Eisenhower chose to elaborate extemporaneously on an aspect of the problem that had not made it into his speech. His comments, while critical of the defense industry, also suggest that its existence was necessary.[32] As with military spending, balance was the key.

Two days after Eisenhower left office, Jack Raymond of the *New York Times* published an analysis of the military-industrial complex. In it he detailed an aspect of the problem that Eisenhower had not specifically mentioned in his speech, but that Williams had included in his first partial draft. After World War II, military men, Eisenhower himself being the best example, had taken positions of leadership in government, universities, and industry. Since then, he said, there had developed a "cross-fertilization of men and ideas" among these institutions. Currently, he said, there were 726 former high-ranking military officers employed by the country's 100 leading defense contractors. Raymond did not name names, but one example was Admiral Arthur Radford, former chairman of the JCS, who was at this time director of the Philco Corporation. "The basic characteristic of military-industrial relations," Raymond said, "is their . . . mutual interest in seeking a large defense establishment, bigger and better weapons and greater national devotion to problems of security." Referring to the comments Eisenhower had made about aerospace advertising at his press conference the day after his speech, Raymond pointed out that earlier in the month, in the same issue of the *Times* that had reported on the president's budget message, there had been "a full-page advertisement of the merits of an airplane for which no new appropriations were being sought."

Raymond confirmed and elaborated on some of the figures that Eisenhower used in his speech. It was true that the government spent 59 percent of its $80.9 billion budget on national security, he said, adding that the Defense Department controlled $32 billion worth of real estate, affecting local economies throughout the country. The majority of defense contracts were held by only a "handful" of large companies, and the federal government supported more than 60 percent of the nation's scientific research. Raymond also defended Eisenhower from critics who claimed his warnings were hypocritical. He reminded readers that two years earlier when Eisenhower had been asked if he would spend more on defense if the nation could afford it, the president had answered flatly "I would not," adding that anyone "with any sense could see that if military spending were not restricted the United States would become a 'garrison state.'"[33]

Raymond's analysis of the military-industrial complex was printed on page four of section two of the *New York Times*. By the time it appeared, the *Times* had largely forgotten Eisenhower's Farewell Address, having turned its attention to John Kennedy whose inaugural address with its lofty exhortation to "ask not what your country can do for you" had captured the nation's imagination. In the years that followed, however, with the country mired in a war in Vietnam—a war that Eisenhower had avoided—the Farewell Address began a new life. It also took on a new meaning. As Ralph Williams—who coined the term "military-industrial complex"—put it, the "subtleties of the original concept . . . became distorted beyond recognition."[34] When antiwar critics used the term, as they often did, they did so as if its meaning was synonymous with the "permanent war economy," a far more radical thesis proposed by Columbia sociologist C. Wright Mills in his book *The Power Elite*, published in 1956.[35] Mills argued that political, military, and economic elites, each acting in their own self-interest, worked together to perpetuate war. As we have seen, the words "whether sought or unsought" were inserted into the Farewell Address to avoid any such suggestion. Furthermore, the speech states that "an alert and knowledgeable citizenry can compel" the proper balance between the military and industry "so that security and liberty may prosper together."

Although Eisenhower's Farewell Address was not particularly well received in 1961, it is well regarded today, particularly his admonition about the military-industrial complex. References to the military-industrial complex surged in the early twenty-first century due to the increase in defense spending triggered by the

September 11, 2001, terrorist attacks and the subsequent wars in Afghanistan and Iraq. More than half of the increase in military spending since Eisenhower left office occurred during the first decade of the twenty-first century. Many of the factors that have contributed to the perpetuation of the military-industrial complex are the same as those that Eisenhower warned us about, but some new factors have contributed as well.

Eisenhower did not blame Congress for the creation of the military-industrial complex, but as he explained in his memoir, it played an important role. Congress continues to perpetuate our unsustainable level of defense spending. For members of Congress, defense spending is about jobs. Forty-three of the world's one hundred largest arms manufacturers are headquartered in the United States. With a combined value of $246 billion, they employ millions of Americans, impacting the economy of every state. Interest in their continued success among members of Congress is, therefore, nationwide and bipartisan.[36]

The "revolving door" between government, the military, and the defense industry, included in an early draft of the farewell address and mentioned in the *New York Times* analysis of the speech, also remains a problem. According to one report, in 2016, the top twenty U.S. defense contractors hired 645 "former senior government officials, military officers, members of congress, and senior legislative staff as lobbyists, board members, or senior executives."[37] The access that these individuals have to current government officials makes them valuable assets to companies seeking government contracts.

Eisenhower believed that an "alert and knowledgeable citizenry" could lessen the negative effects of the military-industrial complex, but the consolidation of American media and its connections to the defense industry and government has made that prospect more difficult. There are currently five conglomerates that control 90 percent of U.S. media. As journalist Helen Johnson has pointed out, these conglomerates are intimately connected to the top defense contractors through interrelated directorships. The resulting "military-industrial-*media* complex," she argues, does not make us more alert and knowledgeable. Instead, it influences our perceptions of war in a positive way.[38] Embedded journalism, the military oversight of journalists in combat zones that became standard practice during the Iraq War, also has a positive influence on our perception of armed conflict. Finally, corporate media has its own revolving door. Those who shape our opinions of a war are often former military officers or former members of the presidential administration that initiated the conflict.

Eisenhower's concerns about the development of a scientific-technological elite have also been substantiated. Federal expenditures on the research and development conducted at colleges and universities has increased from about $4 billion in 1960 (after adjusting to 2020 dollars) to more than $46 billion in 2020.[39] Research universities that rely on federal funding for their graduate programs in science and technology hire faculty whose research is best suited to compete for this funding, validating Eisenhower's fear that federal grants would become a substitute for intellectual curiosity. Eisenhower was also concerned that public policy would become captive to a scientific-technological elite. This perception played into many people's distrust of government health directives during the COVID-19 pandemic.

Eisenhower's Farewell Address, like that of his predecessor George Washington, has become part of our national consciousness. It is unfortunate that in both cases we remember their admonitions primarily because of our failure to heed them.

Conclusion

WHY EISENHOWER STILL MATTERS

On Eisenhower's last full day in office the *New York Times* published an evaluation of his presidency by Washington bureau chief James Reston. His appraisal serves as a time capsule of views commonly held by Eisenhower's critics at the beginning of the 1960s. Recognizing that more perspective was necessary for an objective evaluation, Reston stated his hope that "in a generation or so, the historians may be able to agree on his place in history." Consensus is rare, but after several generations there are some aspects of Eisenhower's presidency that historians largely agree on. Some of Reston's conclusions have stood the test of time and are now shared by most historians, while others have been largely refuted.

Reston's appraisal focused primarily on foreign affairs and national security. Although he gave Eisenhower credit for avoiding war, his praise was lukewarm at best: "The Eisenhower administration has come to a close with a series of truces in Korea, Indochina, the Taiwan Strait and Berlin. Nothing has been settled but nothing vital to the free world has been lost." Given the potential each of these Cold War hot spots had for triggering a wider war, historians generally give Eisenhower higher marks for having avoided one. During the Vietnam War, Eisenhower's decision to put prohibitive conditions on U.S. intervention there seemed prophetic. Reston was correct, however, when he said that Eisenhower "would have liked to secure the peace he did so much to win as a soldier."

On the subject of character, Reston said that Eisenhower had "upheld the dignity and honor of his office." He was also "orderly, patient, conciliatory and a thoughtful team player—all admirable traits of character." These traits, Reston said, were not enough for "his critics [who] saw him not merely as an attractive human being with decent instincts and sound objectives, but as a leader of the free world who was confronted by a unique and cunning challenge which he underestimated from the beginning." The president, Reston elaborated, had been "preoccupied" with other things. His focus was not on "the new situation in post-Stalin Russia." Instead, it was on "Republican objectives" such as "reducing the budget, cutting the nation's commitments overseas, increasing the deterrent of atomic weapons, wiping out inflation, and reducing the authority of the central government."

Reston was furthest from the mark when he criticized Eisenhower's leadership. He said that the president relied on his cabinet and staff to make decisions, making them himself "only when his subordinates could not agree." This view, as we have seen, was widely held at the time but has now been rejected by historians. Overall, Reston concluded, Eisenhower "presided over an era of prosperity and good feeling within the nation," and had "avoided war and depression," an "important if limited objective."[1]

The following day, almost lost among coverage of Kennedy's inauguration, the *New York Times* editorial board weighed in with its own, much shorter, appraisal of the Eisenhower years. Like Reston, they gave Eisenhower high marks for character. He had conducted his office with "dignity," displayed "equanimity" in the face of repeated crises, accepted criticism with "graciousness and good humor," and shown great "personal courage" facing serious illness. In part because of these traits, they said, Eisenhower "will retire from office with the respect and good will of his countrymen." As with Reston, however, they used complements of Eisenhower's character as openings for criticism: "As we look back upon the record of these eight years, however, we cannot fail to note that the convictions he brought with him into office, though each was excellent in its own place, were nevertheless to prove to be the chief elements of weakness in the record of his administration." Among these were his deference to the separation of powers, which made him reluctant to "exert the executive pressure" necessary to win passage of legislation; his dependence on the chain of command, which led him to place important decisions "in the hands of subordinate officials"; and his preference for conciliation, which led him to seek consensus rather than impose a decision on the minority. "The net reliance upon such convictions," they concluded, "has been in some important instances an absence of strong and consistently positive leadership."[2]

The argument that Eisenhower's convictions were both his greatest strength and his greatest weakness is an interesting one that is not without merit. Eisenhower did indeed have a high regard for the constitutionally mandated separation of powers. This conviction, although it may have inhibited him from exerting executive pressure in support of his administration's legislative agenda, was far less relevant to whether it eventually passed than the lack of support often shown for it by his own party, as we saw in chapter 3. Eisenhower's military background had instilled in him a commitment to the chain of command. This commitment can be seen in the organization of the White House, particularly the NSC. As we have seen, however, the chain of command was designed to provide Eisenhower with the best possible information for decision-making, not to relieve him from the responsibility of making decisions. Eisenhower's preference for conciliation is the most interesting of the three "convictions" criticized by the *Times*. On the surface conciliation is a virtue, but being overly conciliatory is, perhaps, at the root of two of Eisenhower's most controversial decisions—his reluctance to publicly criticize Joseph McCarthy, and his reluctance to publicly support *Brown v. Board*.

Those who describe themselves as moderates are often portrayed as unwilling to take a stand or lacking in political sophistication. This was not the case with Eisenhower. His attempts to find balance were part of a carefully considered philosophy, one that he applied consistently throughout his political career. "The middle of the road is derided" by the right and the left, Eisenhower said in a speech to the American Bar Association, long before he seriously considered running for president. "They deliberately misrepresent the central position as a neutral, wishy-washy one. Yet here is the truly creative area in which we may obtain agreement for constructive social action compatible with basic American principles and with the just aspirations of every sincere American. It is the area in which is rooted the hopes and allegiance of the vast majority of our people."[3] In a letter to his friend Bradford Chynoweth during the first term of his presidency, Eisenhower defended his policies as "a practical working basis between extremists." He added, "anything that affects or is proposed for masses of humans is wrong if the position it seeks is at either end of possible argument."[4] Finally, in 1961, in his last speech as president, Eisenhower counseled the American people that when meeting future crises, "whether foreign or domestic, great or small," they should weigh each proposal "in the light of a broader consideration: the need to maintain balance in and among national programs. . . . Good judgment seeks balance and progress; lack of it eventually finds imbalance and frustration."[5] As we have seen, these words were not mere political rhetoric; Eisenhower applied them consistently as president.

In this book, I have argued that the "need to maintain balance" defines the Eisenhower presidency. In his decision to run for president, he sought balance between his personal aversion to politics and his sense of duty to his country. In his social welfare proposals, he sought a Middle Way between conservatives who wanted to reduce federal responsibility and liberals who wanted to increase it. In his creation of the New Look, he sought to provide the nation with the maximum security possible without implementing economic controls that would threaten individual liberty. In his decision not to intervene in the French-Indochina War, he sought a course between the "unattainable" goal of an independent, noncommunist Southeast Asia and the "unacceptable" alternative of communist control. Eisenhower never considered supporting Joseph McCarthy, but he was eventually forced to take a position between ignoring the senator—which he preferred—and publicly condemning him. Eisenhower's preference was to leave public-school desegregation to the states, but when Arkansas governor Orval Faubus violated federal court orders, he was forced to intervene—although he did so without publicly stating his support for *Brown v. Board*. In his response to the Soviet Union's launch of Sputnik, Eisenhower was faced with a practical application of the Great Equation, which sought balance between military security and economic prosperity. Although he believed that the military budget was more than sufficient to provide for the nation's defense, he agreed to increase it, but not to the level proposed by those who claimed the existence of a "missile gap."

While writing the final chapter of this book I was teaching a course called "Eisenhower and the 1950s." During that course I presented each of the eight topics covered in this book to my class of thirteen upper-level history majors. The students seemed particularly interested in figuring out which political party Eisenhower would be in if he were alive today. Some students argued that, given his adherence to the Middle Way, he would be unlikely to win a primary in the current Republican Party. Others conceded this point but were equally adamant that he would not be comfortable with the spending proposals of the current Democratic Party. After briefly indulging their determination to decide whether Eisenhower would be a liberal Republican or a conservative Democrat, I attempted to direct them toward a more productive discussion of what their interest in this topic says about our current political polarization. The fact that most of us only hear about Susan Collins (R-ME) or Joe Manchin (D-WV) when one of them threatens to spoil the aspirations of their own party strongly suggests we have lost sight of the balance that Eisenhower sought in his own presidency. So does the fact that Eisenhower, currently sixth in the most respected ranking of U.S. presidents, would be unlikely to win an election as a member of either political party today.[6]

Eisenhower's centrism is very appealing to many. So are his sense of duty, honor, and integrity—apparent in the topics covered in this book. Duty, honor, and integrity are words rarely used by academic historians, given the difficulty of using them objectively. The fact that so many of our elected officials fall short of our expectations for good character suggests that we should use them more often. This is not to say that Eisenhower is above criticism. As historian Richard Damms has pointed out, accepting that Eisenhower was "intelligent, articulate, and fully in command of his own administration's major domestic and foreign policies" is not to say that one approves of "the wisdom of his policy choices, the effectiveness of his decision-making, and the long-term legacies of his actions."[7] The same is true regarding his character. To say that he was a person of good character is not to say that he would conform to our current views on, for example, race and gender.

Americans are living in a time of extreme partisanship. Democrats and Republicans in Congress are farther apart today than at any time in the past fifty years. Both parties have moved away from the ideological center, leaving only a small number of moderates in Congress who are amenable to bipartisan negotiations.[8] Recent polls, however, show that 37 percent of Americans identify themselves as political moderates, and half believe that it is important for their political leaders to compromise.[9] These Americans are frustrated by the increasing ideological inflexibility of the two major parties, both of which prioritize the views of their more partisan members. The inability or unwillingness of Republicans and Democrats to find common ground often means that victories for one side come only at the expense of the other. What is best for the country is too often lost. In his Farewell Address, Eisenhower asserted that "good judgement seeks balance." This is the most valuable lesson his presidency left for our time.

A Note on Online Sources

Endnote references to documents at the Eisenhower Presidential Library that include an NAID are available online. All endnote references to *Foreign Relations of the United States*, the *New York Times*, *The Papers of Dwight David Eisenhower*, and *Public Papers of the Presidents* refer to the online versions of those sources. Page numbers are those used in the print publication. Links to the websites are listed below. These links, and all of those referenced in the endnotes, were checked on August 1, 2022.

Dwight D. Eisenhower Presidential Library
https://www.eisenhowerlibrary.gov/research/online-documents

Foreign Relations of the United States
https://history.state.gov/historicaldocuments/eisenhower

New York Times
https://timesmachine.nytimes.com
https://www.nytimes.com

The Papers of Dwight David Eisenhower
https://eisenhower.press.jhu.edu

Public Papers of the Presidents, Dwight D. Eisenhower
https://babel.hathitrust.org/cgi/mb?a=listis;c=1429005971

Abbreviations Used in the Notes

ACW	Ann Cook Whitman
COHP	Columbia Oral History Project
DDE	Dwight David Eisenhower
DDEL	Dwight David Eisenhower Presidential Library
FRUS	*Foreign Relations of the United States*
NAR	Nelson Aldrich Rockefeller
NYT	*The New York Times*
OH	Oral History
PACGO	President's Advisory Committee on Government Organization
PDDE	*Papers of Dwight David Eisenhower*
PPP	*Public Papers of the Presidents of the United States*
PSI	Permanent Subcommittee on Investigations
RAC	Rockefeller Archive Center
RG	Record Group

Notes

Introduction. Good Judgment Seeks Balance

1. "Farewell Radio and Television Address to the American People, January 17, 1961," in *PPP, 1960–1961*, 1035–40.

2. George Santayana, *The Life of Reason*, vol. 1, *Reason in Common Sense* (New York: Charles Scribner's Sons, 1905), 284.

3. Arthur Schlesinger Sr., "Our Presidents: A Rating by 75 Historians," *NYT*, July 29, 1962.

4. Siena College Research Institute, "Siena's 6th Presidential Expert Poll 1982–2018," February 13, 2019, https://scri.siena.edu/2019/02/13/sienas-6th-presidential-expert-poll-1982-2018/.

5. For a prominent example, see Marquis Childs, *Eisenhower: Captive Hero. A Critical Study of the General and the President* (New York: Harcourt Brace, 1958).

6. Fred Greenstein, *The Hidden-Hand Presidency: Eisenhower as Leader* (New York: Basic Books, 1982).

7. Among the most important is Stephen Ambrose, *Eisenhower*, vol. 2, *The President, 1952–1969* (New York: Simon and Schuster, 1984).

8. Chester J. Pach and Elmo Richardson, *The Presidency of Dwight D. Eisenhower* (Lawrence: University Press of Kansas, 1991), xiii.

9. Richard Damms, "Leadership and Decision-Making," in *A Companion to Dwight D. Eisenhower*, ed. Chester Pach (Malden, MA: John Wiley and Sons, 2017), 181.

10. Peter Lyon, *Eisenhower: Portrait of the Hero* (Boston: Little, Brown and Co., 1974), 851.

1. Brief Biography

1. Stephen Ambrose, *Eisenhower*, vol. 1, *Soldier, General of the Army, President-Elect, 1890–1952* (New York: Simon and Schuster, 1983), 73.

2. Ambrose, *Eisenhower*, 1:273.

3. "Eisenhower's Letter Stating He Would Not Run," *NYT*, January 24, 1948.

4. Secretary of Agriculture Ezra Taft Benson and Postmaster General Arthur Summerfield both served eight years, as did press secretary James Hagerty. Secretary of defense and secretary of health, education, and welfare were the only cabinet positions to have more than two occupants during Eisenhower's tenure as president.

5. DDE, "Radio and Television Address to the American People on the Achievements of the 83d Congress, August 23, 1954," in *PPP, 1954*, 746–56.

6. "Text of Eisenhower Talk in Salt Lake City," *NYT*, October 11, 1952.

7. DDE, *The White House Years: Waging Peace, 1956–1961* (New York: Doubleday, 1965), 652.

2. A Transcending Duty

1. DDE to James Duff, October 14, 1951, published in its entirety in William Bragg Ewald Jr., "Ike's First Move," *New York Times Magazine*, November 14, 1993.

2. Stephen Ambrose, *Eisenhower*, vol. 1, *Soldier, General of the Army, President-Elect, 1890–1952* (New York: Simon and Schuster, 1983), 489–90.

3. William B. Pickett, *Eisenhower Decides to Run: Presidential Politics and Cold War Strategy* (Chicago: Ivan R. Dee, 2000), xiv–xvi.

4. DDE, *Crusade in Europe* (New York: Doubleday, 1948), 444.

5. *Ike's Letters to a Friend, 1941–1958*, ed. Robert W. Griffith (Lawrence: University Press of Kansas, 1984), 33–34.

6. The volume of Truman's diary that includes this entry was not discovered at the Truman Presidential Library until 2003. National Archives, "Truman Library Discovers 1947 Truman Diary," press release, July 10, 2003, https://www.archives.gov/press/press-releases/2003/nr03-54.html.

7. *The Eisenhower Diaries*, ed. Robert H. Ferrell (New York: W. W. Norton, 1981), 139.

8. "Eisenhower's Letter Stating He Would Not Run," *NYT*, January 24, 1948.

9. "Eisenhower's Letter Stating He Would Not Run."

10. Pickett, *Eisenhower Decides to Run*, 79–80.

11. "Text of Eisenhower's Speech Pledging His Regime's Support to Keep Our Basic Freedom," *NYT*, October 13, 1948.

12. William I. Hitchcock, *The Age of Eisenhower: America and the World in the 1950s* (New York: Simon and Schuster, 2018), 38–39.

13. Hitchcock, *The Age of Eisenhower*, 42.

14. *Eisenhower Diaries*, 153.

15. *Eisenhower Diaries*, 168–69.

16. Hitchcock, *The Age of Eisenhower*, 37.

17. DDE diary entry, December 13, 1948, in *PDDE*, 10:365–67.

18. *Eisenhower Diaries*, 178.

19. *Ike's Letters to a Friend*, 82.

20. DDE, *At Ease: Stories I Tell to Friends* (New York: Doubleday, 1967), 370–71.

21. DDE, *At Ease*, 371.

22. DDE, *At Ease*, 371–72.

23. Pickett, *Eisenhower Decides to Run*, 89–91.

24. Pickett, *Eisenhower Decides to Run*, 91.

25. In a footnote to DDE to Lucius Clay, May 30, 1951, in *PDDE*, 12:308.

26. DDE to Clay, May 30, 1951, in *PDDE*, 12:307.

27. DDE to Monroe Mark Sweetland, September 5, 1951, in *PDDE*, 12:522.

28. DDE, *The White House Years: Mandate for Change, 1953–1956* (New York: Doubleday, 1963), 16–17.

29. DDE, *Mandate for Change*, 17.

30. DDE, *Mandate for Change*, 18.

31. Pickett, *Eisenhower Decides to Run*, 127.

32. Pickett, *Eisenhower Decides to Run*, 128.

33. Ewald, "Ike's First Move."

34. Ewald, "Ike's First Move."

35. *Eisenhower Diaries*, 203.

36. DDE to Edward Robinson, October 31, 1951, in *PDDE*, 12:672.

37. DDE to Milton Stover Eisenhower, October 31, 1951, in *PDDE*, 12:674.

38. DDE to Arthur Hays Sulzberger, November 10, 1951, in *PDDE*, 12:701.

39. DDE to Clifford Roberts, November 8, 1951, in *PDDE*, 12:691.

40. DDE to Clifford Roberts, December 8, 1951, in *PDDE*, 12:763–64.

41. In footnote to DDE to Henry Cabot Lodge, December 12, 1951, in *PDDE*, 12:779.

42. *Eisenhower Diaries*, 206.

43. DDE to Lodge, December 12, 1951, in *PDDE*, 12:777.

44. In footnote to DDE to Lodge, December 29, 1951, in *PDDE*, 12:829.

45. DDE to Lodge, December 29, 1951, in *PDDE*, 12:829.

46. In footnote to DDE to Harry Truman, January 1, 1952, in *PDDE*, 12:830–31.

47. DDE to Truman, January 1, 1952, in *PDDE*, 12:830–31.

48. "Text of Lodge-Adams Letters, *NYT*, January 7, 1951.

49. Clayton Knowles, "Lodge to Enter Eisenhower in New Hampshire Primary; Sure General is Republican," *NYT*, January 7, 1952.

50. "Text of Eisenhower Statement," *NYT*, January 8, 1952.

51. DDE to Lucius Clay, January 8, 1952, in *PDDE*, 13:860–63.

52. *Eisenhower Diaries*, 209.

53. DDE to Edward Robinson, January 19, 1953, in *PDDE*, 12:890.

54. James Hagerty, "A 'Serenade to Ike' Is Theme at Rally of 15,000 in Garden," *NYT*, February 9, 1952.

55. DDE to Philip Young, February 11, 1952, in *PDDE*, 13:970.

56. *Eisenhower Diaries*, 214.

57. DDE to Lucius Clay, February 12, 1952, in *PDDE*, 13:974.

58. DDE to Philip Dunham Reed, February 12, 1952, in *PDDE*, 13:983.

59. DDE to Edward Robinson, February 12, 1952, in *PDDE*, 13:984–91.

60. DDE to Lucius Clay, February 20, 1952, in *PDDE*, 13:998.

61. DDE to Clay, February 20, 1952, in *PDDE*, 13:999; Eisenhower, *Mandate for Change*, 21.

62. Pickett, *Eisenhower Decides to Run*, 178.

63. C. L. Sulzberger, "The General May Act," *NYT*, March 21, 1952.

64. Herbert Brownell, *Advising Ike: The Memoirs of Attorney General Herbert Brownell* (Lawrence: University Press of Kansas, 1993), 99–100.

65. DDE to Clifford Roberts, March 19, 1952, in *PDDE*, 13:1091–92.

66. DDE to Lucius Clay, March 26, 1952, in *PDDE*, 13:1119–20.

67. DDE to Harry Truman, April 2, 1952, in *PDDE*, 13:1154–56.

68. "Text of Eisenhower's Speech at Abilene, Opening His Political Campaign," *NYT*, June 5, 1952.

69. "Eisenhower Outlines Campaign Issues," *NYT*, June 6, 1952.

70. John Robert Greene, *I Like Ike: The Presidential Election of 1952* (Lawrence: University Press of Kansas, 2017), 110.

3. Pursuing the Middle Way

1. DDE to Bradford G. Chynoweth, July 13, 1954, in *PDDE*, 15:1185–86.

2. Marquis Childs, *Eisenhower: Captive Hero. A Critical Study of the General and the President* (New York: Harcourt Brace, 1958), 228–29, 292.

3. Herbert Parmet, *Eisenhower and the American Crusades* (New York: Collier-Macmillan, 1972), 574.

4. Stephen Ambrose, *Eisenhower*, vol. 2, *The President, 1952–1969* (New York: Simon and Schuster, 1984).

5. Exceptions include presidential nominations and budget reconciliation measures that have been excluded from the filibuster.

6. Eisenhower's path to victory at the 1952 Republican National Convention was complicated; for a more complete explanation, see John Robert Greene, *I Like Ike: The Presidential Election of 1952* (Lawrence: University Press of Kansas, 2017), 92–103.

7. DDE, *The White House Years: Mandate for Change, 1953–1956* (New York: Doubleday, 1963), 44–45.

8. "Taft Gives Winner His Pledge of Aid," *NYT*, July 12, 1952.

9. DDE, "Radio and Television Address to the American People on the Achievements of the 83d Congress, August 23, 1954," in *PPP, 1954*, 746–56.

10. "Text of Eisenhower Talk in Salt Lake City," *NYT*, October 11, 1952.

11. For more on the Middle Way and its application in other areas of policy, see my book, *Eisenhower Republicanism: Pursuing the Middle Way* (DeKalb: Northern Illinois University Press, 2006). I would like to thank Northern Illinois University Press for permission to use edited excerpts from that book.

12. Campaign speech in Wheeling, West Virginia, September 24, 1952, Excerpts 1952 Campaign Speeches, Box 1, Chronological Campaign Subseries, Campaign Series, DDE Papers as President, 1953–61, DDEL.

13. "Text of Eisenhower's Speech on 'Middle Way,'" *NYT*, August 21, 1952.

14. "Summary of Policy Statements Made by General Eisenhower; As Excerpted from Major Speeches Carried by the *NYT* and Other Papers from June until November 4th [1952]," Volume 5, HEW, Washington, DC Files, RG 4, NAR Personal, RAC.

15. PACGO, Volume 67, Washington DC Files, RG 4, NAR Personal, RAC.

16. SCGO to DDE, March 5, 1953, Folder 439, Box 49, Reorganization Advisory Committee, Washington, DC Files, RG 4, NAR Personal, RAC.

17. "Special Message to the Congress Transmitting Reorganization Plan I of 1953 Creating the Department of HEW, March 12, 1953," in *PPP, 1953*, 94.

18. Cary Reich, *The Life of Nelson A. Rockefeller* (New York: Doubleday, 1996), 526.

19. "Texts of Addresses by Eisenhower at Bridgeport and Worcester," *NYT*, October 21, 1952.

20. Yonkers, New York, October 29, 1952, "Summary of Policy Statements Made by General Eisenhower," Volume 5, HEW, Washington, DC files, RG 4, NAR Personal, RAC; see also "Aims of the Eisenhower Administration, 1952," Volume 5, HEW, Washington, DC files, RG 4, NAR Personal, RAC.

21. "Annual Message to the Congress on the State of the Union, February 2, 1953," in *PPP, 1953*, 12–34.

22. Donald Bruce Johnson and Kirk H. Porter, eds., *National Party Platforms, 1840–1972* (Urbana: University of Illinois Press, 1975), 503.

23. Congressional Quarterly, *Congress and the Nation, 1945–1964: A Review of Government and Politics in the Postwar Years* (Washington DC: Congressional Quarterly Service, 1965), 1238, 1247.

24. Minutes of Cabinet meeting, November 20, 1953, *Minutes and Documents of the Cabinet Meetings of President Eisenhower (1953–1961)*, 10 reels (Washington, DC: University Publications of America, 1980), reel 1.

25. Congressional Quarterly, *Congress and the Nation*, 1246.

26. DDE to Edward Hutton, October 7, 1953, in *PDDE*, 14:562.

27. "Special Message to the Congress on Old Age and Survivors Insurance and on Federal Grants-in-Aid for Public Assistance Programs, January 14, 1954," in *PPP, 1954*, 62–68; "Annual Budget Message to the Congress, Fiscal Year 1955, January 21, 1954," in *PPP, 1954*, 79–192.

28. New York City Speech, February 2, 1954, Volume 2, HEW, Washington DC Files, RG 4, NAR Personal, RAC.

29. "General Summary of Provisions of Old-Age and Survivors Insurance Bill," Volume 39, HEW, Washington DC Files, RG 4, NAR Personal, RAC; Legislation, Box 25, Oveta Culp Hobby Papers, DDEL.

30. "President Signs Law Extending Social Security to 10,000,000," *NYT*, September 2, 1954.

31. "Aims of the Eisenhower Administration," 1952, Volume 5, HEW, Washington DC Files, RG 4, NAR Personal, RAC.

32. Johnson and Porter, *National Party Platforms*, 503–4.

33. Los Angeles campaign speech, October 10, 1952, "Aims of the Eisenhower Administration," Volume 5, HEW, Washington DC Files, RG 4, NAR Personal, RAC.

34. "Limited Federal Reinsurance Service: Fact Sheet Issued in Connection with Legislative Proposals of 1954," March 1954, Volume 59, HEW, Washington DC Files, RG 4, NAR Personal, RAC.

35. Press Conference, Secretary Hobby, March 11, 1954, March 1954, Volume 59, HEW, Washington DC Files, RG 4, NAR Personal, RAC.

36. Health, Box 7, Campaign Series, DDE Papers as President, DDEL.

37. "Principal Features of Proposed Legislation on Health Service Prepayment Plans," March 10, 1954, Volume 39, HEW, Washington DC Files, RG 4, NAR Personal, RAC.

38. Minutes of Cabinet meeting, December 10, 1954, *Minutes and Documents of the Cabinet Meetings*, reel 2.

39. "Special Message to the Congress on the Health Needs of the American People, January 18, 1954," in *PPP, 1954*, 69–77; and New York City Speech, February 2, 1954, Volume 2, HEW, Washington DC Files, RG 4, NAR Personal, RAC.

40. Minutes of Cabinet meetings, February 16 and 26, 1954, *Minutes and Documents of the Cabinet Meetings*, reel 2.

41. "Reinsurance Bill Fought by A.M.A.," *NYT*, April 6, 1954, 31.

42. Memorandum from Secretary Hobby to DDE, "Luncheon with Insurance Company Executives," May 14, 1954, Hobby (4), Box 19, Administration Series, DDE Papers as President, DDEL.

43. Transcript of television speech, Folder 493 (Health 54–55), Box 57, HEW, Washington DC Files, RG 4, NAR Personal, RAC; and Meeting with AMA officials regarding reinsurance bill, July 7, 1954, Reinsurance, Box 17, Oveta Culp Hobby Papers, DDEL.

44. Roswell B. Perkins to Secretary Hobby, "AMA Attacks on Reinsurance Bill," July 2, 1954, Reinsurance, Box 17, Oveta Culp Hobby Papers, DDEL.

45. Meeting with AMA officials regarding reinsurance bill, July 7, 1954, Reinsurance, Box 17, Oveta Culp Hobby Papers, DDEL.

46. Congressional Quarterly, *Congress and the Nation*, 1153.

47. *The Diary of James C. Hagerty: Eisenhower in Mid-Course, 1954–1955*, ed. Robert H. Ferrell (Bloomington: Indiana University Press, 1983), 89.

48. "President's News Conference, July 14, 1954," in *PPP, 1954*, 633.

49. *Diary of James C. Hagerty*, 94.

50. "President's News Conference, July 14, 1954," in *PPP, 1954*, 633; and "Special Message to the Congress Recommending a Health Program, January 31, 1955," in *PPP, 1955*, 216–23.

51. Minutes of Cabinet meeting, April 22, 1955, *Minutes and Documents of the Cabinet Meetings*, reel 3.

52. Robert Goldberg, *Goldwater* (New Haven: Yale University Press, 1995), 105.

53. Barry Goldwater, *With No Apologies* (New York: Berkley Books, 1979), 89.

54. Edgar Eisenhower to DDE, November 1, 1954, Edgar 1954 (2), Box 11, Name Series, DDE Papers as President, DDEL.

55. DDE to Edgar Eisenhower, November 8, 1954, in *PDDE*, 15:1386.

56. June 21, 1955, 1953 (1), Box 2, Legislative Meetings Series, DDE Papers as President, DDEL.

57. *Diary of James C. Hagerty*, 129.

58. *The Eisenhower Diaries*, ed. Robert H. Ferrell (New York: W. W. Norton, 1981), 288–89.

59. *Diary of James C. Hagerty*, 129.

60. DDE to Gabriel Hauge, September 30, 1954, in *PDDE*, 15:1322.

61. Sherman Adams, *Firsthand Report: The Story of the Eisenhower Administration* (New York: Harper, 1961), 28.

62. Ambrose, *Eisenhower*, 2:152.

63. *Eisenhower Diaries*, 289.

64. DDE to Edgar Eisenhower, May 2, 1956, in *PDDE*, 17:1322.

65. Paul Hoffman visit, June 1, 1955, June 1955 (6), Box 6, Ann Whitman Diary Series, DDE Papers as President, DDEL.

66. *Diary of James C. Hagerty*, 53, 106; see also Minutes of Cabinet meeting, December 15, 1953, *Minutes and Documents of the Cabinet Meetings*, reel 1.

67. DDE diary entry February 13, 1956, Ann Whitman Diary, February 1956, Box 8, Ann Whitman Diary Series, DDE Papers as President, DDEL. Henry Cabot Lodge encouraged these views; see Lodge to Eisenhower, October 15, 1953, Brownell, Herbert, Jr. 1952–54 (5), Box 8, Administration Series, DDE Papers as President, DDEL.

68. Drew DeSilver, "The Polarization in Today's Congress Has Roots that Go Back Decades," Pew Research Center, March 10, 2022, https://www.pewresearch.org/short-reads/2022/03/10/the-polarization-in-todays-congress-has-roots-that-go-back-decades/.

4. A New Look for National Security

1. "The President's News Conference of April 23, 1953," in *PPP, 1953*, 239–40.

2. Robert A. Divine, *Eisenhower and the Cold War* (New York: Oxford University Press, 1981), 153–55.

3. John Lewis Gaddis, *Strategies of Containment* (New York: Oxford University Press, 1982), 162. See also Saki Dockrill, *Eisenhower's New-Look National Security Policy, 1953–61* (New York: St. Martin's Press, 1996), 267–75.

4. Robert R. Bowie and Richard H. Immerman, *Waging Peace: How Eisenhower Shaped an Enduring Cold War Strategy* (New York: Oxford University Press, 1998), 1–5.

5. National Security Act, July 26, 1947, Public Law 80-253, National Archives Catalog, https://catalog.archives.gov/id/299856.

6. Bowie and Immerman, *Waging Peace*, 88.

7. "Memorandum for the President by the Special Assistant to the President for National Security Affairs (Cutler), 16 March 1953," in *FRUS, 1952–1954*, vol. 2, pt. 1: doc. 50.

8. Robert Cutler, *No Time for Rest* (Boston: Little, Brown and Co., 1966), 293–307, 310–13; Robert Cutler, "The Development of the National Security Council," *Foreign Affairs* 34, no. 3 (April 1956): 441–58.

9. "Memorandum of Discussion at the 168th Meeting of the NSC, Thursday, October 29, 1953," in *FRUS, 1952–1954*, vol. 2, pt. 1: doc. 100.

10. Cutler, *No Time for Rest*, 307–8.

11. Cutler, *No Time for Rest*, 308–9.

12. "Memorandum for the Record by Cutler, May 9, 1953," in *FRUS, 1952–1954*, vol. 2, pt. 1: doc. 63.

13. "Memorandum by the President to the Secretary of State, May 20, 1953," in *FRUS, 1952–1954*, vol. 2, pt. 1: doc. 67.

14. Telegram, George Kennan to James Byrnes, February 22, 1946, Ideological Foundations of the Cold War Collection, Harry Truman Administration File, Harry S. Truman Presidential Library, https://www.trumanlibrary.gov/node/312883; X [George Kennan], "The Sources of Soviet Conduct," *Foreign Affairs* 25, no. 4 (July 1947): 566–82.

15. William Pickett, ed., *George F. Kennan and the Origins of Eisenhower's New Look: An Oral History of Project Solarium* (Princeton, NJ: Princeton Institute for International and Regional Studies, 2004), 19.

16. "Report to the NSC by the Executive Secretary (Lay), June 10, 1953," in *FRUS, 1952–1954*, vol. 2, pt. 1: doc. 74.

17. "Memorandum of Discussion at the 136th Meeting of the NSC, March 11, 1953," in *FRUS, 1952–1954*, vol. 8: doc. 566. The Big Four were the Allies in World War II: the United States, USSR, France, and the United Kingdom.

18. Emmet John Hughes, *The Ordeal of Power: A Political Memoir of the Eisenhower Years* (New York: Atheneum, 1963), 103–4.

19. "Address 'The Chance for Peace' Delivered Before the American Society of Newspaper Editors, April 16, 1953," in *PPP, 1953*, 179–88.

20. "The Ambassador in the Soviet Union (Bohlen) to the Department of State, April 25, 1953," in *FRUS, 1952–1954*, vol. 8: doc. 587.

21. "Memorandum to the NSC by the Executive Secretary (Lay), July 22, 1953," in *FRUS, 1952–1954*, vol. 2, pt. 1: doc. 80.

22. Pickett, *Oral History of Project Solarium*, 20, 24.

23. "Memorandum by Cutler, July 16, 1953," in *FRUS, 1952–1954*, vol. 2, pt. 1: doc. 79.

24. Pickett, *Oral History of Project Solarium*, 20–24, 32.

25. "Memorandum by Cutler, July 16, 1953," in *FRUS, 1952–1954*, vol. 2, pt. 1: doc. 79.

26. Pickett, *Oral History of Project Solarium*, 24–25.

27. "Memorandum by Cutler, July 16, 1953," in *FRUS, 1952–1954*, vol. 2, pt. 1: doc. 79.

28. Pickett, *Oral History of Project Solarium*, 10–11.

29. Pickett, *Oral History of Project Solarium*, 29–30.

30. "Memorandum of Discussion at the 157th Meeting of the NSC, July 30, 1953," in *FRUS, 1952–1954*, vol. 2, pt. 1: doc. 81.

31. "Memorandum of Discussion at the 157th Meeting of the NSC, July 31, 1953," in *FRUS, 1952–1954*, vol. 2, pt. 1: doc. 82.

32. "Editorial Note," in *FRUS, 1952–1954*, vol. 2, pt. 1: doc. 78.

33. Bowie and Immerman, *Waging Peace*, 184–85.

34. "Memorandum of Discussion at the 160th Meeting of the NSC, August 27, 1953," in *FRUS, 1952–1954*, vol. 2, pt. 1: doc. 85.

35. "Memorandum by Cutler to the Secretary of State, September 3, 1953," in *FRUS, 1952–1954*, vol. 2, pt. 1: doc. 87.

36. "Memorandum of Discussion at the 165th Meeting of the NSC, October 7, 1953," in *FRUS, 1952–1954*, vol. 2, pt. 1: doc. 94.

37. "Report [NSC 162/2] to the NSC by Lay, October 30, 1953," in *FRUS, 1952–1954*, vol. 2, pt. 1: doc. 101.

38. "Text of an Address by Admiral Radford on the Defense Plans of the Nation," *NYT*, December 15, 1953.

39. "Annual Message to the Congress on the State of the Union, January 7, 1954," in *PPP, 1954*, 6.

40. "Text of Dulles' Statement on Foreign Policy of Eisenhower Administration," *NYT*, January 13, 1953.

41. John Foster Dulles, "Policy for Security and Peace," *Foreign Affairs* 32, no. 3 (April 1954): 359.

42. Susan Eisenhower, "50 Years Later: A Reflection on the Farewell Address," *Washington Post*, January 16, 2011, https://www.susaneisenhower.com.

5. Indochina and the Domino Theory

1. "The President's News Conference of April 7, 1954," in *PPP, 1954*, 382–83.

2. Chalmers Roberts, "The Day We Didn't Go to War," *Washington Post*, June 7, 1954.

3. Kathryn Statler, "Eisenhower, Indochina, and Vietnam," in *A Companion to Dwight D. Eisenhower*, ed. Chester Pach (Malden, MA: John Wiley and Sons, 2017), 494–516.

4. Robert A. Divine, *Eisenhower and the Cold War* (New York: Oxford University Press, 1981); Stephen Ambrose, *Eisenhower*, vol. 2, *The President, 1952–1969* (New York: Simon and Schuster, 1984).

5. Melanie Billings-Yun, *Decision against War: Eisenhower and Dien Bien Phu, 1954* (New York: Columbia University Press, 1988); Geoffrey Perret, *Eisenhower* (New York: Random House, 1999).

6. George Herring and Richard Immerman, "Eisenhower, Dulles, and Dien Bien Phu: 'The Day We Didn't Go to War' Revisited," *Journal of American History* 71, no. 2 (September 1984): 363.

7. "The President's News Conference of April 29, 1954," in *PPP, 1954*, 427.

8. DDE, *At Ease: Stories I Tell to Friends* (New York: Doubleday, 1967), 167–68.

9. *The Eisenhower Diaries*, ed. Robert H. Ferrell (New York: W. W. Norton, 1981), 190.

10. "Inaugural Address, January 20, 1953," in *PPP, 1953*, 4.

11. "Annual Message to the Congress on the State of the Union, February 2, 1953," in *PPP, 1953*, 16.

12. James Reston, "Foreign Diplomats Puzzled by Dulles' Off-Cuff Speech," *NYT*, January 29, 1953.

13. "Text of Secretary Dulles' Warning against Communist Encirclement of the West," *NYT*, January 28, 1953.

14. "Memorandum of Conversation, by the Secretary of State, March 24, 1953," in *FRUS, 1952–1954*, vol. 13, pt. 1: doc. 202.

15. "Minutes of the Meeting Between President Eisenhower and the Prime Minister of France on the Presidential Yacht *Williamsburg*, March 26, 1953," in *FRUS, 1952–1954*, vol. 13, pt. 1: doc. 208.

16. George Allen, *None So Blind: A Personal Account of the Intelligence Failure in Vietnam* (Chicago: Ivan Dee, 2001), 46.

17. "Memorandum of Discussion at the 143rd Meeting of the NSC, May 6, 1953," in *FRUS, 1952–1954*, vol. 13, pt. 1: doc. 268.

18. "Special Message to Congress on the Mutual Security Program," in *PPP, 1953*, 258.

19. Fredrik Logevall, *Embers of War: The Fall of an Empire and the Making of America's Vietnam* (New York: Random House, 2012), 354–55.

20. "Lieutenant General John O'Daniel to the Commander in Chief, Pacific (Radford), June 30, 1953," in *FRUS, 1952–1954*, vol. 13, pt. 1: doc. 317; "Substance of Discussions of State-JCS Meeting at the Pentagon, July 17, 1953," in *FRUS, 1952–1954*, vol. 13, pt. 1: doc. 348.

21. "Editorial Note," in *FRUS, 1952–1954*, vol. 13, pt. 1: doc. 409.

22. James R. Arnold, *The First Domino: Eisenhower, the Military, and America's Intervention in Vietnam* (New York: William Morrow, 1991), 119.

23. "Remarks at the Governors' Conference, Seattle Washington, August 4, 1953," in *PPP, 1953*, 540–41.

24. "Report to the NSC by the Department of State, August 5, 1953," in *FRUS, 1952–1954*, vol. 13, pt. 1: doc. 367; "Record of Actions by the NSC at its 158th Meeting, August 6, 1953," in *FRUS, 1952–1954*, vol. 13, pt. 1: doc. 368.

25. "Memorandum of Discussion at the 161st Meeting of the NSC, September 9, 1953," in *FRUS, 1952–1954*, vol. 13, pt. 1: doc. 396.

26. Arnold, *The First Domino*, 131–33.

27. "Memorandum of Discussion at the 179th Meeting of the NSC, January 8, 1954," in *FRUS, 1952–1954*, vol. 13, pt. 1: doc. 499.

28. "Report to the NSC by the Executive Secretary, January 16, 1954," in *FRUS, 1952–1954*, vol. 13, pt. 1: doc. 509.

29. "Memorandum of Discussion at the 181st Meeting of the NSC, January 21, 1954," in *FRUS, 1952–1954*, vol. 13, pt. 1: doc. 516.

30. "Memorandum of the Meeting of the President's Special Committee on Indochina, January 29, 1954," in *FRUS, 1952–1954*, vol. 13, pt. 1: doc. 525.

31. "The President's News Conference of February 3, 1954," in *PPP, 1954*, 226–27.

32. Arnold, *The First Domino*, 142–43.

33. "The President's News Conference of February 10, 1954," in *PPP, 1954*, 245–55.

34. "The President's News Conference of March 10, 1954," in *PPP, 1954*, 299–309.

35. "The Secretary of State to the President, February 6, 1954," in *FRUS, 1952–1954*, vol. 13, pt. 1: doc. 539.

36. "Memorandum of Discussion at the 186th Meeting of the NSC, February 26, 1954," in *FRUS, 1952–1954*, vol. 13, pt. 1: doc. 585.

37. Bernard Fall, *Hell in a Very Small Place* (New York: Vintage Books, 1968), 137.

38. Arnold, *The First Domino*, 152–53.

39. "Memorandum of Discussion at the 189th Meeting of the NSC, March 18, 1954," in *FRUS, 1952–1954*, vol. 13, pt. 1: doc. 620.

40. "Editorial Note," in *FRUS, 1952–1954*, vol. 13, pt. 1: doc. 622.

41. "Memorandum for the Record, March 21, 1954," in *FRUS, 1952–1954*, vol. 13, pt. 1: doc. 626.

42. "Memorandum for the Record, March 23, 1954," in *FRUS, 1952–1954*, vol. 13, pt. 1: doc. 629.

43. "Memorandum of Conversation, by the Secretary of State, March 24, 1954," in *FRUS, 1952–1954*, vol. 13, pt. 1: doc. 636.

44. "Memorandum of Discussion at the 190th Meeting of the NSC, March 25, 1954," in *FRUS, 1952–1954*, vol. 13, pt. 1: doc. 646.

45. Logevall, *Embers of War*, 457–58. See also Stephen Jurika, ed., *From Pearl Harbor to Vietnam: The Memoirs of Admiral Arthur W. Radford* (Stanford: Hoover Institution Press, 1980), 394–401.

46. "Memorandum by the JCS to the Secretary of Defense, March 31, 1954," in *FRUS, 1952–1954*, vol. 13, pt. 1: doc. 666.

47. "Memorandum of Discussion at the 190th Meeting of the NSC, March 25, 1954," in *FRUS, 1952–1954*, vol. 13, pt. 1: doc. 646.

48. "Text of Address by Secretary of State Dulles on United States Policy in the Far East," *NYT*, March 30, 1954.

49. "Draft Prepared in the Department of State, April 2, 1954," in *FRUS, 1952–1954*, vol. 13, pt. 1: doc. 677.

50. "Memorandum of Conversation, by the Secretary of State, April 2, 1954," in *FRUS, 1952–1954*, vol. 13, pt. 1: doc. 676.

51. "Memorandum for the File of the Secretary of State, April 5, 1954," in *FRUS, 1952–1954*, vol. 13, pt. 1: doc. 686.

52. Sherman Adams, *Firsthand Report: The Story of the Eisenhower Administration* (New York: Harper, 1961), 122.

53. "The Ambassador in France to the Department of State, April 4, 1954," in *FRUS, 1952–1954*, vol. 13, pt. 1: doc. 691.

54. "Memorandum of Presidential Telephone Conversation, April 5, 1954," in *FRUS, 1952–1954*, vol. 13, pt. 1: doc. 694.

55. "Memorandum of Discussion at the 192nd Meeting of the NSC, April 6, 1954," in *FRUS, 1952–1954*, vol. 13, pt. 1: doc. 705.

56. "The Secretary of State to the Embassy in the United Kingdom, April 4, 1954," in *FRUS, 1952–1954*, vol. 13, pt. 1: doc. 692.

57. "Secretary of State to the President, April 13, 1954," in *FRUS, 1952–1954*, vol. 13, pt. 1: doc. 744; Logevall, *Embers of War*, 482–84.

58. "The First Secretary of Embassy in France to Department of State, April 14, 1954," in *FRUS, 1952–1954*, vol. 13, pt. 1: doc. 747.

59. "The Secretary of State to the Department of State, April 22, 1954," in *FRUS, 1952–1954*, vol. 13, pt. 1: doc. 769.

60. "The Secretary of State to the Department of State, April 23, 1954," in *FRUS, 1952–1954*, vol. 13, pt. 1: doc. 779.

61. "The Secretary of State to the Department of State, April 24, 1954," in *FRUS, 1952–1954*, vol. 13, pt. 1: doc. 791.

62. "The Secretary of State to the Department of State, April 23, 1954," in *FRUS, 1952–1954*, vol. 13, pt. 1: doc. 780.

63. "Memorandum of Discussion at the 194th Meeting of the NSC, April 29, 1954," in *FRUS, 1952–1954*, vol. 13, pt. 2: doc. 818.

64. "Memorandum of Discussion at the 194th Meeting of the NSC, April 29, 1954," in *FRUS, 1952–1954*, vol. 13, pt. 2: doc. 818.

65. "The President's News Conference of April 29, 1954," in *PPP, 1954*, 427.

66. "Memorandum of Discussion at the 194th Meeting of the NSC, April 29, 1954," in *FRUS, 1952–1954*, vol. 13, pt. 2: doc. 818.

67. "Memorandum by the Special Assistant to the President for National Security Affairs to the Under Secretary of State, April 30, 1954," in *FRUS, 1952–1954*, vol. 13, pt. 2: doc. 819.

68. "Memorandum of Conversation, by the Secretary of State, May 11, 1954," in *FRUS, 1952–1954*, vol. 13, pt. 2: doc. 866.

69. "Memorandum of Discussion at the 196th Meeting of the NSC, May 8, 1954," in *FRUS, 1952–1954*, vol. 13, pt. 2: doc. 849.

70. "Secretary of State to the Embassy in France, May 11, 1954," in *FRUS, 1952–1954*, vol. 13, pt. 2: doc. 867.

71. Logevall, *Embers of War*, 569–71.

72. "Memorandum of Discussion at the 202nd Meeting of the NSC, June 17, 1954," in *FRUS, 1952–1954*, vol. 13, pt. 2: doc. 980.

73. "Memorandum of Conversation, by the Coordinator of the U.S. Delegation at the Geneva Conference, July 13, 1954," in *FRUS, 1952–1954*, vol. 13, pt. 2: doc. 1051.

74. "Secretary of State to the Under Secretary of State, July 16, 1954," in *FRUS, 1952–1954*, vol. 13, pt. 2: doc. 1061.

75. "Editorial Note," in *FRUS, 1952–1954*, vol. 13, pt. 2: doc. 1073.

76. "The President's News Conference of July 21, 1954," in *PPP, 1954*, 642.

77. DDE, *The White House Years: Waging Peace, 1956–1961* (New York: Doubleday, 1965), 366.

78. Jurika, *From Pearl Harbor to Vietnam*, 446.

79. "President to Supreme Allied Commander, April 26, 1954," in *FRUS, 1952–1954*, vol. 13, pt. 2: doc. 808.

6. Dealing with McCarthyism

1. "Address at the Columbia University National Bicentennial Dinner, New York City, May 31, 1954," in *PPP, 1954*, 523–24.

2. *The Diary of James C. Hagerty: Eisenhower in Mid-Course, 1954–1955*, ed. Robert H. Ferrell (Bloomington: Indiana University Press, 1983), 59.

3. "Address at Columbia University, May 31, 1954," in *PPP, 1954*, 524.

4. Charles Grutzner, "Eisenhower Warns U.S. of Demagogues Greedy for Power," *NYT*, June 1, 1954.

5. Robert Griffith, *The Politics of Fear: Joe McCarthy and the Senate* (Rochelle Park, NJ: Hayden Book Co., 1970), 199.

6. Fred Greenstein, *The Hidden-Hand Presidency: Eisenhower as Leader* (New York: Basic Books, 1982), 157. This interpretation is echoed in David Oshinsky, *A Conspiracy So Immense: The World of Joe McCarthy* (New York: Free Press, 1983).

7. See for example Larry Tye, "The President and the Bully: In Dealing with Senator Joe McCarthy, Eisenhower Chose Conciliation over Confrontation," *Saturday Evening Post*, October 15, 2020, https://www.saturdayeveningpost.com/2020/10/the-president-and-the-bully-joseph-mccarthy-vs-dwight-eisenhower/.

8. "The President's News Conference of June 17, 1953," in *PPP, 1953*, 426.

9. Oshinsky, *A Conspiracy So Immense*, 107.

10. Oshinsky, *A Conspiracy So Immense*, 109. Ten days later McCarthy submitted a copy of the speech to the *Congressional Record*. In this version the number of communists in the State Department had been changed to fifty-seven.

11. Harold Hinton, "Marshall U.S. Foe, McCarthy Charges," *NYT*, June 15, 1951.

12. DDE, *The White House Years: Mandate for Change, 1953–1956* (New York: Doubleday, 1963), 317.

13. Sherman Adams, *Firsthand Report: The Story of the Eisenhower Administration* (New York: Harper, 1961), 30–31.

14. "Sixth Draft" of Eisenhower speech given on October 3, 1952, in Milwaukee, Wisconsin, deleted section defending Marshall, Stephen Benedict Papers, Box 4, 10–3–52 Milwaukee, Wisc. (1), NAID #16614761, DDEL.

15. DDE, *Mandate for Change*, 318–19; see also DDE to Harold Edward Stassen, October 5, 1952, in *PDDE*, 13:1372.

16. DDE, *Mandate for Change*, 213.

17. Richard M. Nixon, *RN: The Memoirs of Richard Nixon* (New York: Simon and Schuster, 1978), 139.

18. *The Eisenhower Diaries*, ed. Robert H. Ferrell (New York: W. W. Norton, 1981), 234.

19. Nixon, *RN*, 139.

20. DDE to Bill Robinson of the *New York Herald Tribune*, July 27, 1953, December 1952 – July 1953 (1), Box 3, DDE Diaries Series, DDE Papers as President, 1953–61, DDEL. The term "Old Guard" referred to the conservative wing of the Republican party.

21. Ferrell, *Eisenhower Diaries*, 234.

22. DDE to Harry Bullis, May 18, 1953, 99-R McCarthy, Joseph, Box 368, Official File, White House Central Files, 1953–61, DDE Records as President, DDEL.

23. DDE to Robinson, July 27, 1953, December 1952 – July 1953 (1), Box 3, DDE Diaries Series, DDE Papers as President, DDEL.

24. DDE to Paul Hoy Helms, March 9, 1954, in *PDDE*, 15:937.

25. DDE to Philip Dunham Reed, June 17, 1953, in *PDDE*, 14:305.

26. *Ike's Letters to a Friend, 1941–1958*, ed. Robert W. Griffith (Lawrence: University Press of Kansas, 1984), 110.

27. Herbert Brownell, *Advising Ike: The Memoirs of Attorney General Herbert Brownell* (Lawrence: University Press of Kansas, 1993), 236–39.

28. "Text of Address by Truman Explaining to Nation His Actions in the White Case," *NYT*, November 17, 1953.

29. "Text of Senator McCarthy's Speech Accusing Truman of Aiding Suspected Red Agents," *NYT*, November 25, 1953.

30. "Daily Notes by C.D. Jackson, November 27, 1953, C. D. Jackson Papers, Box 68, Log 1953 (3), NAID #16702995, DDEL.

31. James Reston, "Eisenhower Staff Interprets McCarthy Speech as Attack," *NYT*, November 26, 1953.

32. "Daily Notes by C.D. Jackson, November 30, 1953, C. D. Jackson Papers, Box 68, Log 1953 (3), NAID #16702996, DDEL.

33. "Daily Notes by C.D. Jackson, December 2, 1953, C. D. Jackson Papers, Box 68, Log 1953 (3), NAID #16702997, DDEL.

34. "The President's News Conference of December 2, 1953," in *PPP, 1953*, 802.

35. "Daily Notes by C.D. Jackson, December 2, 1953, C. D. Jackson Papers, Box 68, Log 1953 (3), NAID #16702997, DDEL.

36. Oshinsky, *A Conspiracy So Immense*, 365–66.

37. Oshinsky, *A Conspiracy So Immense*, 366–68.

38. Oshinsky, *A Conspiracy So Immense*, 368–70. The Fifth Amendment to the U.S. Constitution provides protection against self-incrimination. It allows witnesses to refuse to answer questions on the grounds that the answer may incriminate them.

39. "Transcript of General Zwicker's Testimony before the McCarthy Senate Subcommittee," *NYT*, February 23, 1954.

40. Oshinsky, *A Conspiracy So Immense*, 377–80.

41. White House Chief of Staff Sherman Adams and Army Counsel John Adams were not related.

42. Brownell, *Advising Ike*, 257–58; Adams, *Firsthand Report*, 153–54; Oshinsky, *A Conspiracy So Immense*, 363.

43. Nixon, *RN*, 141–42.

44. W. H. Lawrence, "Stevens Bows to McCarthy at Administration Behest; Will Yield Data on Peress," *NYT*, February 25, 1954.

45. *Diary of James C. Hagerty*, 19–21.

46. W. H. Lawrence, "Army Secretary Denies Surrender—Senator Charges Falsehood," *NYT*, February 26, 1954.

47. "The President's News Conference of March 3, 1954," in *PPP, 1954*, 288–91.

48. W. H. Lawrence, "President Chides McCarthy on 'Fair Play' at Hearings; Senator Defiant in Retort," *NYT*, March 4, 1954.

49. Lawrence, "President Chides McCarthy on 'Fair Play' at Hearings," *NYT*, March 4, 1954.

50. "Text of Stevenson Address to the Southeastern Democratic Conference at Miami Beach," *NYT*, March 7, 1954.

51. Nixon, *RN*, 144–46. The term "pink" was often used at this time to describe someone who was not quite red (a communist).

52. "Text of Nixon Reply to Stevenson Attack on the Administration," *NYT*, March 14, 1954.

53. W. H. Lawrence, "McCarthy Strives 'To Shatter' G.O.P., Flanders Asserts," *NYT*, March 10, 1954.

54. W. H. Lawrence, "Army Charges McCarthy and Cohn Threatened It in Trying to Obtain Preferred Treatment for Schine: Stevens a Target," *NYT*, March 12, 1954.

55. Senate Committee on Government Operations, Permanent Subcommittee on Investigations, *Special Senate Investigation on Charges and Countercharges Involving: Secretary of the Army Robert T. Stevens, John G. Adams, H. Struve Hensel and Senator Joe McCarthy, Roy M. Cohn, and Francis P. Carr*, 83rd Cong., 2nd Sess., 1954 [hereafter PSI, *Army-McCarthy Hearings*], 5:135, https://hdl.handle.net/2027/uc1.b5138098.

56. W. H. Lawrence, "McCarthy Charges Army 'Blackmail,' Says Stevens Sought Deal with Him," *NYT*, March 13, 1954; Oshinsky, *A Conspiracy So Immense*, 405–6.

57. "The President's News Conference of March 24, 1954," in *PPP, 1954*, 339.

58. Oshinsky, *A Conspiracy So Immense*, 406–10.

59. Oshinsky, *A Conspiracy So Immense*, 416.

60. PSI, *Army-McCarthy Hearings*, 5:969.

61. *Diary of James C. Hagerty*, 52.

62. PSI, *Army-McCarthy Hearings*, 6:1059.

63. Oshinsky, *A Conspiracy So Immense*, 442.

64. Adams, *Firsthand Report*, 149.

65. Brownell, *Advising Ike*, 257–58.

66. *Diary of James C. Hagerty*, 53.

67. DDE to Secretary of Defense Charles Wilson, May 17, 1954, in *PDDE*, 15:1075.

68. "The President's News Conference of May 19, 1954," in *PPP, 1954*, 489–90.

69. W. H. Lawrence, "McCarthy Hearing Off a Week as Eisenhower Bars Report," *NYT*, May 18, 1954.

70. Anthony Leviero, "President Wants McCarthy Inquiry to Go On—It Will," *NYT*, May 20, 1954.

71. "Dare to Indict Him Made by McCarthy," *NYT*, May 28, 1954.

72. *Diary of James C. Hagerty*, 58.

73. HUAC, *Report on the National Lawyer's Guild: Legal Bulwark of the Communist Party*, 81st Cong., 2nd sess., 1950, Report no. 3123.

74. Robert Marcus and Anthony Marcus, *On Trial: American History Through Court Proceedings and Hearings*, vol. 2 (Hoboken, NJ: Brandywine, 1998), 136–51; "'Have You No Sense of Decency?': The Army-McCarthy Hearings," History Matters: The U.S. Survey Course on the Web, American Social History Project, City University of New York, http://historymatters.gmu.edu/d/6444/.

75. *Diary of James C. Hagerty*, 68.

76. Senate Resolution 301, 83rd Cong., 2nd Sess., July 30, 1954, Report no. 2508.

77. "The Censure Case of Joseph McCarthy of Wisconsin (1954)," United States Senate, https://www.senate.gov/about/powers-procedures/censure/133Joseph_McCarthy.htm.

78. "Text of McCarthy Speech for Delivery Today in Censure Debate," *NYT*, November 10, 1954.

79. Anthony Leviero, "Final Vote Condemns McCarthy, 67–22, for Abusing Senate and Committee; Zwicker Count Eliminated in Debate," *NYT*, December 3, 1954.

80. Of the Republican leadership in the Senate, only Leverett Saltonstall (MA) voted in favor of censure. William Knowland (CA), Styles Bridges (NH), Eugene Millikin (CO), and Everett Dirksen (IL) all voted against.

81. *Diary of James C. Hagerty*, 126.

82. "Texts of Statement by McCarthy and Some Replies," *NYT*, December 8, 1954.

83. *Diary of James C. Hagerty*, 128; "Memo by Ann Whitman regarding events leading up to so-called 'break' made by McCarthy," December 7, 1954, DDE's Papers as President, Admin. Series, Box 25, McCarthy Letters, NAID #16702984, DDEL.

84. Brownell, *Advising Ike*, 261.

85. "Staff Notes on McCarthyism, June 21, 1955," Notes by L. Arthur Minnich, Assistant White House Staff Secretary, White House Office of the Staff Secretary, L. Arthur Minnich Series, Box 1, Miscellaneous McC, NAID #16703048, DDEL.

7. *Brown v. Board* and the Little Rock Desegregation Crisis

1. "Radio and Television Address to the American People on the Situation in Little Rock, September 24, 1957," in *PPP, 1957*, 689–90.

2. "The President's News Conference of July 17, 1957," in *PPP, 1957*, 134.

3. Arthur Schlesinger Jr., *A Thousand Days: John F. Kennedy in the White House* (Boston: Houghton Mifflin, 1965); Theodore Sorenson, *Kennedy* (New York: Harper and Row, 1965).

4. Earl Warren, *The Memoirs of Earl Warren* (New York: Doubleday, 1977), 289–91.

5. See James Duram, *A Moderate among Extremists: Dwight D. Eisenhower and the School Segregation Crisis* (Chicago: Nelson-Hall, 1981); and Robert Burk, *The Eisenhower Administration and Black Civil Rights* (Knoxville: University of Tennessee Press, 1984).

6. Stephen Ambrose, *Eisenhower*, vol. 2, *The President, 1952–1969* (New York: Simon and Schuster, 1984), 620.

7. David A. Nichols, *A Matter of Justice: Eisenhower and the Beginning of the Civil Rights Revolution* (New York: Simon and Schuster, 2007), 273.

8. DDE, *The White House Years: Waging Peace, 1956–1961* (New York: Doubleday, 1965), 150.

9. Quoted in William I. Hitchcock, *The Age of Eisenhower: America and the World in the 1950s* (New York: Simon and Schuster, 2018), 215.

10. DDE, *Waging Peace*, 149.

11. Memorandum for the record, August 19, 1953, Brownell 1952–1954 (c), ACW Administration Series, DDE Papers as President, DDEL.

12. DDE to Governor James F. Byrnes, December 1, 1953, DDE Diary December 1953 (2), Box 4, DDE Diaries Series, DDE Papers as President, NAID #12171150, DDEL.

13. *Brown v. Board of Education of Topeka, Kansas*, 347 U.S. 483 (1954).

14. "The President's News Conference of May 19, 1954," in *PPP, 1954*, 491–92.

15. These were the southern states of Texas, Florida, Tennessee, and Virginia, and the border states of Oklahoma, Missouri, and Maryland.

16. Frederic Morrow to Dr. Gabriel Hauge, March 21, 1956, March 1956 Misc. (2), Box 24, DDE Diaries Series, DDE Papers as President, DDEL.

17. "The President's News Conference of May 19, 1954," in *PPP, 1954*, 491–92.

18. Herbert Brownell, *Advising Ike: The Memoirs of Attorney General Herbert Brownell* (Lawrence: University Press of Kansas, 1993), 165–67.

19. Edgar Eisenhower to DDE, September 28, 1953, and DDE to Edgar Eisenhower, October 1, 1953, Eisenhower, Edgar-1953 (1), Box 11, Name Series, DDE Papers as President, DDEL.

20. One example is Gayle B. Montgomery and James W. Johnson, *One Step from the White House: The Rise and Fall of Senator William F. Knowland* (Berkeley: University of California Press, 1998), 152.

21. Brownell, *Advising Ike*, 173; Herbert Brownell Oral History, Recorded at the DDEL, 1977.

22. Telegram from DDE to Walter White, June 29, 1954, for delivery at the Forty-fifth Annual Meeting of the NAACP, Box 47, President's Personal Files, DDE Records as President, White House Central Files, 1953–61, DDEL; Duram, *A Moderate among Extremists*, 116.

23. *Ike's Letters to a Friend, 1941–1958*, ed. Robert W. Griffith (Lawrence: University Press of Kansas, 1984), 134–35.

24. Brownell, *Advising Ike*, 196–98.

25. "The President's News Conference, November 23, 1954," in *PPP, 1954*, 1065–66.

26. Brownell, *Advising Ike*, 196–98; Duram, *A Moderate among Extremists*, 118–19.

27. *Brown v. Board of Education of Topeka, Kansas*, 349 U.S. 294 (1955).

28. August 14, 1956, August 1956 Diary-ACW (1), Box 8, ACW Diary Series, DDE Papers as President, DDEL.

29. *Ike's Letters to a Friend*, 186.

30. Minutes of Cabinet meeting, March 9, 1956, in *Minutes and Documents of the Cabinet Meetings of President Eisenhower (1953–1961)*, 10 reels (Washington, DC: University Publications of America, 1980), reel 4.

31. Minutes of Cabinet meeting, March 9, 1956, *Minutes and Documents of the Cabinet Meetings*, reel 4.

32. Brownell, *Advising Ike*, 183.

33. Duram, *A Moderate among Extremists*, 145–46.

34. Duram, *A Moderate among Extremists*, 146–48.

35. "Telegram to the Governor of Arkansas in Response to His Request for a Meeting, September 11, 1957," in *PPP, 1957*, 673–74.

36. "Notes dictated by the President on October 8, 1957 concerning visit of Governor Orval Faubus of Arkansas to Newport on September 14, 1957," Little Rock, Arkansas (1), Box 23, Administration Series, DDE Papers as President, NAID #17366732, DDEL; "Statement by the President Following a Meeting with the Governor of Arkansas, September 14, 1957," in *PPP, 1957*, 674–75.

37. "Governor Faubus Assures President He'll Obey Integration Order, but Asks for Patience by US," *NYT*, September 15, 1957.

38. Brownell, *Advising Ike*, 210.

39. "Statement by the President on the Developments at Little Rock, September 21, 1957," in *PPP, 1957*, 678–79.

40. Brownell, *Advising Ike*, 211; "Statement by the President Regarding Occurrences at Central High School in Little Rock, September 23, 1957," in *PPP, 1957*, 689.

41. For a firsthand account from the point of view of one of the Little Rock Nine, see Melba Patillo Beals, *Warriors Don't Cry* (New York: Washington Square Press, 1995).

42. Telegram, Woodrow Wilson Mann, Mayor of Little Rock, to President Eisenhower, September 23, 1957, DDE Records as President, Official File, Box 615, OF 142-A-5-A (2), NAID #12237734, DDEL.

43. "Statement by the President Regarding Occurrences at Central High School in Little Rock, September 23, 1957," in *PPP, 1957*, 689.

44. Press release, Proclamation 3204, Obstruction of Justice in the State of Arkansas, by the President of the United States of America, September 23, 1957, Kevin McCann Collection of Press and Radio Conferences and Press Releases, Box 20, September 1957, NAID #17366742, DDEL.

45. Telegram, Woodrow Wilson Mann, Mayor of Little Rock, to President Eisenhower, September 24, 1957, DDE Records as President, Official File, Box 615, OF 142-A-5-A (2), NAID #17366836, DDEL.

46. Press release, Executive Order 10730, Providing for the Removal of an Obstruction of Justice within the State of Arkansas, September 24, 1957, Kevin McCann Collection of Press and Radio Conferences and Press Releases, Box 20, September 1957, NAID #17366749, DDEL.

47. Eisenhower to General Alfred M. Gruenther, September 24, 1957, September 1957, Box 9, ACW Diary Series, DDE Papers as President, DDEL.

48. "Radio and Television Address to the American People on the Situation in Little Rock, September 24, 1957," in *PPP, 1957*, 690.

49. "The President's News Conference, September 3, 1957," in *PPP, 1957*, 646.

50. Anthony Lewis, "Washington Studies Little Rock Dispute," *NYT*, September 4, 1957.

51. "Telegram to Senator Russell of Georgia Regarding the Use of Federal Troops at Little Rock, September 28, 1957," in *PPP, 1957*, 695–96.

52. Duram, *A Moderate among Extremists*, 161–63.

53. "Statement by the President Concerning the Removal of the Soldiers Stationed at Little Rock, May 8, 1958," in *PPP, 1958*, 387.

54. DDE, *Waging Peace*, 175.

55. Frederick E. Morrow, *Black Man in the White House: A Diary of the Eisenhower Years by the Administrative Officer for Special Projects, the White House, 1955–1961* (New York: Coward-McCann, 1963), 179.

56. Emmett John Hughes, *The Ordeal of Power: A Political Memoir of the Eisenhower Years* (New York: Atheneum, 1963), 261, 349.

57. DDE, *Waging Peace*, 150.

58. DDE to Bradford G. Chynoweth, July 13, 1954, in *PDDE*, 15:1185–86.

59. Angie Maxwell and Todd Shields, *The Long Southern Strategy: How Chasing White Voters in the South Changed American Politics* (New York: Oxford University Press, 2019).

60. Anne Kornblut, "Bush and Party Chief Court Black Voters at Two Forums," *NYT*, July 15, 2005.

61. "Trump Refuses to Condemn White Supremacists," *NYT*, September 19, 2020.

62. Astead Herndon and Katie Glueck, "Biden Apologizes for Saying Black Voters 'Ain't Black' if They're Considering Trump," *NYT*, May 22, 2020.

8. Sputnik and the Race for Space

1. "Text of Johnson's Statement on Status of Nation's Defenses and Race for Space," *NYT*, January 8, 1958.

2. Robert A. Divine, *The Sputnik Challenge* (New York: Oxford University Press, 1993), vii–viii. See also David L. Snead, *The Gaither Committee, Eisenhower, and the Cold War* (Columbus: Ohio State University Press, 1999).

3. Yanek Mieczkowski, *Eisenhower's Sputnik Moment: The Race for Space and World Prestige* (Ithaca, NY: Cornell University Press, 2013), 2, 20, 23.

4. "Senators Attack Missile Fund Cut," *NYT*, October 5, 1957.

5. "Senators Attack Missile Fund Cut."

6. Richard Witkin, "U.S. Delay Draws Scientists' Fire," *NYT*, October 5, 1957.

7. Mieczkowski, *Eisenhower's Sputnik Moment*, 36–37, 57.

8. "Memorandum of Conference with the President on October 8, 1957, 8:30 a.m." DDE Papers as President, DDE Diary Series, Box 27, October '57 Staff Notes (2), NAID #12043774, DDEL.

9. Mieczkowski, *Eisenhower's Sputnik Moment*, 55–56.

10. "Memorandum of Conference with the President on October 8, 1957, 5:00 p.m.," DDE Papers as President, DDE Diary Series, Box 27, October '57 Staff Notes (2), NAID #12043783, DDEL.

11. "Statement by the President Summarizing Facts in the Development of an Earth Satellite by the United States, October 9, 1957," in *PPP, 1957*, 733–35.

12. "The President's News Conference, October 9, 1957," in *PPP, 1957*, 719–31.

13. Mieczkowski, *Eisenhower's Sputnik Moment*, 27.

14. "Text of Khrushchev Interview on Wide Range of Issues Between East and West," *NYT*, October 10, 1957.

15. Summary of Discussion, 339th Meeting of the NSC, October 10, 1957, DDE Papers as President, NSC Series, Box 9, NAID #12093096, DDEL.

16. Mieczkowski, *Eisenhower's Sputnik Moment*, 27.

17. DDE, *The White House Years: Waging Peace, 1956–1961* (New York: Doubleday, 1965), 211.

18. Memorandum of Conference with the President on American Science Education and *Sputnik*, October 15, 1957, DDE Papers as President, DDE Diary Series, Box 27, October '57 Staff Notes (2), NAID #12043792, DDEL.

19. "Radio and Television Address to the American People on Science in National Security, November 7, 1957," in *PPP, 1957*, 789–99.

20. "Radio and Television Address to the American People on Science in National Security, November 7, 1957," in *PPP, 1957*, 789–99.

21. James R. Killian, *Sputnik, Scientists, and Eisenhower: A Memoir of the First Special Assistant to the President for Science and Technology* (Cambridge: Massachusetts Institute of Technology Press, 1977), 29.

22. "Radio and Television Address to the American People on Science in National Security, November 7, 1957," in *PPP, 1957*, 789–99.

23. "Radio and Television Address to the American People on 'Our Future Security,' November 13, 1957," in *PPP, 1957*, 807–16.

24. Divine, *Sputnik Challenge*, 45.

25. Divine, *Sputnik Challenge*, 58–60.

26. "National Security Council Report (Gaither Committee Report)," November 7, 1957, in *FRUS, 1955–1957*, vol. 19: doc. 158.

27. "Memorandum of Discussion at the 343rd Meeting of the NSC," November 7, 1957, in *FRUS, 1955–1957*, vol. 19: doc. 156.

28. DDE, *Waging Peace*, 221–22.

29. Snead, *The Gaither Committee*, 189–90.

30. Quoted in Killian, *Sputnik, Scientists, and Eisenhower*, 98.

31. Divine, *Sputnik Challenge*, 41.

32. *Ike's Letters to a Friend, 1941–1958*, ed. Robert W. Griffith (Lawrence: University Press of Kansas, 1984), 190.

33. "The President's News Conference, October 9, 1957," in *PPP, 1957*, 724.

34. "Memorandum of Conference with the President on October 8, 1957, 8:30 a.m.," DDE Papers as President, DDE Diary Series, Box 27, October '57 Staff Notes (2), NAID #12043774, DDEL.

35. Divine, *Sputnik Challenge*, 62–64.

36. DDE, *Waging Peace*, 221–22.

37. DDE to Frank Altschul, October 25, 1957, in *PDDE*, 18:514.

38. Mieczkowski, *Eisenhower's Sputnik Moment*, 43.

39. DDE, *Waging Peace*, 206.

40. "Memorandum of Discussion with the President," November 22, 1957, in *FRUS, 1955–1957*, vol. 19: doc. 165.

41. DDE, *Waging Peace*, 225.

42. "Vanguard Rocket Burns on Beach; Failure to Launch Test Satellite Assailed as Blow to U.S. Prestige," *NYT*, December 7, 1957.

43. Killian, *Sputnik, Scientists, and Eisenhower*, 121.

44. DDE, *Waging Peace*, 255–57.

45. Mieczkowski, *Eisenhower's Sputnik Moment*, 49.

46. Killian, *Sputnik, Scientists, and Eisenhower*, 9.

47. Divine, *Sputnik Challenge*, xvi.

48. Reminiscences of Marion B. Folsom, 1968, COHP. Secretary Hobby resigned in August 1955.

49. Minutes of Cabinet meetings, November 15 and December 2, 1957, *Minutes and Documents of the Cabinet Meetings of President Eisenhower (1953–1961)*, 10 reels (Washington, DC: University Publications of America, 1980), reel 6.

50. DDE, *Waging Peace*, 241.

51. Minutes of Cabinet meeting, December 2, 1957, *Minutes and Documents of the Cabinet Meetings*, reel 6.

52. "Special Message to the Congress on Education, January 27, 1958," in *PPP, 1958*, 127–32.

53. Congressional Quarterly, *Congress and the Nation, 1945–1964: A Review of Government and Politics in the Postwar Years* (Washington, DC: Congressional Quarterly Service, 1965), 1208.

54. Congressional Quarterly, *Congress and the Nation*, 1208.

55. DDE, *Waging Peace*, 243.

56. "Statement by the President Upon Signing the National Defense Education Act, September 2, 1958," in *PPP, 1958*, 671.

57. Divine, *Sputnik Challenge*, 99–100.

58. Divine, *Sputnik Challenge*, 100–102.

59. Divine, *Sputnik Challenge*, 102–3.

60. Alice Buchalter and Patrick Miller, *The National Advisory Committee for Aeronautics: An Annotated Bibliography* (Washington, DC: NASA, 2014), iii; available at https://www.nasa.gov/sites/default/files/files/NACA_Annotated_Bibliography.pdf.

61. Divine, *Sputnik Challenge*, 104.

62. "Special Message to the Congress Relative to Space Science and Exploration, April 2, 1958," in *PPP, 1958*, 269.

63. Mieczkowski, *Eisenhower's Sputnik Moment*, 172–73.

64. DDE to Arthur Eisenhower, November 8, 1957, in *PDDE*, 18:551.

65. "Public Opinion Index, April 14, 1958," DDE Records as President, Official Files, Box 625, OF 146-F-2 Earth Circling Satellites (2), NAID #12060495, DDEL.

66. The World Bank, "World Bank Open Data," https://data.worldbank.org.

67. Congressional Budget Office, "The Federal Budget in Fiscal Year 2020," April 30, 2021, https://www.cbo.gov/publication/57170.

68. Diego Lopes Da Silva, Nan Tian, and Alexandra Marksteiner, "Trends in World Military Expenditure, 2020," Stockholm International Peace Research Institute, April 2021, https://sipri.org/sites/default/files/2021-04/fs_2104_milex_0.pdf.

69. Peter G. Peterson Foundation, "Budget Basics: Spending," https://www.pgpf.org/finding-solutions/understanding-the-budget/spending.

9. Eisenhower and the Farewell Address

1. "Farewell Radio and Television Address to the American People, January 17, 1961," in *PPP, 1960–1961*, 1035–40. This is the source for all quotes from the Farewell Address throughout the chapter.

2. Chester Pach, ed., *A Companion to Dwight D. Eisenhower* (Malden, MA: John Wiley and Sons, 2017), 2.

3. James Ledbetter, *Unwarranted Influence: Dwight D. Eisenhower and the Military Industrial Complex* (New Haven, CT: Yale University Press, 2011), 121–27.

4. Delores Janiewski, "Eisenhower's Paradoxical Relationship with the 'Military Industrial Complex,'" *Presidential Studies Quarterly* 41, no. 4 (December 2011): 676, 682.

5. DDE, *The White House Years: Waging Peace, 1956–1961* (New York: Doubleday, 1965), 614–15.

6. Interview with Captain Ralph Williams on June 3, 1988, OH 503, DDEL, 17–21.

7. Milton Eisenhower, *The President Is Calling* (New York: Doubleday, 1974), 322–23.

8. Williams, OH 503, DDEL, 40.

9. DDE to Milton Eisenhower, May 25, 1959, Arthur Larson and Malcolm Moos Records, Box 17, Presidential Speech Planning, NAID #12614784, DDEL.

10. Interview with Malcolm Moos on November 2, 1972, COHP, 33.

11. Memo regarding George Washington's Farewell Address, April 5, 1960, Arthur Larson and Malcolm Moos Records, Box 16, Farewell Address (1), NAID #12615069, DDEL.

12. George Washington, "Farewell Address, September 17, 1796," George Washington Papers, Series 2, Letterbooks, Letterbook 24, Library of Congress, https://www.loc.gov/item/mgw2.024/.

13. "Memorandum for the Record regarding the State of the Union 1961," October 31, 1960, Ralph Williams Papers, Box 1 Chronological (1), NAID #16972132, DDEL.

14. Moos, COHP, 34.

15. Williams, OH 503, DDEL, 27.

16. Moos, COHP, 35.

17. Janiewski, "Eisenhower's Paradoxical Relationship with the 'Military Industrial Complex,'" 678.

18. "Annual Message to the Congress on the State of the Union, January 12, 1961," in *PPP, 1961*, 913–31.

19. Draft of the Speech with handwritten editing by Milton Eisenhower, January 7, 1961, DDE Papers as President, Speech Series, Box 38, Final TV talk (1), NAID #16972219, DDEL.

20. Janiewski, "Eisenhower's Paradoxical Relationship with the 'Military Industrial Complex,'" 679.

21. Williams, OH 503, DDEL, 32–35.

22. "Radio Address to the American People on the National Security and its Costs, May 19, 1953," in *PPP, 1953*, 307, 310.

23. Harold Stassen and Marshall Houts, *Eisenhower: Turning the World toward Peace* (St. Paul, MN: Merril/Magnus Publishing, 1990), 236–37, 240.

24. Williams, OH 503, DDEL, 32–33, 36.

25. James R. Killian, *Sputnik, Scientists, and Eisenhower: A Memoir of the First Special Assistant to the President for Science and Technology* (Cambridge: Massachusetts Institute of Technology Press, 1977), 238, 230.

26. DDE, *Waging Peace*, 615.

27. Charles Griffin, "New Light on Eisenhower's Farewell Address," *Presidential Studies Quarterly* 22, no. 3 (Summer 1992): 476.

28. Janiewski, "Eisenhower's Paradoxical Relationship with the 'Military Industrial Complex,'" 684.

29. Janiewski, "Eisenhower's Paradoxical Relationship with the 'Military Industrial Complex,'" 684.

30. DDE to Milton Eisenhower, May 25, 1959, NAID #12614784, DDEL.

31. Pach, *A Companion to Dwight D. Eisenhower*, 1–2.

32. "The President's New Conference, January 18, 1961," in *PPP, 1960–1961*, 1045.

33. Jack Raymond, "The 'Military-Industrial Complex': An Analysis," *NYT*, January 22, 1961.

34. Quoted in Janiewski, "Eisenhower's Paradoxical Relationship with the 'Military Industrial Complex,'" 685.

35. C. Write Mills, *The Power Elite* (New York: Oxford University Press, 1956).

36. Aude Fleurant et al., "The SIPRI Top 100 Arms-Producing and Military Services Companies, 2018," Stockholm International Peace Research Institute, December 2019, https://www.sipri.org/sites/default/files/2019-12/1912_fs_top_100_2018_0.pdf.

37. Project on Government Oversight, "Brass Parachutes: Defense Contractors' Capture of Pentagon Officials through the Revolving Door," November 5, 2018, https://s3.amazonaws.com/docs.pogo.org/report/2018/POGO_Brass_Parachutes_DoD_Revolving_Door_Report_2018-11-05.pdf.

38. Helen Johnson, "The (Im)proper Meshing of the Corporate Media and the Military-Industrial Complex," *The Miscellany News*, May 13, 2021.

39. National Science Foundation, "Higher Education Research and Development: Fiscal Year 2020," December 27, 2021, https://ncses.nsf.gov/pubs/nsf22311.

Conclusion. Why Eisenhower Still Matters

1. James Reston, "The Eisenhower Era: President Is Called the Most Popular and Most Criticized Man in the Nation," *NYT*, January 19, 1961.

2. "The Eisenhower Years," *NYT*, January 20, 1961.

3. "Text of General Eisenhower's Address before Bar Association," *NYT*, September 5, 1949.

4. DDE to Bradford G. Chynoweth, July 13, 1954, in *PDDE*, 15:1185–86.

5. "Farewell Radio and Television Address to the American People, January 17, 1961," in *PPP, 1960–1961*, 1035–40.

6. Siena College Research Institute, "Siena's 6th Presidential Expert Poll 1982–2018," February 13, 2019, https://scri.siena.edu/2019/02/13/sienas-6th-presidential-expert-poll-1982-2018/.

7. Richard Damms, "Leadership and Decision-Making," in *A Companion to Dwight D. Eisenhower*, ed. Chester J. Pach (Malden, MA: John Wiley and Sons, 2017), 181.

8. Drew DeSilver, "The Polarization in Today's Congress Has Roots that Go Back Decades," Pew Research Center, March 10, 2022, https://www.pewresearch.org/short-reads/2022/03/10/the-polarization-in-todays-congress-has-roots-that-go-back-decades/.

9. Lydia Saad, "U.S. Political Ideology Steady; Conservatives, Moderates Tie," *Gallup*, January 17, 2022, https://news.gallup.com/poll/388988/political-ideology-steady-conservatives-moderates-tie.aspx; Frank Newport, "Bring about More Compromise in Congress," *Gallup*, October 10, 2018, https://news.gallup.com/opinion/polling-matters/243566/bringing-compromise-congress.aspx.

Suggested Reading

Memoirs, Diaries, and Letters

Adams, Sherman. *Firsthand Report: The Story of the Eisenhower Administration.* New York: Harper, 1961.

Brownell, Herbert. *Advising Ike: The Memoirs of Attorney General Herbert Brownell.* Lawrence: University Press of Kansas, 1993.

Cutler, Robert. *No Time for Rest.* Boston: Little, Brown and Co., 1966.

Eisenhower, Dwight D. *At Ease: Stories I Tell to Friends.* New York: Doubleday, 1967.

Eisenhower, Dwight D. *The Eisenhower Diaries.* Edited by Robert H. Ferrell. New York: W. W. Norton, 1981.

Eisenhower, Dwight D. *Ike's Letters to a Friend, 1941–1958.* Edited by Robert W. Griffith. Lawrence: University Press of Kansas, 1984.

Eisenhower, Dwight D. *The White House Years: Mandate for Change, 1953–1956.* New York: Doubleday, 1963.

Eisenhower, Dwight D. *The White House Years: Waging Peace, 1956–1961.* New York: Doubleday, 1965.

Eisenhower, Milton. *The President Is Calling.* New York: Doubleday, 1974.

Hagerty, James C. *The Diary of James C. Hagerty: Eisenhower in Mid-Course, 1954–1955.* Edited by Robert H. Ferrell. Bloomington: Indiana University Press, 1983.

Hays, Brooks. *A Southern Moderate Speaks.* Charlotte: University of North Carolina Press, 1959.

Killian, James R. *Sputnik, Scientists, and Eisenhower: A Memoir of the First Special Assistant to the President for Science and Technology.* Cambridge: Massachusetts Institute of Technology Press, 1977.

Morrow, Frederick E. *Black Man in the White House: A Diary of the Eisenhower Years by the Administrative Officer for Special Projects, the White House, 1955–1961*. New York: Coward-McCann, 1963.

Nixon, Richard M. *RN: The Memoirs of Richard Nixon*. New York: Simon and Schuster, 1978.

Books and Articles

Ambrose, Stephen. *Eisenhower*. Vol. 1, *Soldier, General of the Army, President-Elect, 1890–1952*. New York: Simon and Schuster, 1983.

Ambrose, Stephen. *Eisenhower*. Vol. 2, *The President, 1952–1969*. New York: Simon and Schuster, 1984.

Ambrose, Stephen. *Nixon*. Vol. 1, *The Education of a Politician, 1913–1962*. New York: Simon and Schuster, 1987.

Arnold, James R. *The First Domino: Eisenhower, the Military, and America's Intervention in Vietnam*. New York: William Morrow, 1991.

Bowie, Robert R., and Richard H. Immerman. *Waging Peace: How Eisenhower Shaped an Enduring Cold War Strategy*. New York: Oxford University Press, 1998.

Broadwater, Jeff. *Eisenhower and the Anti-Communist Crusade*. Charlotte: North Carolina University Press, 1992.

Damms, Richard. *The Eisenhower Presidency, 1953–1961*. New York: Routledge, 2014.

D'Este, Carlo. *A Soldier's Life*. New York: Henry Holt and Company, 2002.

Divine, Robert A. *Eisenhower and the Cold War*. New York: Oxford University Press, 1981.

Dockrill, Saki. *Eisenhower's New-Look National Security Policy, 1953–61*. New York: St. Martin's Press, 1996.

Duram, James. *A Moderate among Extremists: Dwight D. Eisenhower and the School Segregation Crisis*. Chicago: Nelson-Hall, 1981.

Eisenhower, Susan. *How Ike Led: The Principles Behind Eisenhower's Biggest Decisions*. New York: Thomas Dunne Books, 2020.

Greene, John Robert. *I Like Ike: The Presidential Election of 1952*. Lawrence: Kansas University Press, 2017.

Greenstein, Fred. *The Hidden-Hand Presidency: Eisenhower as Leader*. New York: Basic Books, 1982.

Griffith, Robert. *The Politics of Fear: Joe McCarthy and the Senate*. Rochelle Park, NJ: Hayden Book Co., 1970.

Hitchcock, William I. *The Age of Eisenhower: America and the World in the 1950s*. New York: Simon and Schuster, 2018.

Jacobs, Travis Beal. *Eisenhower at Columbia*. New Brunswick, NJ: Transaction Publishers, 2001.

Logevall, Fredrik. *Embers of War: The Fall of an Empire and the Making of America's Vietnam*. New York: Random House, 2012.

Nichols, David A. *Ike and McCarthy: Dwight Eisenhower's Secret Campaign against Joseph McCarthy*. New York: Simon and Schuster, 2017.

Nichols, David A. *A Matter of Justice: Eisenhower and the Beginning of the Civil Rights Revolution*. New York: Simon and Schuster, 2007.

Oshinsky, David M. *A Conspiracy So Immense: The World of Joe McCarthy*. New York: Free Press, 1983.

Pach, Chester, ed. *A Companion to Dwight D. Eisenhower*. Malden, MA: John Wiley and Sons, 2017.

Pach, Chester J., and Elmo Richardson. *The Presidency of Dwight D. Eisenhower*. Lawrence: University Press of Kansas, 1991.

Perret, Geoffrey. *Eisenhower*. New York: Random House. 1999.

Pickett, William B. *Eisenhower Decides to Run: Presidential Politics and Cold War Strategy*. Chicago: Ivan R. Dee, 2000.

Polsky, Andrew J., ed. *The Eisenhower Presidency: Lessons for the Twenty-First Century*. Lanham, MD: Lexington Books, 2015.

Shinkle, Peter. *Ike's Mystery Man: The Secret Lives of Robert Cutler*. Hanover, NH: Steerforth Press, 2018.

Snead, David L. *The Gaither Committee, Eisenhower, and the Cold War*. Columbus: Ohio State University Press, 1999.

Wagner, Steven. *Eisenhower Republicanism: Pursuing the Middle Way*. DeKalb: Northern Illinois University Press, 2006.

Index

Milton Keynes UK
Ingram Content Group UK Ltd.
UKHW041959160324
439502UK00004B/159